Afghan
Hounds

Lynda Race

contents

Foreword 4

Acknowledgements 5

chapter 1   History of the Afghan Hound 6

chapter 2   The Afghan in Recent Years 20

chapter 3   Contemporary British Kennels 39

chapter 4   Afghan Hounds World-Wide 60

chapter 5   The Breed Standard 91

chapter 6   Starting Out 108

chapter 7   Care and Basic Training 120

chapter 8   Grooming 133

chapter 9   Afghan Hound Activities 144

chapter 10   Breeding 162

chapter 11   Whelping and Rearing 171

chapter 12   Health Care 186

appendix a   Kennel Club Registrations (1945-97) . 211

appendix b   Afghan Hound Champions 212

Bibliography and Abbreviations 236

Useful Addresses 237

Index 238

Foreword

It gives me great pleasure to write the foreword to this book which I feel will prove a most valuable asset to all who have recently become acquainted with or have an interest in the breed. Whether you are a judge, breeder or novice, or just someone contemplating the addition of an Afghan Hound to your life, this book represents a wealth of knowledge and information, which is derived from Lynda's experience accumulated over the past 26 years.

In this book Lynda Race covers thoroughly all aspects of the care and management of the breed and, in the sections about breeding and stud work, there is useful advice on what to do when things do not go according to plan. Lynda also guides the enthusiast from choosing a puppy through all the stages of its development and training. The chapter on grooming explains in detail how to set about the task from start to finish and, in the section on showing, there are useful tips on how to make the best of your dog in the ring. Lynda's insight into the interpretation of the breed standard provides a mental picture of the ideal Afghan for both judge and exhibitor.

With more enthusiasts now than ever before expressing interest in the breed world-wide, the chapter about Afghan Hounds around the world covers interesting aspects of the breed in many other countries.

The Health Care chapter alone makes this book distinct from other breed books I have read. I can confidently recommend it as a worthwhile addition to the bookshelves of anyone interested in Afghan Hounds.

Sheila Devitt Gilleney
Carloway

Acknowledgements

In writing this book I have sought assistance from many different quarters and I am grateful for the help that has been so freely given. In particular, my sincere thanks must go to fellow enthusiasts, both at home and abroad, who have responded to my requests for all manner of information and entrusted me with precious photographs.

In addition, I must thank all the overseas contributors who have so kindly put time and effort into writing about our breed in their country.

I should like to tender my special thanks to the following:

- May Singleton for her excellent artwork and line drawings throughout the book.
- Avril Lancashire and Wendye Slatyer for many hours' work in checking proofs.
- Peter Harcourt Brown, whose *Afghan Hound Year Book* has been an excellent source of reference.
- Miss Gillian Averis BVMS, MRCVS for her help with the section on Artificial Insemination.
- The Afghan Hound Association for kind permission to use photographs from its archives.
- The staff at The Kennel Club for providing access to breed records and statistics.
- Thereséa Grist, Pat Latimer and Liz O'Connor for recording litter weights.
- Pam Blay at *Dog World* for compiling a list of competition winners.
- Mick O'Hanlon and Sandra Stapp of the Oddbodds Training Group.
- Lastly, a special 'thank you' to Jacquie Singleton and to my husband John, for their help and encouragement throughout.

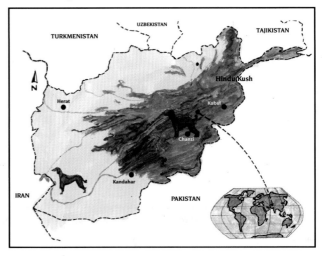

chapter one
History of the Afghan Hound

About Afghanistan

Since the dawn of history there has been a constant coming and going of different people to and from Afghanistan, for reasons of conquest, migration, religion or trade. Being situated in the middle of the major overland trade routes linking the Middle East with Central Asia, the country has been a temporary home to every manner and race of people, speaking a myriad of languages and dialects. Because of the intricate maze of contending armies, various tribes and wandering nomads who have always been a part of the

Where the two types of Afghans originated.

Afghan scene, it would seem that no permanent ancient civilisation ever flourished in Afghanistan, a fact sustained by the absence of archaeological remains of any great antiquity. Little wonder then that the history of the Afghan Hound is a mixture of fact, fiction, legend and conjecture.

To trace the history of the Afghan Hound we must look to the Middle East, where early tomb paintings provide evidence that long-legged, long-tailed, deep-chested, slender-built, Greyhound-type hounds existed before 5000 BC. That the Afghan Hound is related to this family of hounds there is no doubt, but it would have taken several centuries for it to find its way eastwards, possibly accompanying the Syrian caravans overland *en route* to Central Asia and India, via Afghanistan. Once there, it adapted to the terrain, climate and local prey by developing greater strength and a heavier coat. As its environment and purpose changed, so did its appearance.

However, to understand and appreciate the Afghan's development it would be helpful to examine in greater depth the Afghanistan in which it roamed many years ago; its spectacular landscape, extremes of climate and varied inhabitants. It is a country as varied as the people who have inhabited it over the centuries, sandwiched between the former

Soviet Union to the north and Pakistan to the south. The central core of the country is dominated by snow-capped mountains and high plateaux. To the north-east, the rugged mountains of the Hindu Kush tower above the scenery. The landscape is tortuous, rough and unwelcoming, with precipitous passes leading down from the sparsely-covered mountains into deep gorges. The climate in the mountains is bitterly cold, especially in winter. Temperatures plummet when the sun sets upon the crisp, sunny days.

Towards sea level, the terrain changes to rolling hills protecting broad, fertile valleys, vast low-lying plains and extensive areas of desert and semi-desert, which characterise southern Afghanistan. Here, the climate is searingly hot by day, but still cold at night.

From these regions, two distinct types of hound evolved: mountain dogs and desert dogs. Those originating from the northern mountainous areas were smaller, stockier and more powerfully built, with thicker coats to protect them from the extreme cold at night. They had short loins, well sprung ribs, well angulated quarters, and large feet to suit the harsh terrain. Necks were shorter and carried more upright Their heads were of a stronger type, with thicker muzzles, more pronounced stops (see diagram on page 92) and front-facing eyes. Whilst purely speculative, it is quite possible that this type of dog resulted from the Afghani shepherds crossing the thickly coated Tibetan-Mastiff-type dogs they used for herding with the Saluki/Greyhound-type originating from the East. This type of hound, the foundation of the Ghazni Kennels, was brought into England by Major and Mrs Amps on their return from Afghanistan.

The desert dogs of the south and low-lying areas were taller, lighter-boned and longer-bodied, with lean heads, little stop and more triangular eyes. Built for speed rather than climbing, their sloping shoulders, sparse silky coats, bare pasterns (see diagram on page 92) and smaller feet are more reminiscent of the purer Eastern Greyhound or Saluki, with not so much outcrossing as is suspected with the mountain types. Temperaments were reputedly quite aloof. When they came to England, this type became known as the Bell-Murray hound, taking its name from the family who imported it.

The hounds, or *Tazis*, were used originally for hunting by the poorer tribesmen and their prey would have included anything from rabbits to gazelles. The hounds belonging to the Chiefs and Shikaris fared better. Used for hunting as a sport and not a necessity, they were extremely well cared for and bred for speed and endurance. It is said they were protected so carefully that they became aloof and shy as a result.

Tribal revolts and turbulent warfare have always dominated the history of Afghanistan, with chieftain fighting chieftain, but it was not until the early 1800s that the British became involved in Afghani affairs. Already established in British India and mistrustful of a Russian advancement southwards via Afghanistan, they settled their troops into Kabul and Kandaha to establish the country as a buffer state. With their wives and families, the officers introduced many customs of the Western world and became so intrigued by the hounds that several were brought back with them on their return to England.

Once over here, the two types of Afghan Hound were blended together, although dogs with a strong ancestral resemblance to one type or the other can still emerge occasionally. Which is the correct type has long been a subject of conjecture but, when all is said and done, the elegant head and Eastern expression of the Bell-Murrays combined with the more profusely coated, balanced body of the Ghaznis has given rise to the glamorous, functional hound we know today.

Early dogs into Great Britain

Several dogs came into Britain from the 1890s onwards, but they were a somewhat mixed bunch of specimens. Not until Captain John Barff's Zardin won the foreign dog class at The Kennel Club Championship Show at Crystal Palace in 1907 did people take notice. He made such an impact that he was summoned to Buckingham Palace to be viewed by Queen Alexandra. On his way to England in 1906 he was successfully exhibited in India, where a report on him in the *Indian Kennel Gazette* gave one of the earliest detailed descriptions of an Afghan Hound. This can be found printed in full in chapter 5 on page 91.

Sadly, in London Zardin was sold by Captain Barff to an animal dealer by the name of Shackleton, and he died in unexplained circumstances. He left no recorded progeny but has since gained immortality by providing the foundation upon which our Breed Standard has been built.

The breed came to a standstill at the beginning of the First World War, and was not revived until 1921, when Major and Mrs G Bell-Murray, accompanied by their governess, Miss Jean Manson, returned to England by tramp steamer, with nine Afghan Hounds. The dogs were of the sparsely-coated, leggy, desert type, with deep saddles and long, chiselled heads – a totally different type from the famous Zardin. Miss Manson founded her kennel in Cove, Scotland, where she continued to breed her hounds, working relentlessly to bring them to the attention of the public.

Meanwhile, Major and Mrs Amps were establishing their **Ghazni** kennels in Afghanistan, having obtained their dogs from the higher mountainous areas around Kabul and Ghazni. Several dogs accompanied them on their return to England in 1925, including the famous Sirdar of Ghazni, who was to become a prolific sire and stamp his mark on the breed. The Ghazni dogs were smaller, cobbier and more profusely coated than the Bell-Murrays, with shorter, thicker-muzzled heads. Their strong resemblance to the famous Zardin, also a mountain type, gave Mrs Amps the upper hand in declaring that hers were of the correct type, referring to those belonging to the Bell-Murrays as impostors.

Open confrontation between the two kennels continued until the late 1920s, by which time many of the other breeders had begun to see the virtues in mixing the bloodlines together. By the early 1930s, both kennels had faded from the scene, and the Bell-Murray/Ghazni era came to a close.

A group of Bell-Murray hounds with Miss Jean Manson and Miss Bell-Murray. Photo courtesy AHA.

Ch Sirdar of Ghazni, owned by Mrs Amps. Photo: Thomas Fall

Until the outbreak of the Second World War in 1939, Mrs Paddy Drinkwater's **Geufron** kennel, the **Westmill** kennel of Mrs Wood, the **Jalalabad** kennel of Miss Ide and the **El Kabul** kennel of Dr Betsy Porter all worked hard to establish type and temperament in their foundation stock. Fortunately, they were all successful in maintaining vital bloodlines throughout the War, although by its end in 1945 the gene pool was considerably reduced.

Another important kennel in this period was Mrs Molly Sharpe's **Chaman** kennel, established in Scotland in 1935. Consistently breeding to type, the kennel won both Challenge Certificates (CCs) at the first championship show after the War. Mrs Sharpe's involvement with Afghans spanned 40 years, during which time she bred and owned 11 champions.

So many other early influential breeders worked tremendously hard to establish important breeding programmes that it seems almost sacrilege to condense their efforts into a passing name or phrase. As the main purpose of this book is to concentrate on the progression of the breed over the past 20 years or thereabouts, many smaller kennels, regretfully, will be omitted.

1945–1979

The immediate post-war years saw a great surge of interest in the breed. The **Bletchingley** kennel of Mrs Peggy Riley consistently produced winners of a lovely type. Her hounds still hold the record for winning the most CCs at Crufts during any one era, with Ch Bletchingley Zara winning in 1948, 1952 and 1953, Ch Tribesman in 1951, Ch Hillsman in 1955 and Ch Talookdar in 1957. Bletchingley bloodlines are behind many of our modern hounds.

The **Khorrassan** kennel of Miss Eileen Snelling gained international repute by exporting hounds to Thailand, Canada, Australia, the United States of America, Belgium, South Africa, Italy and India. Miss Snelling loved the Bell-Murray type and is most remembered for producing exquisitely-headed ivories and creams. She bred 10 champions in all, one of her last litters producing the first champion of the **Pooghan** Kennels owned by Dennis McCarthy: Ch Zaza of Khorrassan

At the same time Mrs Abson (later Mrs Morton) established her **Netheroyd** kennel in Huddersfield, achieving great success with her black-and-tan dog Ch Netheroyd Alibaba by winning Reserve Best In Show (RBIS) at Crufts in 1953. Alibaba was the first Afghan to win a Kennel Club Junior Warrant and gained 19 CCs.

In addition to the larger kennels, many smaller supporters sustained the breed during the early post-war period. For instance, Mrs D Hall of the **Barbille** affix in Preston achieved success with the all-black Kosalas Khan el Kabul and later with Ch Barbille Houri of Carloway. The kennels were always a family affair and her son, Bill, has remained deeply committed to the breed, becoming Breed Correspondent for *Dog World* in 1973.

Charles and Muriel Harrisson founded their small **Vishnu** kennels and made up their first champion, Ch Khanabad Azravi of Vishnu, in 1959. Charles' book, *The Afghan Hound*, coincided with the popularity explosion of the breed in the early 1970s, a situation about which he was genuinely concerned.

Another well-known lady of this era was Mrs Claire Race of the **Rifka** affix who, in addition to other champions, bred the famous twins Ch Rifka's Musqat D'Rar and Ch Rifka's Tabaq D'Rar. The bitch, Musqat, established a new record in the country by winning 20 CCs, beating the previous record holder, Ch Netheroyd Alibaba. Presented annually in her memory to the Best of Breed (BOB) at Crufts is the Claire Race Memorial Trophy.

By the early 1960s the breed had caught the imagination of the general public and, no longer seen as a peculiarity, started to replace the Poodle as a status symbol. Up until this point most of the large kennels had been established in the South, but the 1960s saw many northern kennels emerging, each producing their own individual strains. The whole show scene changed. Where previously the majority of enthusiasts would only show in their own part of the country, they were now getting into their motor cars and venturing further afield. Attending a long-distance show was no longer a two-day affair.

Other prolific kennels founded in this era, namely **Badakshan**, **Bondor**, **Davlen**, **Khonistan** and **Shanshu**, are still active and feature in more detail in the following chapter.

Probably the most famous bitch to be bred in the **Pooghan** kennel of writer and broadcaster Dennis McCarthy was the glamorous masked cream Ch Tzara of Pooghan, who was also campaigned to her Irish title. A complete extrovert, she appeared in the Best In Show (BIS) ring on many occasions. She won 21 CCs and four Green Stars, breaking the CC record previously held by Ch Rifka's Musqat D'Rar.

Other significant northern kennels of this period were the **Khyber** kennel of Mr and Mrs Walmsley, particularly noted for their American import Mandith Patriot of Khyber, who features behind the present-day **Karnak** and **Sharazah** kennels.

The **Kushra** kennel of Mrs Morgan and Mr Hedges produced Ch Chandi Bibi of Kushra and also Dk Ch Kushra Ben Jashmal, sire of Ch Mashour Kataghan Khan, bred and owned by Miss J Singleton and Mr B Farnell.

Arthur and Beryl Appleton founded their **Anzani** kennel in the North East in 1954, based on Carloway and Horningsea bloodlines. Bred and owned were the litter brother and sister Ch Marquis of Anzani and Ch Dame Johanne of Anzani.

Mr and Mrs Barlow owned the small **Taiwara** kennel in Worksop and produced, among others, Ch Taiwara Nazzari Chare and Ch Taiwara Saroya from their lovely brindle bitch Ch Miyasht Chare Toqmar, bred by Mrs Ann Andrews.

Recognised for her interest in the blue lines as well as the golds, Mrs Hazel Kinread produced two home-bred champions at her **Hazuki** kennel at Ripon, Jahana and Jalaluddin of Hazuki.

Active in the breed from the late 1950s, Mrs Barbara Taylor of the **Koolaba** affix produced her first home-bred champion in the free-moving brindle bitch Ch Koolaba Tajma Zai, born in 1970. However, it was Ch Koolaba Horningsea Eboni Earl who brought the kennel to the forefront in the 1970s, by his great contribution to the breed as a stud dog. The sire of 10 champions, 'Darkle' is behind many of today's pedigrees and, although used only at limited stud, will be remembered as one of the most prolific sires of the 1970s–1980s. When mated to Ch Koolaba Tajma Zai, he produced yet another champion for Koolaba: Ch Zanek Tarf, owned by Mrs Obo.

Daphne and Richard Gie founded their **Jagai** kennel in the late 1950s based on Khorrassan/Carloway lines, and champions bred by them include Rasta of Jagai, Begum Kanda of Jagai, Ranjitsinhji of Jagai (owned by Jo Holden-Ereira) and Vishnu Sitara of Jagai (owned by Charles and Muriel Harrisson). The kennel also produced many overseas champions. Daphne and Richard now live in Queensland, Australia, where they remain actively involved with the breed.

The **Moonswift** kennel, established in 1957 by Diana Bowdler-Townsend, was founded entirely upon Carloway stock. Eleven champions came from here, the first being Ch

Ch Koolaba Horningsea Eboni Earl (standing) and Ch Koolaba Tajma Zai.

Conygar Janze of Carloway in 1962. Two prolific sires were Ch/Ir Ch Moonraker of Moonswift (owner-bred) and his son Ch Moonswift Moonglade (owned by Mike Lancashire and Jenny Arkill), who sired seven and nine champions respectively. Important brood bitches included Amudarya Mikhala of Moonswift (dam of Ch Amudarya Khala and Ch The Pagan, themselves top producers) and Ch Millionairess of Moonswift (dam of Champions Moonswift Mitzouko and Majidque). The last litter to carry the Moonswift affix, born in 1989, included Ch Moonswift Medici, owned by the author, and Ch Moonswift Mhirtara at Altside, owned by Domenico Traversari and Chris Greenwood. Diana still retains an interest in the breed, although she is now more active breeding and showing Chinese Crested dogs.

Another kennel to be founded on Carloway lines was **Alyshan**, owned by Carole Walkden, starting in 1963 with Alyshan Rifka's Trendsetter (Ch Rifka's Tarquin of Carloway

ex Rifka's Rajeena of Carloway). Her first home-bred champion was Ch Alyshan Hassan Shabbah, made up in 1972, followed by Ch Alyshan Michelle in 1974, both dogs also gaining their Irish titles. In 1978, Alyshan Ysabel, a daughter of Ch Hassan, also gained her title. Currently, Carole is Chairperson of the Afghan Hound Breed Council.

Owned by Mrs Anne Hattrell and her daughter Sarah, the **Khinjan** kennel was founded in the late 1960s. Their first home-bred champion was Ch Khinjan Lorcah, a combination of Horningsea and Carloway breeding,

Ch Moonswift Medici.

who was to sire four champions. Other home-bred champions include Mr and Mrs Arris' Ch Khinjan Angelique of Sharazah and Miss J Nicholl's Ch Khinjan Sudi Shan. Sarah has since achieved great success showing and breeding Standard Schnauzers.

Among the early northern pioneers were Sid and Joan Pollock with their **Tarril** hounds. Sid's first sight of an Afghan was during the war, when he saw a pair of them racing full speed across an extremely steep mountainside in the Himalayas. Attracted by their grace, power and sure-footedness, he tried to purchase one in India, but without success. It was not until the late 1940s that he acquired his first dog, Budmash Khan, by Ch Taj Amrit of Chaman, who provided great interest to the uninitiated when taken around the northern shows. Another of their earlier dogs was a rich mahogany who sported pewter grey splashes in his ear fringes. Drawn to this fascinating colour, Sid was determined to breed a silver grey with black mask and points, which he achieved four generations later with Chandi B'Har of Tarril. When mated to the American import Ch Wazir of Desertaire, she produced their first champion, Kismati Khan of Tarril. A tremendous winner for the kennel, Kismati Khan took the Hound Group at Crufts in 1966. He was recognised as a significant stud, and his grandson was Ch Ghuura Khan of Tarril, also a black-masked silver-grey with black points, who in turn sired Ch Sacheverell Zukwala, breed CC record holder for many years. Principally using Carloway and Chaman lines in their breeding programme, Sid and Joan produced more than 20 Tarril champions.

Another northern kennel was **Sharikhan**, owned by Fred and Jean Severn. Their first dog was The Caliph, born in 1964, who gained his title in 1970. In 1965 they purchased Kalbikhan Kara, who gained her title in 1968, from Ruth Hughes. Other notable dogs from the kennel were Ch Kharisar Solomon of Sharikhan, bred by the Harcourt-Brown family in 1977, and the home-bred Ch Sharikhan Khadine of Brandeswood, owned by Peter and Jean Wright.

Jenny Dove founded her **Saringa's** kennel with two litter-mates, Rifka's Kazinga and Rifka's Seronera (Ch Rifka's Tabaq D'Rar ex Ch Rifka's Moti of Carloway), given to her by her godmother, Claire Race. Kazinga's first litter in 1970, to Ch Horningsea Tiger's Eye, produced Ch Saringa's Amira, Ch Saringa's Andante and Ch Saringa's Abracadabra, who made history in 1976 by siring a litter from frozen semen to a Calahorra bitch in Australia. Other champions produced by the kennel in 1975 were litter-mates Saringa's Jeramiah and Saringa's Jemimah (Ch Saringa's Abracadabra ex Ahmedazi Dainty Dinah). Jemimah also gained her Indian title.

The **Landhavi** affix owned by Mike and May Lancashire was started in 1977 and proved very successful before being disbanded in 1983. Ch Moonswift Moonglade (co-owned by Mike Lancashire and Jenny Arkill) gained his title in 1976 and was the sire of nine champions, including Ch Khamseen Mannetass of Landhavi, Ch Barnesmore The Baron of Landhavi and Ch Severndene Marionette of Landhavi, all owned and campaigned by Mike and May. Ch Baron and Ch Marionette, mated together, produced Ch Landhavi Love Bug of Dalparva, owned by Mr and Mrs Waistnidge.

Across the water in Ireland, the late 1960s and early 1970s were dominated by the **Veldspringer** breeding of Mrs Thelma Borst. Diana Bowdler-Townsend also lived in Ireland for a while during this period, her Ch/Ir Ch Moonraker of Moonswift siring a number of litters to Irish bitches. The achievements of other significant Irish kennels can be found in Chapter 3.

Afghan registrations

Up until 1960, the number of Afghans registered annually with The Kennel Club remained below 300, but all was to change by the end of the decade. The critical years for the breed were 1969–1975, when indiscriminate breeding sent registrations sky high, peaking at 4890 in 1974. In 1975, The Kennel Club introduced a new two-tier registration system, whereby breeders were discouraged to register all but a few of their progeny and consequently the majority of puppies bred for the pet market were never accurately accounted for. A table of post-war Kennel Club registrations can be found in Appendix A.

Three influential kennels

Whether you have owned an Afghan for a number of years or are a recent newcomer to the breed, there is a good chance that, provided your dog has some English breeding, one or more of the above kennels will feature in the background of his pedigree. The following three ladies were amongst the most successful breeders of the golden years of Afghans and their affixes were held in high esteem throughout the world. It is therefore appropriate that their breeding programmes and achievements be discussed more thoroughly.

Carloway – Mrs Sheila Devitt Gilleney

Sheila Bremner saw her first Afghan at a pre-war show, but did not own one until 1945, when she was given a bitch, Kosthi of Westover, as an engagement present. Her engagement was short-lived, but her love of Afghans is still as strong as ever, although she is now retired and living quietly in Malta.

The Carloway affix was first registered just before the Second World War by Sheila's mother, who had decided that the breeding of Lakeland Terriers would be a 'suitable occupation' for her daughter when she returned home from boarding school. The War intervened, and Sheila was posted north to the city of Chester, where she managed to keep a Lakeland Terrier as a companion throughout the War.

At the end of the War she returned home, acquired her engagement present, Kosthi, and started her kennel, which was to have the strongest influence on the breed in the post-war era. At her very first show she went BIS with Kosthi, which, by her own admission was due more to good luck than anything else. Nevertheless, this influenced her decision that it was Afghan Hounds, and not Lakeland Terriers, that she wanted to breed. She was a great fan of a young shaded masked gold dog called Kohistan Shahudin, owned by Dr B Unkauf, and in 1947 was fortunate to add a youngster sired by Shahudin to her kennel, namely Jalalabad Barwala of Carloway. Shahudin is particularly significant to the Carloway story in that Sheila credits him for establishing in her kennel the type for which her affix has been synonymous.

Barwala features in the pedigree of almost every Carloway registered. It was unfortunate that as a youngster he contracted chorea, a distemper-related disease, which left him with a slipped disc in his spine and ended his show career. He was, however, very much in demand as a sire and his first mating to Peggy Riley's top winning bitch of the day, Ch Bletchingley Zara, was a great boost for the Carloway kennel. The resulting litter produced Ch Bletchingley Hillsman, retained by Mrs Riley, and Bletchingley Barzara of Carloway, sire of Sheila's Ch Muphytt of Carloway, Mrs McGregor-Cheers' Ch Baluch Ranee Ashraf and Helen Barnes' first champion, Fantasia of Carloway.

Sheila then mated Barwala to another of her foundation bitches, Winstyle Dera Khan, producing Dulli Khan, the sire of Zog of Carloway. Zog, when line-bred back to Dulli Khan's sister Dana Khan, produced Ch Yussef of Carloway.

Barwala also sired Sheila's first champion, Carloway Sharmain of Virendale, who, after a year of winning Reserve CCs to Ch Bletchingley Zara, became the top winning bitch in 1952–1953. Success then followed, with seven more Carloway champions gaining their titles by the end of the 1950s.

Yussef sired nine British champions and his black-and-tan son, Ch Pasha of Carloway,

A Carloway group. Left to right: Bletchingley Barzara of Carloway, Ch Jalalabad Barwala of Carloway, Booji of Carloway, Zog of Carloway and Ch Carloway Sharmain of Virendale. Photo: Sussex Photo Agency

won six CCs and a Hound Group as well as siring six champions. Yussef's other famous sons were Ch Khymn, owned by Sheila, Ch Rifka's Tarquin of Carloway, who was Claire Race's first champion, Ch Conygar Janze of Carloway, who became Diana Bowdler-Townsend's first champion, Ch Alphonse of Khyber, owned by Derek and Doreen Walmsley, and Ch Kalbikhan Ali Bey of Carloway, owned by Ruth Hughes. Yussef's daughters included Ch Mandodari of Carloway and the top winning bitch for 1956–1957 Ch Tijah of Carloway who, when mated back to her sire, produced Ilexis of Carloway. Ilexis in turn was the dam of Ch Waliwog of Carloway, Ch Takkabor Tiaga and Ch Takkabor Golden Eagle (all by different sires). Her sister, Indira, was the dam of Ch/Ir Ch Moonraker of Moonswift.

Ch Pasha's six champion children included Empress of Carloway, owned by Mrs Gent, Bondor Lezah, owned by Messrs Brooks and Swallow, Tara of Pooghan, owned by Dennis McCarthy, Rifka's Moti of Carloway, owned by Claire Race, and Mazari of Carloway, owned by Sheila and later exported to David Roche in Australia. Following his transfer to Richard and Daphne Gie, Ch Pasha sired Ch Begum Kanda of Jagai.

Watsatari of Carloway (Zog of Carloway ex Winstyle Dera Khan) was born in 1954 and remained with Sheila until she left England in 1965. Quite a shy dog, he sired the champion sisters Jil and Jinga (to Undine of Carloway) and, mated to Leila of Carloway (Ch Yussef ex Ch Sharmain), he sired the famous 'Yaz' litter: Yazeena, dam of Ch Bondor Serenade, and Yazmin, dam of the last Carloway champion, Xzari. When mated to Horningsea Samsie (litter sister to Ch Horningsea Sheer Khan), Watsatari sired Ueda of Carloway, owned by Anne Andrews, later to become the dam of Anita Doe's Ch Miyasht Empress.

Sheila and Claire Race were great friends and would often travel to shows together, and Sheila recalls the two of them enjoying a lively social scene when the showing was over. Whilst on a trip to America in 1960, Claire visited the Crown Crest kennels of Kay Finch and the Grandeur kennels of Sunny Shay in search of a dog to bring back to England, whose breeding would complement the Carloway lines. Together Sheila and Claire imported Crown Crest Zardeeka, in whelp to the legendary Am Ch Crown Crest Mr Universe, whose litter was subsequently born in quarantine. Tragically, the puppies contracted hardpad shortly after they were released and the whole litter was lost. As compensation for the loss of Zardeeka's litter, Kay Finch sent out the black-masked silver Wazir of Desertaire, a son of Mr Universe. He was of a completely different type to that of the Carloways: Sheila described him as 'big, jolly and hairy, with a head like a bucket!' The plan was to mate all of the Carloway bitches to him once and then go back into the Carloway lines. As it happened, other breeders of the day rushed to use him and eventually doubled up on his breeding, which was never Sheila's plan.

Around this time Sheila mated Ilexis (Ch Yussef ex his daughter, Ch Tijah) to Marna Dods' very successful Ch Horningsea Sheer Khan. She retained the black-masked red, Ch Waliwog of Carloway, who gained his title in 1963. Ch Waliwog sired three champions: Ch Xzari of Carloway, bred by Diana Bowdler-Townsend and owned by Bob Allison, and the litter-mates Ch Rasta and Ch Ranjitsinhji of Jagai, bred by Daphne Gie.

In 1965, Sheila married Michael Gilleney and went to live in Malta. Her dogs were distributed amongst breeders in Great Britain and abroad. Champions Mazari and Waliwog, accompanied by Sheila's kennel manageress Joyce West, went out to live with David Roche in Adelaide, where they soon became Australian champions.

Sheila's last Afghan, 'Musti', died in 1991.

Horningsea – Mrs Marna Dods

Marna came into Afghans in the late 1940s, and her highly successful kennel and team of stud dogs greatly influenced the breed over the next 20 years. She chose not to line-breed as closely as the Carloways, generally preferring to outcross and introduce new lines. Her knowledge and understanding of bloodlines, together with her famed puppy-rearing abilities, ensured that she remained at the top until her untimely death in 1976.

A significant foundation bitch of the Horningsea kennel was the deep red Ch Marika of Threestreams, who was obtained from Mr Parker when he was disbanding his kennel. At the time, Marna was showing a self-masked cream dog called Horningsea Turridu, whom she duly mated to Ch Marika, thereby producing her first champion, Ch Horningsea Majid, in 1956. An elegant black-masked cream, Ch Majid, sired two champions when mated to Margaret Niblock's Khanabad Azrar: Ch Khanabad Azravi of Vishnu and Ch Khanabad Aztrajid. A further brother, Azreefa, initially went to Marna, but was later sold on to America where he was campaigned to his American title. The next home-bred champion sired by Ch Majid (ex Tilluh of Carloway) was Ch Horningsea Sheer Khan, who was himself an influential sire, providing the foundation stock of three well-known kennels: Ch Safiya of Sacheverell (bred and owned by Monica Booth), Ch/Ir Ch Moonraker of Moonswift (bred and owned by Diana Bowdler-Townsend) and Ch Horningsea Mittani (home-bred by Marna and owned by Bettie McClark). Ch Sheer Khan was also the sire of Ch Waliwog of Carloway. Marna then branched out into the 'colours' by mating Horningsea Sardi, a Ch Suvaraj daughter, to Misses Kean and McKenzie's American-bred import, Ajman Branwen Kandahar (Am Ch Chinah of Grandeur ex Suriyeh of Grandeur). The result was the grey brindle dog, Ch Horningsea Tiger's Eye, who was used extensively at stud to become the sire of eight champions, including Marna's eighth home-bred champion, Ch Horningsea Tiger Doll.

Marna also incorporated Ch Wazir of Desertaire into her lines who, when mated to Horningsea Seriya, produced the black-and-brindle dog, Horningsea Sagittarius. Sagittarius in turn sired the black-and-tan male Ch Horningsea Mustagh Ata (ex Horningsea Marue) and Ch Horningsea Kayacci (dam of Ch Koolaba Horningsea Eboni Earl). Both were owned by Marna. A further champion sired by Sagittarius was Jenny Nicholls' Ch Khinjan Sudi Shan, bred by Mrs Hattrell.

Ch Horningsea Khanabad Suvaraj (Horningsea Salim Dar ex Khanabad Azra) spearheaded the Horningseas to the forefront in 1962, when he achieved the ultimate acclaim by becoming the only Afghan in the history of the breed to date to win Dog of the Year All Breeds. To qualify for this award he had won BIS at seven championship shows,

Mrs Marna Dods with (left to right) Horningsea Surivor, Ch Horningsea Tiger's Eye, Ch Horningsea Tiger Doll and Ch Horningsea Kayacci.

with three RBISs and fifteen CCs. He was subsequently retired from the ring and went on to sire four champions, namely Ch Aryana Shalym, owned by Father Ford and Miss Barnes and later exported to become an American and Canadian champion, Ch Masquerade of Moonswift, bred by Diana Bowdler-Townsend, and Claire Race's famous twins, Ch Rifka's Tabaq D'Rar and Ch Musqat D'Rar.

In 1963, Marna and Sheila Devitt co-bred the stylish Ch Barbille Houri of Carloway (Ch Conygar Janze of Carloway ex Horningsea Samsie), owned by Mrs Hall.

After visiting America in 1974, Marna brought back a son of Ch Horningsea Mustagh Ata (ex Red Rock Duhst) from the kennels of Mrs P Ide. Am Ch Huzzah Excelsis of Horningsea became her pride and joy and, in 1975, became the first import since Ch Wazir of Desertaire to gain an English title.

Marna was a valued member of the Afghan Hound Association (AHA) Committee for many years. She instigated the Code Of Ethics and co-wrote the pamphlet on *Hereditary Defects*, a subject about which she was deeply concerned and extremely knowledgeable.

Khanabad – Miss Margaret Niblock
Margaret acquired her first Afghan in 1947, a bitch, Bletchingley Berberine, from the kennels of Mrs Peggy Riley. When mated to Jalalabad Barwala of Carloway, Berberine produced Khanabad Abdul Hamzavi, significant in that he was the sire of Khanabad Azrar, a bitch who was to become a famous brood for the Khanabads.

Khanabad Azrar was mated to Ch Horningsea Majid and the litter produced the first two Khanabad champions. Ch Khanabad Azravi of Vishnu was owned by Charles and Muriel Harrisson, whilst Ch Khanabad Aztrajid was retained by Margaret. Another brother, Azreefa, went to the United States as a junior and later gained his American title.

Azrar was then mated to Horningsea Salim Dar to produce the two brothers Khanabad Suradar and Suvarov, along with a black-masked red sister, Ch Patchouli Khanabad Surasu, the foundation bitch of Joyce Purdue's Patchouli kennels. But probably the most famous brother of this union was Ch Horningsea Khanabad Suvaraj, owned by Marna Dods, whose success has already been documented. However, Margaret deserves recognition for having bred him.

Ch Azravi was mated to Rahane of Ladysmyle, owned by Ann and Ron Adams, to produce their first Badakshan champion, Rani.

In 1964, Margaret's interest in breeding blues became reality when she imported two silver-blue males from Mrs Madigan's Branwen kennels in Spain, namely Khanabad Branwen Sheen Khalifa and his litter brother Khurram (Branwen Kadar ex Branwen Karuna of Grandeur). Khurram sired the first British blue bitch champion, Khanabad Blue Pearl (co-owned with Mrs M Baster), whilst Khalifa went on to sire the first British blue dog champion, Khanabad Diablo of Whodeanie, owned by Mr D McCann. Khalifa was also the sire of Margaret's all-white Ch Khanabad White Warrior. Another blue, Khanabad Azure Azami, sired the self-cream champion bitches Khanabad Peach Blossom and Khanabad Honeydew, both owned by Gloria North.

Margaret was a firm believer in natural rearing methods and would free-run her hounds together as a pack on the farm she ran with Miss Rene Sawyer. Around 30 hounds were kept until the mid-1980s, when her modest breeding programme scaled down even further, resulting in fewer youngsters being retained.

Miss Margaret Niblock with five home-bred Khanabad champions. (Left to right) White Warrior, Honeydew, Peach Blossom, Blue Pearl and Diablo of Whodeanie. Photo: Alan S Kimpton

Margaret was involved in formulating the Afghan Hound Association (AHA) scheme to examine junior judges, which in turn was adopted by the other clubs and the Afghan Hound Breed Council. Her excellent definitive study of the breed was published in 1980. Margaret was a life-long supporter and President of the AHA and was also President of the Afghan Hound Club of Wales.

It was a great loss when Margaret died in April 1995; her candid viewpoint and knowledge of the breed are irreplaceable.

chapter two
The Afghan in Recent Years

Ch Balkasha Barabbas.

To bring the history of the breed up to date, I shall give a year-by-year summary of the major awards won by Afghan Hounds, recalling memorable events and mentioning some of the people and dogs who have shaped the breed and enriched our lives. A full list of champions for each year can be found in Appendix B.

The 1980s

1980

Miss Niblock's long-awaited book *The Afghan Hound – A Definitive Study* was available at Crufts, where the dog CC and BOB went to Mr and Mrs Dryden-Bell's Ch Balkasha Barabbas. Notably, at 17 months old, Barabbas was the youngest male ever to become a champion. The bitch CC went to Mr McAthy and Mrs Doe's Ch Izmars Enchanting Empress, who gained her title on the same day. Judges were Mr Allan Brooks (dogs) and Mrs Joan Pollock.

Litter brother and sister, Mr and Mrs Szyczewski's Karnak Shamrock and Mr and Mrs Thornton's Karnak Juniper, won both CCs at the East of England Championship Show, with another 'double' being won by Mike and May Lancashire's Khamseen Mannetass of Landhavi and Severndene Marionette of Landhavi at the Midland Afghan Hound Club Championship Show.

At Leeds Championship Show, Ch Sacheverell Madam Zinnia took the BIS award, a great moment for her owner/breeder Monica Booth. Birmingham's dog CC winner was Terry and Carol Hall's Koolaba Hareeb, who became their second champion in seven years. It was a great shock for exhibitors to learn of Terry's sudden and tragic death only three weeks later.

Later in the year Bill Hall awarded the Bitch CC to Richard Kirkham's puppy, Khorlynton Keltic Karibou. Soon to become a champion, Karibou was one day under twelve months old at the time and the youngest on record to win such an award.

In the *Dog World* Pedigree Chum Competition, the Top Winning Afghan was Ch Sacheverell Madam Zinnia.

1981

Mrs Anna Paton and Mrs Carole Sturgeon-Walkden judged at Crufts, where BOB was awarded by the Referee, Mr Bobby James, to May and Jim Thompson's Karnak Bay of Imrahn, making it a special day for the Karnak kennel as Ch Karnak Shamrock, owned by Stan Szyczewski, won the RCC.

Pauline and Marita Gibbs' Dutch-bred import, Montravia Dun-Dun v Bornia State, became the first import to become a British champion since Marna Dods' Ch/Am Ch Huzzah Excelsis in 1975. Dun-Dun gained his title at the Afghan Hound Association (AHA) Show, under judge Mrs Margaret Baster. American judges Pat Ide and Carol Esterkin drew a mammoth entry of 475 exhibits at the East of England Club Championship Show, where Ch Karnak Shamrock and Ch/Indian Ch Saringa's Jemimah took the top awards.

The Birmingham Afghan Hound Club celebrated its 10th anniversary in style by achieving Kennel Club recognition, bringing the number of breed clubs in Great Britain to 12. Later in the year, when judging at Richmond Championship Show, Dennis McCarthy was of the opinion that none of the exhibits merited the CC or RCC and, as a consequence, withheld both.

The breed lost two of its great ambassadors when Ch Koolaba Horningsea Eboni Earl and Ch Amudarya The Pagan died.

Top Winning Afghan was Ch Montravia Kaskarak Hitari.

1982

Once again, the Referee's services were required at Crufts when the two judges, Mrs Barbara Taylor and Mrs Daphne Gie, could not decide between the dog, Ch Montravia Kaskarak Hitari, owned by Pauline Gibbs and handled by daughter Marita, and the bitch, Ch Khorlynton Keltic Karibou, owned by Richard Kirkham. Mr Joe Braddon selected the bitch to go forward to the Hound Group.

The Hound Association Championship Show saw yet another 'double' when Hazel and Derek Arris won both CCs with their exhibits, Ch Sharazah Milwalki Stroller (dog) and Ch Sharazah Blackberry Silk (bitch).

Margaret Niblock and Jenny Dove judged the 34th AHA Championship show and between them drew an entry of 510 dogs (705 entries). The BIS award went to the winner of the Limit dog class, the Irish-bred Barnesmore The Baron of Landhavi, with RBIS going to the bitch, Harlextan The Mad Nun.

Ch Amudarya Shalar, owned by Linda Aldous, surpassed the previous record held by Ch Yussef of Carloway

Ch Sharazah Blackberry Silk and Ch Sharazah Milwalki Stroller at the Hound Association Show 1982. Photo: McFarlane

in the 1960s, to become the Top Sire in the history of the breed. By the end of the year he had eleven British champions to his credit and was also the Top Sire in the Hound Group.

The breed lost two more outstanding hounds: Ch Amudarya Khala, who had kept the flag flying in the Group and BIS rings, and Ch Sacheverell Zukwala, the CC record holder at the time.

Top Winning Afghan was Ch Moonswift Mitsuoko.

1983

Jillian Knight-Messenger and Monica Booth-Thomson chose Mrs Pauline Gibbs' silver brindle dog Ch Montravia Kaskarak Hitari, bred by the author, for BOB at Crufts. 'Alfie', as he was known at home, went on to win BIS under Mr W Parkinson and thereby took his place in history as the first Afghan ever to become Best In Show at Crufts. By the end of the year he was to win many more Groups and BISs. Winner of the bitch CC was Tulak Gin Fizz of Kakara, owned by Mr and Mrs Smith.

At Southern Counties Championship Show, Marita Gibbs awarded the CC to Graham and Christine Parsell's 14-month-old Playfere's Petticoat Wag at Harlextan. A wonderful year followed for this bitch and she went on to gain her title at 17½ months, becoming one of the youngest champions to date.

During the year, four overseas judges officiated in Great Britain. Carla Molinari from Portugal and Harry Spira from Australia both awarded the CC to Ch Montravia Kaskarak Hitari,

Ch Montravia Kaskarak Hitari with the Crufts BIS trophy.

Milan Anteglievic from South Africa chose Warrenoak Timpani, whilst Carol Esterkin's choice was Ch Zendushkas Pan-Celli.

Another import to our shores, Finnish-bred Tuohi-Tikan Loiske at Mirsamir, owned by Isobell Dyke, won the CC at Paignton under judge Mrs J Wilson Stringer.

Sadly, the breed was to lose Mr Gerry Hitchens of the Ashihna Hounds and Mrs Margaret Pickard, owner of Ch Kohsan's Mr Inigo Jones.

Top Winning Afghan was Ch Montravia Kaskarak Hitari. *Dog World* Pedigree Chum began a new competition for Top Afghan Stud Dog, and the winner was Ch Amudarya Shalar.

1984

Judges Mr Bill Hall (dogs) and Mrs Diana Bowdler-Townsend (bitches) chose Chris and Julie Amoo and Meriel Hitchens' Ch Ashihna Raoul as BOB at Crufts. Davlen Tijuana Silk, owned by Rev Ford, Miss Barnes and Mrs Haywood, won the bitch CC.

Molly Sharpe awarded CCs for the last time at the Border Counties Hound Show, where

Ch Amudarya Shalar (aged 10), Top Afghan Stud Dog to date.
Photo: John M Hope

BOB went to Ch Montravia Kaskarak Hitari, who was to finish the year as the new Breed CC record holder; the previous record of 27 CCs up until this time had been held by his sire, Ch Sacheverell Zukwala.

Another record to be broken was by Ch Amudarya Shalar, when at 10 years old he became Top Sire All Breeds, with 23 champions to his credit.

Isobell Dyke's Finnish-bred Ch Tuohi-Tikan Loiske at Mirsamir became the first imported bitch for several decades to become a champion. Also during the year, the Harcourt-Brown family imported a puppy from the United States, Coastwind Apphia at Kharisar, whose breeding comprised mainly American, Australian and old English lines.

A sad event was the death of Jim Thompson, husband of May, of the Imrahn affix.

The breed was to also lose Ch Bondor Sayonara of Fiazabad, Ch Moonswift Moonglade, and one of the last remaining Horningseas, Ch Horningsea Balubianka.

Top Winning Afghan was Ch Sharazah Night Gambler. Top Stud Dog was Ch Amudarya Shalar.

1985

BOB at Crufts for the second year running was Ch Ashihna Raoul, who went on to win the Hound Group. The bitch CC was won by Ch Katree Miss Schiapparelli, owned by John Bland and Eve Bishop. The judges were Mr Arthur Hedges (dogs) and Mr Dennis McCarthy (bitches).

The Birmingham Afghan Hound Club held its first championship show, judged by its President, George Masters, and Club Committee Member, John Bunce. Their choice for BOB from the 281 dogs entered was Clive and Susan Winters' Harlextan The Rifleman.

Following a 10-year stay in Italy, Hermione Bruton returned to England, bringing back with her Int Ch Joe Mirzabad.

Our own Kaskarak kennels exported a red puppy bitch, namely Kaskarak Best Of British, to Wendye and Stuart Slatyer in Australia, sired by Ch Montravia Kaskarak Hitari. Her dam was litter sister to Ch Kaskarak Kochise.

Ch Amudarya Shalar died aged 11½ years old. His record as the Top British Afghan Sire, with 23 champions to his credit, still remains unbeaten in 1998.

A shock to the breed was the sudden death of Rev David Ford, co-owner of the Davlen affix with Miss Helen Barnes. Active in the breed since the early 1950s, David was greatly respected by all who knew him.

Top Winning Afghan was Ch Montravia Kaskarak Hitari. Top Sire was Ch Amudarya Shalar.

1986

Crufts judges Mr Bill Eccles (dogs) and Mrs Dorothea Edge (bitches) awarded BOB to Ian and Mary Fishers' Ifmarif Go-Man-Go, with Sandra Miles' Sana's Moon Jade winning Best Bitch.

Ch Sharazah Night Gambler went to join the Calahorra Kennels in Australia, where only a few months after his release from quarantine he won Runner-Up All Breeds BIS at a major show and quickly gained his Australian title. Prior to his export, Gambler had won six CCs in total and an All-Breeds BIS.

Bo Bengtson was invited to judge the East of England Afghan Club Show, where he awarded the CC to the winner of the Veteran class, the seven-year-old Ch Montravia Kaskarak Hitari. Heather Crowe judged bitches, her CC choice being Hashtana Lucy Limelight.

Daphne and Richard Gie emigrated to Australia, taking with them a few of their Jagai hounds.

Hermione Bruton's Int Ch Joe Mirzabad gained his British title and finished the year with five CCs to his credit. Other imports to our shores were Dk Ch Boxadan Junior Jumper, co-owned by Jillian Knight (Messenger) with Bob and Ann Savage, and the Spanish-bred duo Sumava's Hdjab at Sumahari and Sumava's Haidalla at Sumahari, owned by Mick and Sue Virgo.

1986 was another sad year, when Mr Ron Adams, Chairman of the AHA and Breed Council, died. He and his wife Ann owned the Badakshan affix, having bought their first puppy in 1955. He had been a member of the AHA since 1956, and his knowledge, personal integrity and love of Afghans are irreplaceable. Two other notable ladies sadly passed away: Mrs Ida Morton of the famous Netheroyds and Mrs Isobel Kershaw, owner of the Fartonia affix.

Top Winning Afghan was Ch Viscount Grant. Top Stud Dog was Ch Karnak Shamrock.

1987

People said it could never happen twice – how wrong they were! At Crufts, Chris and Julie Amoo's home-bred Ch Viscount Grant went Best In Show, to become the breed's second Crufts Supreme Champion. A great year ahead followed for this young dog, who was to win four Hound Groups and two BIS awards. The bitch CC was awarded to Ledger and Thornton's Ch Karnak Jasmine. Mrs Joan Wonnacott judged dogs and Mrs Isobell Dyke bitches.

When reprinting the Afghan Hound Breed Standard, the KC made certain changes to the wording of the description of the forequarters, which were not at all well received by serious enthusiasts. Bill Hall, *Dog World* Breed Correspondent and devotee of 50 years standing, successfully spear-headed a campaign to redress the situation.

Sadly, Mr Albert Munro, President of the Southern Afghan Club, was to pass away in his 90th year, as was Mrs Nona Thorpe, a past Secretary of the Midland Afghan Hound Club and co-owner of the Xanaghan affix. Another staunch supporter and author of a book on our breed, Cathy Sutton, was also to die. Cathy is probably better remembered as one of the great all-breed judges of the era.

Top Winning Afghan was Ch Viscount Grant. Top Stud Dog was Ch Karnak Shamrock.

(Above) Ch Viscount Grant winning BIS Crufts.
Photo: Dave Freeman
(Below) Ch Ratheeli Jadu. Photo: Martin Leigh

1988

BOB at Crufts was won by Tony and Pat Cleak's Ch/Ir Ch Ratheeli Jadu, the bitch CC being awarded to Elaine and Mike Wyatt's Ch Lissue Storm Cloud. Mr Vic Hammon judged the dogs and Mrs Anita Doe the bitches. Undecided between a choice of two outfits especially purchased for the occasion, Anita compromised by changing into the second outfit during the lunch break - and very smart she looked too!

Sue and Mick Virgo's Spanish-bred Sumava's Haidalla at Sumahari went to join the Grandeur Kennels in America, where, handled by Michael Canalizo, she quickly gained her American title. By the end of the year she was brought back into British quarantine, to resume her show career.

Finnish Ch Mandrills Myltha Izmar Tragband was imported into Great Britain in whelp to Int Ch Choice Be A Pepper. She was owned by Anita Doe, John Watson and Andrew Brace, and her litter of 10 puppies was born in quarantine.

Mr Eric Swallow, founder partner of the famous Bondor kennels, died in Australia, where he had resided for a number of years. News of the sudden death of the great all-rounder Mr Bobby James was also to shock the dog world. A good friend of the breed, Bobby certainly knew his Afghans and was scheduled to judge them at Crufts in 1989.

Top Winning Afghan was Ch Solomon's Seal from Karnak. Top Stud Dog was Ch Karnak Shamrock.

1989

Replacing the late Bobby James at Crufts, Mrs Doreen Walmsley awarded the dog CC to Mr and Mrs Ledger's Ch Karnak Mulberry. Judging bitches, Miss Christabel Holmes chose Pauline Mullins and Jill McBride's Ch Ratheeli Mahzuzh. The dog was BOB.

John Charlesworth came over from Canada and judged bitches at the East of England Club Show, with Best Bitch going to Karaburan Tokyo Rose, shown by Rose-Marie Boyd. Dogs were judged by Miss Jacquie Singleton, who found her CC winner in Pat and Pete Dollman's Khorramabad Fire Fox.

Australian judges officiated at the Yorkshire Afghan Hound Society Championship Show, where Carmyn Kingston gave the CC to the top winning dog, Ch Solomon's Seal from Karnak. Wendye Slatyer chose Ch Shanshu Casa Biere from Khados, the bitch going BIS.

The Midland Afghan Hound Club celebrated its Silver Jubilee Year in great style. Everyone connected with the Club, both past and present, helped make the Championship Show a most memorable occasion, with sponsorship received from enthusiasts at home and abroad. The two judges, Jacquie Singleton and myself, agreed upon Jill and Clari Cross' Gilari Goldstrike for BIS with Best Bitch being awarded to Carmel and Pete Barnett's Zoreba Nodashti of Kindjara.

Leeds Championship Show invited Erika Rödde from West Germany to judge the dogs, her choice being Lesley and Alan Busby's Jahadi Bosch at Wilbus. Her co-judge, Jillian Knight-Messenger, found her bitch CC winner in Miamarna Michelle, owned by Mrs Shirley Gill.

The Breed lost two very knowledgeable ladies when Miss Pauline Leyder and Mrs Marjorie Doody sadly passed away.

Top Winning Dog was Ch Solomon's Seal from Karnak. Top Stud Dog was Ch Barnesmore Imperial Wizard. *Dog World* Pedigree Chum introduced a new competition for Top Brood Bitch and the winner was Ch Maljan Golden Samarina from Sharazah.

The 1990s

Up until the 1990s, imports into Britain were quite a rarity but, as the breed becomes more cosmopolitan and more new bloodlines come into the country, it is impossible to mention every single one by name. I have therefore included an account of influential imports later in this chapter.

Likewise, overseas breed specialist judges officiating at our shows have previously been few and far between, but these too are becoming more popular.

Entries at championship shows began to fall and, in view of this, The Kennel Club reduced the allocation of CCs on offer to the breed. A rotation system was agreed amicably between the 12 breed clubs and the present situation is that each Breed Club will forego its Championship show once in every 12 years. However, there is no guarantee that the present number of CCs will not be reduced further if this downward trend continues. Added to this, more and more societies have begun to opt for one judge only, whereas in the past we have had a separate judge for each sex.

1990

At Crufts, dogs were judged by Mr Keith Thornton and bitches by Mrs Ann Adams. Best of Breed was won by Brian Gilchrist's Ch Solomon's Seal from Karnak with the bitch CC going to Richard Jamrozik's Zardalu Maleke.

Marie Howitt returned to Britain with three of her young dogs, having emigrated to Australia in 1950.

Mrs Fukie Yoshimoto from Japan judged the breed at the Afghan Hound Club of Wales Show, and her choice for the dog CC was Pat and Dawn Kirwan's Padaki Qala-E-Shah. Mrs Ruth Hughes awarded the bitch CC to Chris and Julie Amoo's Sadé Solace, who also won BIS.

Am Ch Sumava's Haidalla at Sumahari gained her British title at the Hound Association under judge Len Hitch. Margaret Niblock, awarding CCs for the last time, awarded the dog CC to Hazel and Derek Arris' Ch Sharazah Sir Vivor.

The breed CC record holder and first Afghan ever to win BIS at Crufts, Ch Montravia Kaskarak Hitari, died aged 10 years.

Further sad losses to the breed were the deaths of Joe Dryden-Bell, co-owner of the Balkasha affix, and Fred Severn, Chairman of the Breed Council and co-owner of the Sharikhan Afghans.

Top Winning Afghan was Ch Sharazah Shannon. Top Stud Dog was Ch Barnesmore Imperial Wizard. Top Brood Bitch was Ch Maljan Golden Samarina from Sharazah

1991

Crufts moved out of London to the National Exhibition Centre at Birmingham. Miss Helen Barnes awarded the dog CC to Chardhuri Chianti for Drishaun, owned by Avril and Mike Lancashire and Pam and Steve Sharman. Mrs Anna Paton, judging bitches, awarded the CC to Bob and Ann Savage's Sashkan Me and My Girl. Referee Mr G Farrand awarded BOB to the bitch.

The first May Ball Supermatch was held, which was to turn into an annual event. Organised by the East of England Afghan Club, the CC winners from the previous year were invited to compete in a knockout competition, with the identity of the judges being concealed until the actual event. Preceded by dinner and followed by dancing, the evening was a great success, especially for the overall winner Ch Dalparva Imperial Daughter, owned by Jean Williams.

Two prolific and significant stud dogs, Ch Barnesmore Imperial Wizard and Ch Karnak Shamrock, died.

Liz O'Connor and Terry Thomas' Myways American Dream of Renza, imported into Great Britain from America in 1990, became the first imported male to gain a Kennel Club Junior Warrant.

In Belfast, Finnish Ch Mandrills Myltha Izmar Tragband gained her third CC under judge Sylvia Evans, whilst her quarantine-born son, Izmar Tragband Finnegan, won the dog CC.

Two ladies involved in the breed for many years, Mrs Ivy Atkins (Koh-I-Noor) and Mrs Hazel Kinread (Hazuki), sadly passed away.

Top Winning Afghan was Ch Sharazah Sir Vivor. Top Stud Dog was Ch Saxonmill Black Currant. Top Brood Bitch was Ch/Ir Ch Playfere's Petticoat Wag at Harlextan.

1992

Two of the youngest and most successful latter-day members of the breed judged at Crufts. Miss Jenny Dove (dogs) and Mrs Marita (Gibbs) Rodgers (bitches), awarded the CCs to Eleanor Wilson's Sochera's Indigo Wizard at Jimellree (BOB) and Bob and Ann Savage's Sashkan Me and My Girl. Winner of the May Ball Supermatch was Ron and Peggy Clifford's all-black Ch Ellistine A Star Is Born.

At Leeds Championship Show, Hazel Arris awarded the CC, his first, to the American import Myways American Dream at Renza, who went on to win Reserve in the Hound Group.

Top Winning Afghan was Ch Solomon's Seal from Karnak. Top Stud Dog was Ch Saxonmill Black Currant. Top Brood Bitch was Ch/Ir Ch Playfere's Petticoat Wag at Harlextan.

1993

Mrs Anne Hattrell and Mr John Bland were the judges at Crufts. Dog CC, BOB and Reserve in the Hound Group went to Ch Karaburan Jelly Roll Morton, owned by Mr and Mrs D Boyd and Miss R Boyd, with the bitch CC being awarded to Mr A Margetts Ch Amanrha Miss Ayesha. Both winners gained their titles on the day. Winner of the May Ball Supermatch was Jackie Harnett's Ch Harlextan Mad Mullah.

At the Afghan Hound Society of Northern Ireland, Ch Solomon's Seal from Karnak broke the Breed CC Record by being awarded his 35th CC. Gaining her title at this show was Susan and Alan Charlton and Richard Kirkham's Ch Jhansi Calandre. Sadly, Calandre was to die a few weeks later.

Ch Karaburan Jelly Roll Morton. Photo: David Paton

Ch Solomon's Seal from Karnak, Breed CC Record Holder.
Photo: John M Hope

Peter Luty, judging dogs at the Northern Afghan Hound Club Show, was informed during his Post Graduate class that he had become the father of a baby girl. Quietly delighted, he carried on judging in a professional manner to award the CC to Shirley Harris' Gezancol Smooth Criminal. His co-judge Ellis Hulme gave the bitch CC to Peter and Jean Wright's Brandeswood Harrier.

From Australia, the Kaskarak Kennels imported Calahorra Kasa Blanca at Kaskarak, in whelp to Aust Ch Khandhu Cracker Jack. Four puppies were subsequently born in quarantine.

At the Afghan Hound Association Championship Show Mr and Mrs Keelan's Am/Ir Ch Pahlavi Pandemonium, from Ireland, gained his English title. His sire was the famous Am Ch Pahlavi Puttin' On The Ritz. A few weeks later, Mr and Mrs Keelan's bitch, Am/Ir Ch Anasazi's Testerossa, also American-bred, won her first CC at Bath.

Also at Bath, Liz O'Connor and Terry Thomas' Myways American Dream of Renza, another American bred son of Puttin' On The Ritz, took the CC and BOB.

The first Afghan Hound World Congress was held on the week-end of Windsor Championship Show. It was organised by the Yorkshire Afghan Hound Society, and speakers were invited from all over the world. The event was declared such a resounding success that Dave and Sandy Frei from the USA announced that their country would be delighted to host a second World Congress in 1995.

Sadly, the breed was to lose two more enthusiasts when Mrs Chris Mahn Lloyd and Mr Jade Larden died.

Top Winning Afghan was Ch Sadé Hi-Ranger to Sharazah. Top Stud Dog was Ch Saxonmill Black Currant. Top Brood Bitch was Ch Sadé Solace.

1994

Arthur and Beryl Appleton were scheduled to judge the breed at Crufts, but withdrew from the engagement for personal reasons. Brought forward to take their place, Hazel and Derek

Arris found their BOB in Kulute Miles Ahead, owned by Debbie Coates-Waite. The bitch CC winner was Ian and Mary Fishers' Sadé Regina at Ifmaraf, who was to gain her title later in the year. Winner of the May Ball Supermatch was Gezancol Smooth Criminal.

Ch Saxonmill Black Currant, sire of 10 British champions, sadly died at the age of 12.

Top Winning Afghan was Ch Sadé Hi-Ranger to Sharazah. Top Stud Dog was Ch Izmar Tragband Finnegan. Top Brood Bitch was Obadar Miss You Nights at Bondor.

Ch Izmar Tragband Finnegan.

1995

BOB at Crufts was Ch Sadé Hi-Ranger to Sharazah owned by Hazel and Derek Arris. Winner of the bitch CC was Maria Niedzwiedz and Frances Mallinsons' Karandikar Wicked Lady, who went on to gain her title during the year. The judges were Gloria North (dogs) and Olive Simpson (bitches). The winner of the May Ball Supermatch was Ch Kulute Miles Ahead.

Ch Tejas Conquistador, owned by Mike Gadsby and Anita Doe, began to make her mark in the show ring. Bred by Ivor and Michelle Keelan in Northern Ireland from American lines, Conquistador gained five CCs during the year.

Jackie and Brian Harnett emigrated to Australia, taking with them nine of their hounds. Jackie has bred many top winners carrying the Tianze affix, probably the most notable being Ch Tianze Kalvados.

Ch/ Finnish Ch Mandrill's Myltha Izmar Tragband, dam of Top Sire for 1994–1997 Ch Izmar Tragband Finnegan, sadly died. Also to die was the current Breed CC record holder, Ch Solomon's Seal from Karnak.

Bo Bengtson came over from America to judge both sexes at the Scottish Kennel Club Championship Show and awarded BOB to Nicky and Linda Bishop's Ch Tejas Sahuara. Reserve bitch CC went to her litter sister Ch Tejas Conquistador. In dogs, Jan and Nobby Beckett's Wilbus Kharjeem of Phinjani gained his first CC and became a champion a few months later.

In June, Afghan enthusiasts from 21 countries gathered in San Diego, California for the Second Afghan Hound World Congress, combined with the 59th Specialty Show of the Afghan Hound Club of America. Here the British learnt to whoop and cheer for their favourites, but the idea never really caught on when they returned home. It was a memorable occasion for everyone who made the trip, especially for Liz O'Connor and Terry Thomas of the Renza affix, who took the opportunity to celebrate their marriage.

A great shock to the breed was the sudden death of Miss Margaret Niblock. A truly knowledgeable lady, her Khanabad affix is renowned world-wide. Mrs Joan Pollock of the famous Tarril Afghans and Mrs Vi Gilligan (Shemsuki) also passed away.

Top Winning Afghan was Ch Tejas Conquistador. Top Stud Dog was Ch Izmar Tragband Finnegan. Top Brood Bitch was Amudarya Shushma's Image.

1996

Judges at Crufts were husband and wife Gus and Anne MacDonald, who agreed upon Ch Tejas Conquistador for BOB. The dog CC winner was Ch Wilbus Kharjeem of Phinjani.

In winning her third CC at Afghan Hound Society of Northern Ireland Show, June Leitch's 17½-month-old Khamis Bhi-Candlelight became the youngest Afghan bitch on record to gain a British title.

Ch Tejas Conquistador, handled by co-owner Mike Gadsby, became unstoppable. Having won five Hound Groups and BIS at Belfast and Darlington, she also took the top spot at the May Ball Supermatch

The Afghan Hound Breed Council organised its first seminar, Afghan '96, which was attended by around 150 enthusiasts. The British speakers and panelists covered a variety of subjects. Ann Adams presented her collection of early slides and John and Jo Ereira showed their excellent video Champions All.

The Southern Afghan Club celebrated its Golden Jubilee year in style, culminating in December at the championship show. Thirty-six champions entered the Champions Parade and, from the 350 exhibits, judges Cindy Heal and Jo Newman gave the BIS award to Ch Wilbus Kharjeem of Phinjani.

A number of long-standing devotees of the breed were to sadly leave us: Mrs Molly Sharpe of the Chaman Afghans; Dennis McCarthy MBE and owner of the Pooghan affix; Mrs Helen Morgan, President of the Northern Afghan Hound Society and co-owner of the Kushra affix; and Mr Bill Eccles, who owned the Mansarovar Afghans with his late wife Enid.

Top Winning Afghan was Ch Tejas Conquistador. Top Stud Dog was Ch Izmar Tragband Finnegan. Top Brood Bitch was Amudarya Shushma's Image.

1997

Another husband and wife team, Dan and Lesley-Anne James, officiated at Crufts and Ch Tejas Conquistador won BOB for the second year running. Paula Woodward's Sashkan Incognito was Lesley-Anne's choice for the dog CC.

The Northern Afghan Hound Society celebrated its Golden Jubilee Year. The judges at the Easter Championship Show were two long-standing supporters of the Club, Bill Hall and Arthur Hedges, who awarded BIS to Hazel and Derek Arris' Cotton Velvet to Sharazah.

The Yorkshire Afghan Hound Society invited two overseas judges for its championship show. Lotte Jorgensen from Denmark and Betsy Hufnagel from the United Staes of America agreed upon Ch Tejas Conquistador for their top award. Lotte, judging dogs, awarded the dog CC to Roberta Hall's home-bred Ch Saxonmill Rum Tum Tigger.

Commemorating its 70th Anniversary and 50th Championship Show, the Afghan Hound Association celebrated in style with many 'specials' on offer to class winners. BIS was won by Saxonmill Jennyanydots, owned by Roberta Hall.

In June, around 200 enthusiasts gathered in Elsinore, Denmark for the third Afghan Hound World Congress, held to coincide with the Afghan Hound Club of Denmark's Silver

Jubilee Show and the European Winners Show in Copenhagen. Many people stayed on a further day to join the Danes in Midsummer's Eve celebrations.

Leeds Championship Show proved to be a great day for the Irish when, for the first time ever, both CCs were awarded to a Southern Irish bred litter brother and sister, Yarabis Jeddah and Ir Ch Yarabis Java, owned and bred by Brian and Zita Fogarty.

Devotee of our breed since 1943, Miss Eileen Snelling (Khorrassan) was to pass away. Shortly afterwards, Mrs Connie Crowther (Karakuli) lost her battle against a long illness. Sadly, the Western Afghan Hound Club lost both its Patron, Maurice Edge, and its Hon Vice President, Bryan Courtney (Zarheid) during the year.

Top Winning Afghan was Ch Tejas Conquistador. Top Stud Dog was Ch Izmar Tragband Finnegan. Top Brood Bitch was Amudarya Shushma's Image.

1998

The services of the Referee, Zena Thorn-Andrews, were required at Crufts when judges Jean Severn (dogs) and Jo Holden-Ereira (bitches) could not agree on BOB. Zena chose Diana Greenfield's Saqlawi Standing Ovation who that day both became a champion and

Ch Tejas Conquistador.
Photo: John M Hope

Ch Saqlawi Standing Ovation winning Hound Group at Crufts.
Photo: Carol Ann Johnson

went on to win the Hound Group. Best Dog was Roberta Hall's Ch Saxonmill Rum Tum Tigger.

Winner of the May Ball Supermatch was Ch Wilbus Kharjeem of Phinjani.

In April, Drishaun Desdemona, owned by Avril and Mike Lancashire, made British breed history by producing the the first Afghan litter to be born by Artificial Insemination (AI) in Great Britain, using frozen semen from Am Ch Gazon Say What You Mean.

Also in April there was a double win for Roberta Hall at WELKS, when half-brother and half-sister Saxonmill Currant Bun and Ch Saxonmill Jennyanydots won both CCs under judge Colin Dann.

At the Scottish Kennel Club Show the bitch CC record was broken when Ch Tejas Conquistador won her 22nd CC. Her 23rd soon followed at Blackpool, under judge Ellis Hulme.

During 1997 The Kennel Club introduced a new system of gaining Junior Warrant points. While more difficult to attain, they now result in the winner gaining a Kennel Club Stud Book Number. Pat and Robert Latimer and Christine Campbell's Aberkal Reflection of Love at Zharook became the first Afghan to win a JW under the new system.

In May, the Western Afghan Hound Club celebrated its 30th Anniversary with a 'Pearl Party', where past and present members gathered to share memories and reminisce fondly over absent friends and hounds.

Preparations are under way for the year 2000, with all the breed clubs planning special events to commemorate the millennium. The AHA and Midland Afghan Hound Club have invited overseas specialists to officiate at their championship shows, while other clubs are all planning something extra special. The year 2000 is guaranteed to be a great year for Afghan enthusiasts world-wide to visit Great Britain.

To end on a sad note: long-standing devotees who sadly passed away this year were Richard and Maureen Barlow (Taiwara), Cynthia Pearce (Ghanistan) and Dorothea Edge.

And today...

Now the Afghan Hound is no longer a fashionable or marketable product, and registrations have, thankfully, remained below the thousand mark since 1982. Considering the damage that was done to the breed as a result of the boom years, my view is that we have come through better than most and are once again on an even keel. Whilst it was a nightmare at the time, the outcome could have been much, much worse.

As to the future, the wind of change is once again upon the British Afghan and the next decade is set to become yet another testing time for the breed. Dogs carrying foreign bloodlines are coming into Britain in ever-increasing numbers, imported by breeders wishing to emulate a type and style of dog they have admired overseas. Whilst such imports have always been available to breeders, never have there been so many, or of such variation, as at the present time. Artificial Insemination (AI) techniques are constantly improving, and it will be extremely interesting to see how this ever-extending gene pool is utilised.

Having said that, there are those staunchly opposed to foreign stock who intend to remain firmly with the British bloodlines, preferring the type and style of dog that these lines produce. Such differing aims and viewpoints make it difficult to predict the future course of the breed in Great Britain. This situation has already been addressed by breeders in many other countries and an account of the progression of the breed world-wide can be found in chapter 4.

Another gradual but significant change is in how the dogs are presented for the show ring. British enthusiasts are renowned the world over for growing coats in which every hair is carefully treasured. Judges visiting our shores from overseas, without exception, remark that our dogs carry far too much coat and a cleaner outline would be preferred. So much so, that presentation skills acquired from our overseas counterparts are beginning to alter the appearance of the breed in our show rings. Whilst some dogs are still shown with natural untouched coats, many have had subtle encounters with the stripping stone and thinning scissors as British exhibitors become more adventurous.

Foreign imports

Quarantine

Pressure is increasing upon the British Government to replace quarantine with vaccinations, blood tests and approved methods of identification in respect of domestic pets coming from countries within the European Union (EU). In terms of modern scientific advances our present laws are extremely out of date, and the stress caused to animals and owners is unjustifiable. When quarantine was introduced no other methods of rabies control were available but, in recent years, vaccines that are virtually 100% effective have been developed. Great Britain and the Republic of Ireland are the only EU countries still using quarantine and they impose stricter regulations than any other island nations in the world. It is ludicrous that a dog on an aeroplane trip from Jersey (Channel Isles) to England, if the flight is diverted to France, can end up in quarantine for six months upon landing in England without having left the confines of the aeroplane. There are no known plans to relax quarantine for domestic animals coming from countries outside the EU, whether the countries be rabies-free or not.

Importing a dog through quarantine is really quite straightforward and the six months spent in confinement will pass by trouble-free if you have first done some research and chosen your quarantine kennel with care. If you are bringing in a puppy, concern about its coat is not as important as the size of the housing and exercise area. Depending upon the time of year and the climate from which the dog is coming, adequate heating must be provided, with the adjoining run preferably covered to prevent the dog from getting too wet. While many breeds do not require much warmth, this cannot be said of a young Afghan, brought in on its own. The young Afghan would stand around getting wet, for fear of missing anything, rather than going into the warmth of its kennel.

Socialisation with the kennel staff is almost as important as warmth, and there should be interesting things happening around to prevent boredom setting in. Because the growing puppy will not be getting much exercise, it will quickly become overweight if not fed on a diet that is high in nutrients, low in carbohydrates.

Choosing a kennel close to your home can have its advantages, in that you can visit regularly and play with your dog, but if a kennel with an excellent reputation happens not to be on your doorstep, don't be afraid to place your puppy (and your trust) in this establishment. The welfare of your Afghan Hound for the next six months will be in the hands of the kennel staff, so they must have your total confidence.

Bringing in a show dog over the age of 12 months has an added stipulation, in that a member of the kennel staff must be competent to maintain its coat. Alternatively, some kennels allow you to use their facilities to bath and groom the dog when you visit. Always check first, as some kennels forward wonderful brochures stating what they will do, but fail miserably when requests are made. Once again, it is wise to be guided by recommendations from exhibitors who have successfully imported a dog of a long-coated breed.

A bitch in whelp requires constant supervision by the kennel owners or their staff, not only throughout the period of whelping but for the first few critical days following the birth of the puppies. Afghan bitches giving birth for the first time in strange surroundings can panic and require a watchful eye if the venture is to be a success. Puppies born in quarantine can be released once they have been separated from their dam for a period of two weeks (usually at around eight weeks old), but Mum must remain to complete the six months duration.

The Balai Directive

Members of the European Union are urging Britain to repeal the quarantine laws on animals from their countries, and it would seem that the Balai Directive has been devised to meet them halfway. Whatever the reasons, this would seem to be a step in the right direction and makes far more sense than putting an animal through six months' quarantine. It is also less expensive. However, it relates only to *traded animals* which, according to Ministry of Agriculture, Food and Fisheries (MAFF) regulations, means dogs or cats that are the subjects of commercial transactions, not family pets.

The Directive contains five requirements that must be met before a dog can be brought into the United Kingdom, the most important being that the animal must have remained on the premises of its birth until the day it is exported, the only exception being for a visit to a vet. In effect, this means that the dog is undergoing quarantine in its country of birth. It must be inoculated against distemper and rabies and be microchipped for identification purposes. The rabies inoculation cannot be administered before a puppy is three months old, with a blood test showing an acceptable level of protection against rabies carried out six months after the initial rabies vaccination. This means that a dog will be at least nine months old before it can be exported. The breeders in the country of origin are required to sign a statement guaranteeing that the dog has never been in contact with any form of wildlife, and it must be transported in a container recognised for the purpose.

MAFF must be notified of the import at least 24 hours before the dog arrives in Great Britain. On arrival, it must be taken directly to the address on the import form and remain there until a MAFF vet visits to take a blood sample (usually within 48 hours of arrival). The blood sample is then tested within the next 10 days, during which time the dog cannot be moved. If the rabies antibody level is correct, the dog can then be taken out.

It is wise to ask your local MAFF office to inform Customs at the point of entry, as there are some officials at ports and airports who have never heard of the Balai Directive. Should any of the regulations not be fully complied with, the dog must go straight into quarantine until the matter is resolved. It is also necessary to have a microchip reader available, as the MAFF vet must be able to read the implanted chip to prove identification.

At present, a dog imported from outside Europe, or one that is not still living at the establishment in which it was born, will still be subjected to quarantine.

Ch Mandrills Myltha Izmar Tragband.
Photo: Lewis Baucutt

Influential imports into Great Britain – 1978 to the present day

Australia: A number of dogs have been imported from Australia, including several from the Calahorra kennels of Wendye and Stuart Slatyer. Probably the most notable of these is Calahorra Kasa Blanca at Kaskarak, imported in whelp to Aust Ch Khandhu Cracker Jack in 1993. Her four quarantine-born puppies included Avril and Mike Lancashire's Kaskarak Alice Springs, who has to date won two CCs and four RCCs.

In 1995, Graham and Christine Parsell imported Dzum My Girl Lollipop at Harlextan from the Dzum kennel of Peter and Kathy Frost, and to date she has won one CC and two RCCs.

Denmark: In 1986, Bob and Ann Savage, in partnership with Jillian Knight-Messenger, imported Dk Ch Boxadan Junior Jumper from the kennels of Lotte Jorgensen. He was to sire five British champions. From the same kennel some years later came Boxadan Give Me A Break at Benatone, imported in accordance with the Balai Directive. To date he has won one CC for his owners, Sarah Jackson and Anita Doe and sired the CC-winning Sumahari Starturn.

Finland: In 1983, Isobell Dyke imported from Finland the litter brother and sister Tuohi-Tikan Luoti at Mirsamir and Tuohi-Tikan Loiske at Mirsamir. The bitch gained her title at two years of age.

In 1988, Fin Ch Mandrills Myltha Izmar Tragband was imported in whelp to Int Ch Choice Be A Pepper, by Anita Doe, John Watson and Andrew Brace. Her quarantine-born puppies included Ch Izmar Tragband Finnegan (Top Stud Dog 1994–1997), Ch Izmar Tragband Finnishing School, Izmar Tragband Finlandia (two CCs) and Izmar Tragband Finnishing Touch (one RCC), who went on to become the dam of Ch Saqlawi Standing Ovation and Saqlawi Secret Passion at Wendells (one CC). Myltha also gained her British title in 1991.

Punapaulan Into Araki, owned by Mr K and Mrs A Sinclair, became a British champion in 1997 – the first Afghan imported via the Balai Directive to gain a title. More recently, Neliapilan Aave Maria at Phelezzi was imported through quarantine by Diana Greenfield. To date she has won one CC, two RCCs and a Junior Warrant.

Germany: In 1978, Dan and Lesley-Ann James imported from West Germany Kunta Kinte von Katwiga from Jahadi and Nausikaa's Djamani from Jahadi. Mated together, they produced Ch Jahadi Achill, and their lines are behind several British champions.

Italy: In 1985, Hermione Bruton returned from Italy, bringing with her Ch/It Ch Joe Mirzabad, who gained his title in 1986.

Spain: In 1986, Sue and Mick Virgo imported the litter brother and sister Sumava's Hdjab at Sumahari and Sumava's Haidalla at Sumahari (see picture overleaf). Haidalla won a RCC before going to the United States, where she quickly gained her American title. Upon her return to England she won four CCs and was then mated to Ch Sharazah Sir Vivor to produce Ch Sumahari Starlight.

Sweden: In 1979 two litter-mates were imported from Sweden. The dog, Amudarya El Khyrias Y'Made in Sweden, was imported by Anna Paton, and the bitch, El Khyrias Y'Swedish Girl at Saqlawi, by June Davies. Y'Made in Sweden sired Ch Amudarya Shh Y'Know Who and Amudarya Shafi (one CC). In 1990, June Davies imported another litter brother and sister. The male, El Khyrias Veni-Vedi-Vici at Saqlawi, went on to sire the litter sisters Ch Saqlawi Standing Ovation and Saqlawi Secret Passion at Wendells (one CC).

United States of America: In 1984, the Harcourt-Brown family imported Coastwind Apphia at Kharisar from Richard Sousa and Mike Dunham. She gained a CC before producing Ch Kharisar Rhia at Cloudside, Kharisar Tobias (one CC) and Kharisar Tickety Boo at Sacheverell (one CC).

In 1990, Liz O'Connor and Terry Thomas brought in Myways American Dream of Renza, who was to win two CCs, both with BOB and Reserve in the Hound Group. Unfortunately, he was forced to retire at four years of age because of a spinal injury.

On their return to Northern Ireland from the United States, Ivor and Michelle Keelan brought with them several American champions, the most notable being Ch/Ir/Am Ch Anasazi's Testarossa and Ch/Ir/Am Ch Pahlavi Pandemonium who, when mated together, produced Ch Tejas Conquistador (Top Afghan 1995–1997) and Ch Tejas Sahuara.

Ch/It Ch Joe Mirzabad. Photo: John M Hope

Ch/Am Ch Sumava's Haidalla at Sumahari. Photo: Sumahari

Pam and Stuart Mottershaw have brought in several dogs from the United States, the most successful being Am Ch K'Amour Seafarer Summerwind BBE, who gained her British title in 1997.

Am/Can Ch Trinity's Backdraft Paladin to Freecloud was imported by Mark Cocozza in 1994 and has produced several winning youngsters, including one CC winner and two RCC winners.

In 1995, Fabelhaft Could It Be Majic at Harlextan, bred by James Dalton and Cindy Chandler, was imported by Graham and Christine Parsell. She currently has three RCCs, the second of which was won at Crufts 1998,

In 1997, aunt and niece Am Ch Seistan's Hearts Afire to Freecloud and Fabelhaft With All My Heart to Khamis were imported by Mark Cocozza and June Leitch respectively. Hearts Afire gained her British title at Leeds Championship Show 1998 and All My Heart has one CC and two RCCs to date.

chapter three
Contemporary British Kennels

A List of Champions 1927–1997, with their breeding and owners, can be found in Appendix B (page 212).

England, Scotland and Wales

Amshura

Sylvia Evans became acquainted with the breed whilst working in Canada in the mid-1960s and acquired her first Afghan, Alyshan Francis Can, upon her return. A second male, Amudarya Shura (by Ch Amudarya The Pagan) joined the household in 1972 and was later to sire Ch Amudarya Khashushma. From Shura's first litter in 1978 to Bowentree Anastasia, a line-bred Bletchingley bitch, Sylvia selected Soames, alias Alexiev of Amshura, who, apart from winning well in the show ring, underwent successful surgical treatment for Laryngeal Paralysis at the age of 11 years. Sylvia's articles on this subject have since helped many owners to recognise the early stages of this debilitating condition.

Ch Amshura Nijinsky. Photo: David Paton

Soames' litter sister, Kalinka of Bowentree, was mated to Amudarya Shafi, the union producing many winners for the kennel, including Alice Faye (one CC) and Sylvia's own Madam Gaye who, when mated to Ch Izmars Tragband Finnegan, produced the home-bred Ch Amshura Nijinsky and the CC-winning bitch Angelina Ballerina. As one of the weekly Breed Columnists for *Our Dogs*, Sylvia keeps Afghan enthusiasts up to date with news and forthcoming events.

Amudarya

Anna Paton founded her kennel in 1958 with Shahzadi of Aryana (sired by Ch Yussef of Carloway), who became the granddam of Ch Ranjitsinghi of Jagai and Ch Rasta of Jagai. In 1966 Anna acquired Mikhala of Moonswift and mated her in 1969 to Horningsea Aramis. From the resulting litter Anna chose the future Ch Amudarya The Pagan. When mated to Bondor Moonmist in 1971 Mikhala also produced Ch Amudarya Khala. Mikhala was granddam to Ch Amudarya Shalar (Top Stud Dog 1983–1985) and Ch Amudarya Shastri. In 1975, Anna selected a puppy sired by The Pagan out of a bitch directly descended from Shahzadi – and Ch Shushma from Amudarya gained her title in 1982.

In 1979 Anna imported El Khyrias Y'Made In Sweden and, although never shown, when mated to Ch Shushma from Amudarya, he sired Ch Amudarya Shh Y'Know Who and the CC-winning

(Left to right) Ch Amudarya Shushila, Amudarya Shushma's Image and Amudarya Shaffire. Photo: David Paton

Amudarya Shafi and Amudarya Shakuntallah. Ch Shh Y'Know Who had one litter by Ch Amudarya Shalar and a bitch, Amudarya Shaffire, was later mated to Amshura The Tsarevitch to produce Amudarya Shushma's Image. When mated to Ch Karnak Mulberry, Shaffire also produced Ch Amudarya Thanks A Million. Also in 1979, Amudarya Khashma was mated to Amudarya Shura (litter brother to Ch Amudarya Shalar) and produced Ch Amudarya Khashushma, who gained her title in 1983. Amudarya Shushma's Image was mated to Ch Izmar Tragband Finnegan in 1992 to complement the El Khyrias lines and the resulting litter included the litter-mates Ch Amudarya Shushila, Ch Amudarya Shashkia and Ch Amudarya Sholti of Zadal.

Badakshan
Ann and Ron Adams bought their first puppy in 1955, Ron first having seen the breed at boarding kennels in 1938. Salterns Sheba and another bitch, Rahane of Ladysmyle, became the foundation bitches of the kennel. Rahane, mated to Ch Khanabad Azravi of Vishnu, gave them their first champion in 1962: Ch Badakshan Rani.

A descendant of Ch Rani, mated to Ch Khanabad White Warrior, produced Ch Badakshan Pink Pearl, who was to become the foundation of the Palamedees kennel. Ch Pink Pearl's daughter by Badakshan Amber Azravi in turn produced Ch Badakshan Persimmon in 1986. After a long absence from the show ring, Ann has recently returned with two promising puppies.

Ann is Patron of the Afghan Hound Association.

Bondor
The Bondor kennel was started in the 1950s by Allan Brooks and Eric Swallow. They loved the Carloway and Horningsea Afghans and purchased their foundation bitch, Yazeena of Carloway, from Sheila Devitt (Gilleney). Yazeena, mated to the imported dog Ch Wazir of

Ch Bondor Lilac Wine.

Desertaire, produced their first home-bred champion, Ch Bondor Serenade (Top Afghan 1964). Their second champion, Ch Bondor Lezah, was Top Afghan in 1966 and won BOB at Crufts in the same year. Ch Serenade had only one litter, by Ch/Ir Ch Moonraker of Moonswift, which included the litter-mates Ch Bondor Kumari Khanum (Bitch CC Crufts 1969), Ch Bondor Dera Ghazi Khan (Top Afghan 1970 and joint Top Afghan 1971) and Ch Bondor Azim Khan (BOB Crufts 1970, with Ghazi RCC).

Bondor Cinnamon (Ch Horningsea Mustaph Ata ex Ch Bondor Lezah), when mated to Ch Horningsea Tiger's Eye, produced Ch Bondor Barbarella (BOB Crufts 1973). Cinnamon's sister, Ch Bondor Sayonara of Fiazabad, and brother, Bondor Moonmist, won both CCs at Richmond in 1970, with Sayonara taking the Group. Moonmist won two CCs and proved very popular at stud, one of his daughters being Ch Amudarya Khala, Top Winning Hound All Breeds. Cinnamon also produced Ch Bondor Lady Marika (by Ch Dera Ghazi). Ch Marika's sister, Bondor Belle of the Ball, mated to Ch Sacheverell Zukwala, produced Ch Bondor Gypsy Casanova. Cinnamon was also mated to Ch Azim Khan, producing Ch Bondor Shades of Serenade and Bondor Naughty Marietta, who were both mated to Ch Karnak Shamrock. Ch Shades produced the litter-mates Ch Bondor Some Like It Hot and Ch Bondor Hot Gossip of Karandikar, while Marietta produced Ch Bondor Lilac Wine .

Allan moved to South Africa in 1985 and, on his return to England in the late 1980s, Stuart Smith joined the partnership. Allan continued his line by mating The Charmer of Bondor (Ch Barnesmore Imperial Wizard ex Ch Bondor Lilac Wine) to Obadar Miss You Nights at Bondor, who was sired by Ch Bondor Lilac Wine's litter brother, producing the litter-mates Ch Bondor I Am What I Am, Bondor Maggie May (two CCs) and Bondor Play Misty For Me (one CC). A repeat mating produced Ch Bondor It's A Kinda Majic and Bondor Matinee Idol (one CC). To date the Bondor kennel has produced 15 British and 17 overseas champions.

Allan is President of the North Eastern Afghan Hound Society.

Calamayor

Thereséa Grist's kennel was founded with Ch Palamedees Anaja of Calamayor who, when mated to Ch Barnesmore Imperial Wizard in 1986, produced the first home-bred champion, Ch Calamayor Ra, and his sister Calamayor Isis (one CC). Success followed when Ch Anaja was mated to Ch Ellistine A Star Is Born in 1990, to produce Ch Calamayor Thor and his brother Ch Calamayor Glyndwr.

Davlen

Helen Barnes and Father David Ford formed their partnership in 1954 and made up their first champion, Fantasia of Carloway, in 1957. They also had Winomara of Carloway, who is behind many of the Davlen champions, including Ch Aryana Shalym, later exported to Canada. In 1964 they acquired Ch Takkabor Tiaga, who sired Copper Coin of Davlen (later exported to Denmark), Ch Shireen B'Har of Tarril and Ch Kismati Khan of Tarril. Ch Kismati's daughter, Khandi B'Har of Tarril, produced three home-bred champions, one of whom was Ch Hajubah of Davlen, David's favourite dog.

In 1970, Gloria Haywood joined Davlen and successfully handled Ch Davlen Flame of the Forest (later exported to Norway), Ch Davlen Tijuana Silk, Ch Davlen the Godfather, Ch Davlen Tamarisk and her own Ch Davlen Petite Etoile to their titles. Gloria also owned Davlen Master Of The Game (two CCs).

Helen is President of the Midland Afghan Hound Club.

Drishaun

Following the dispersal of the Landhavi kennels and partnership in 1983, Mike Lancashire formed a new partnership with Avril (Peary), whose Avibar kennel was founded in 1972, and together they created the Drishaun kennels. Two dogs founded the kennel: Severndene Ghostbuster for Drishaun (one RCC) (Ch Barnesmore The Baron of Landhavi ex Ch Severndene Marionette of Landhavi) and his half-brother Chardhuri Chianti for Drishaun (Ch Barnesmore The Baron of Landhavi ex Severndene Spellbinder of Chardhuri), who gained his title in 1991. Ch Chianti sired

Ch Chardhuri Chianti for Drishaun (aged 10).

three very typical champion daughters, Ch Karandikar Wicked Lady and the home-bred Ch Drishaun Delores and Ch Drishaun Danielle. The litter sisters Drishaun Desdemona and Ch Delores both have successful children, including the currently campaigned Drishaun D'Licious (one CC) (Ch Dalparva Regal Raider of Hashtana ex Desdemona) and Ch Drishaun Djudgement Day for Bichoux (Zharook Scarlet Pimpernel ex Ch Delores).

In 1993, Mike and Avril purchased the quarantine-born brindle bitch Kaskarak Alice Springs (Aust Ch Khandhu Cracker Jack ex Calahorra Kasa Blanca at Kaskarak (Australian import)) with the intention of blending her new bloodlines with the tightly line-bred Drishaun stock. A consistent winner, Alice has already gained two CCs.

Gardwright

Christian Gardiner acquired his first Afghan in 1972 from the Countess de Melville, who was a regular client at the Vidal Sassoon Salon where he has worked since 1969. Later, he purchased Dietrich from Alyshan from Carole Walkden. Dietrich, mated to Ch Amudarya Shalar, produced one surviving puppy who became Ch Gardwright Damascus from Shechem and in turn went on to sire Ch Shechem Santinella, Ch Shanshu Casa Biere from Khados and Ch Gardwright Gloria. Ch Gardwright Bibi at Shanshu gained her title in 1984, followed by Ch Zoreba Indian at Gardwright in 1992. The same year, a son of Gardwright Grace, Ch Sochera's Indigo Wizard at Jimellree, gained his title. Grace also produced a champion daughter, Ch Sochera's Diva from Gardwright.

Gilari

Jill and Clari Cross founded their kennel in 1971. Their first litter was born in 1973 from an Isfahan-bred bitch, Kalafrana Kaldora. Later, they acquired Sana's Bewitching Star of Gilari (Ch Tuttlebees Stargazer ex Ch Tuttlebees Moonstar) and Sana's Moon Wizard of Gilari. Bewitching Star had two litters and, from the second, to Ch Barnesmore The Baron of Landhavi, they retained Gilari Goldstrike, who gained his title in 1989, becoming their first champion. In 1994 they purchased Rhazmakh Medeia of Gilari (Ch Dalparva Mr Bojangles ex Shimalma Genevieve of Rhazmakh)(one CC).

Harlextan

Graham and Christine Parsell produced their first home-bred champion, Harlextan Dick Deadeye (Ch Sacheverell Zukwala ex Takabbor Joao), in 1973. In 1976, Ch Sacheverell Zukwala was used again, this time on Harlextan Mad Margaret, to produce Ch Harlextan Mad Miranda, who gained her title in 1981. Mad Margaret (mated to Ch Amudarya Shalar in 1978) also produced Ch Harlextan The Mad Nun. In 1982, they purchased Playfere's Petticoat Wag at Harlextan (Ch Karnak Shamrock ex Ch Harlextan Mad Miranda) who gained her title before she was two years old. Ch Petticoat Wag went on to produce Harlextan The Ice Man (two CCs) by Ch Montravia Kaskarak Hitari, and the litter-mates Ch Harlextan Mad Mullah, Ch Harlextan Padishah, Ch Harlextan Mad Marsala and Ch Harlextan Piara at Saxonmill by Ch Saxonmill Black Currant.

In 1995 they imported from Australia Dzum My Girl Lollipop at Harlextan (Aust Ch Dzum The Bees Knees ex Aust Ch Dzum Goodbye Lollipop) (one CC and two RCCs) and from the United States the following year, Fabelhaft Could It Be Majic at Harlextan (Am Ch Tifarah's Hi-Flying Victory ex Am Ch Applause Majic Show) (three RCCs).

Graham is President of the Birmingham Afghan Hound Club.

Hashtana

Sam Forrest saw his first Afghan at an agricultural show in 1969. At the time he was still living at home with his parents who, being farmers, would only permit dogs 'that could earn their keep', such as sheepdogs and terriers. He purchased his first Afghan, Sasmar Megan Estelle, in 1976 and, when mated to Severndene Starbound, she produced the kennel's first two champions: Ch Hashtana Lucy Limelite and Ch Hashtana Red Alert (picture overleaf). He then purchased a male puppy who gained his title in 1993, becoming Ch Dalparva Regal Raider of Hashtana (Ch Barnesmore Imperial Wizard ex Ch Landhavi Love Bug of Dalparva).

Ch Hashtana Red Alert. Photo: Lewis Baucutt

The kennel has remained within British bloodlines so far, and the current home-bred Ch Hashtana Red Revolution gained his title in 1995.

Isfahan

Joan Wonnacott saw her first Afghan in Plymouth in 1958 and purchased Bletchingley Sarhang from Peggy Riley in 1959. Her son Richard Jamrozik showed Sarhang in Junior Handling classes, demonstrating an early interest in the breed that has continued to this day.

From her foundation bitch Helmunds Cherade (mainly Khorrassan breeding) Joan has bred selectively to maintain a distinctive type over the years.

Although never heavily campaigned, Isfahan dogs have been successful in the show ring, with Ahmagh of Isfahan winning the Dog CC at Crufts in 1977 and Ch Isfahan Feisal Ibn Sadiq of Kushbudar gaining his title in 1984. Isfahan Hurree Babu and Isfahan Zardalu Maleke took both CCs at the Afghan Hound Association Championship Show in 1990, this win giving Maleke her title.

Joan is Vice President of the AHA.

Izmar

Anita Doe started in the early 1960s with Lotos of Khamora and later purchased Miyasht Empress (Horningsea Aramis ex Ch Ueda of Carloway), who gained her title in 1970 to become Anita's first champion. Mated to Ch Hajubah of Davlen in 1972, Empress produced the first home-bred champion, Ch Izmars Cherokee of Davlen, and in a second litter she produced Ch Izmar Enchanting Empress, by Ch

Ch Isfahan Zardalu Maleke.

Alyshan Hassan Shabbah. Ch Enchanting Empress, mated to Ch Kharisar Kharibh Khan, produced Ch Portia from Izmar, who made history by producing 18 puppies when mated to Ch Kharisar Nicomedes of Phinjani. Two of these puppies gained their titles, becoming

Ch Izmars Alibech and Ch Izmars Lucrezia. Ch Kharisar Kharibh Khan also produced Ch Izmars Rebecca when mated to Izmars Hannah. Izmars Empress Messalina, mated to her half-brother Izmars Jerimiah, produced Ch Izmars Dizzy Dolly, who also excelled on the race track.

More recently, in partnership with Andrew Brace and John Watson, Anita imported Finnish Ch Mandrills Myltha Izmar Tragband in whelp to Int Ch Choice Be A Pepper, and Myltha gained her British title in 1991. Her son, Ch Izmar Tragband Finnegan, was Top Hound Stud in 1994 and Top Afghan Stud 1994–1997. Ch Myltha was also the dam of Ch Izmar Tragband Finnishing School, Izmar Tragband Finlandia (two CCs) and Izmar Tragband Choice Finnish, who in turn produced Ch Izmar by Moonlight of Meredith and NZ Ch Izmar Tamasar Finnesse, by Ch Saxonmill Black Currant.

NZ Ch Izmar Tamasar Finnesse.

In 1991 Tejas Conquistador was purchased and, after producing two litters to Ch Finnegan, she began her show career in partnership with Mike Gadsby and was the Top Winning Afghan in 1995–1997. In 1998 she became the Bitch CC record holder. Her daughter, Ch Izmar Now Or Never, gained her title in 1998.

Jahadi
Dan and Lesley-Ann James founded this kennel in 1961. Their first Afghan, Jahadi Ghalaxy of Carloway (Watsatari of Carloway ex Crown Crest Zardeeka (imported)), carried both American and English bloodlines. Several litters and Afghans later, their desire to bring back Ghazni bloodlines and type, which had disappeared in the 1930s, to England became reality, when in 1978 they imported from West Germany Kunta Kinte von Katwiga and Nausikaa's Djamani. Mated together, their son became Ch Jahadi Achill, who was used selectively at stud to protect his bloodline. Successful offspring included Ch Jahadi Bosch at Wilbus, Ch Padaki Qala-E-Shah and Ch Palamedees Kallista. Several kennels have incorporated these unique lines into their breeding programmes.

In 1991, Dan and Lesley-Anne purchased the adult dog Harlextan Padishah, who quickly became a United Kingdom champion, adding to the Irish title he already carried.

Jhansi
Richard Kirkham owned his first Afghan in the early 1970s, but it was not until several years later that he acquired the bitch who was to be the foundation stone of the kennel: Moonswift Mitsouko (Ch Moonswift Moonglade ex Ch Millionairess of Moonswift). She gained her title in 1982 and, when mated to Ch Karnak Shamrock, produced the kennel's first home-bred champion, Ch Jhansi Indiana Opium, and SA Ch Jhansi Royal Performance.

A sister, Jhansi Chinah Rose, produced Ch Zoreba Indian at Gardwright and Ir Ch Zoreba Nodashti, from her mating with Ch Kaskarak Kochise, and a further brother, Jhansi Avalon, sired Ch Shadia Kimara from Marnadee.

Ch Opium produced Ch Jhansi Calandre and Ir Ch Jhansi Armani in her first litter to Karachi Khan (litter brother to Ch Mahogonny Moon of Jhansi), and a later litter, to Ch Chardhuri Chianti for Drishaun, produced Ch Drishaun Danielle.

Alongside Mitsouko, Richard was also campaigning Khorlynton Keltic Karibou (Ch Amudarya Shalar ex Ch/Ir Ch Khorlynton Kirjatharba). This bitch had an incredible show career, winning her first CC at less than 12 months old and gaining her title before the age of two, culminating with BOB at Crufts in 1982. Unfortunately, she never produced puppies, but Richard was able to keep her lines through her sister who, when mated to Ch Barnesmore Imperial Wizard, produced Ch Mahogonny Moon of Jhansi (co-owned with Bob Allison). In 1997, Ch Jhansi Touched By Magic (Davlen Master Of The Game ex Jhansi Magic Noire) gained her title.

Karaburan

Dennis, Elizabeth and Rose-Marie Boyd founded their kennel in 1979 with Rudbeckia Karah Bazzman at Karaburan. Mated in 1985 to Toptani's Barracuda of Karaburan, she produced Karaburan Tokyo Rose (one CC) and Karaburan Raving Red Rita. Rita was mated to Ch Viscount Grant in 1987 and the resulting litter included Karaburan Billie Holiday (one CC). Karaburan Cleopatra (Toptani's Barracuda of Karaburan ex Sacheverell Anouska) was mated to Ch Saxonmill Black Currant in 1989, producing Ch Karaburan Pretty Boy Floyd of Shirobana, and a repeat mating in 1991 produced Ch Karaburan Tina Turner.

Sacheverell Anouska was mated again in 1990 to Karaburan Count Baisey, brother to Billie Holiday, and produced Ch/Ir Ch Karaburan Jelly Roll Morton (BOB Crufts 1993 and Reserve in the Hound Group). A repeat mating in 1991 produced Ch Karaburan Be Be King, co-owned with Mr and Mrs Woodward.

Karnak

Keith and Brenda Thornton owned their first Afghan in 1963: Caliph of Kushra. In 1971, Keith met Mr and Mrs Tate, who owned Pandora of Khyber (Mandith Patriot of Khyber (United States import) ex Ormerod Sherrendale Tara), a bitch he handled and later owned. Pandora was mated to Ch Koolaba Horningsea Eboni Earl and in 1975 she produced Ch Oregano Tarragon of Karnak and Ch Oregano Angellica of Sharazah. Amongst his many awards, Tarragon won two Groups, 18 CCs, 17 BOBs and the Final of the Pedigree Chum Veteran Stakes. His champion progeny include Ch Ashihna Raoul (Hound Group Crufts 1995) and the litter-mates Ch Xerkhan Apollo, Ch Xerkhan Aurora of Taltonia and Ch Xerkhan Adonis. Ch Raoul's son, Ch Solomon's Seal from Karnak, is the present CC breed record holder.

Ch Tarragon's sister, Oregano Rosemary of Karnak, when mated to Ch Amudarya Shalar in 1978, produced the *Famous Five* champions; Ch Karnak Juniper, Ch Karnak Bay of Imrahn, Ch Karnak Chillie, Ch Karnak Thyme and Ch Karnak Shamrock (Top Stud Dog 1986–1988). Juniper went on to produce Ch Karnak Jasmine and Ch Karnak Turmeric of Jazar.

A repeat of the mating between Rosemary and Ch Amudarya Shalar in 1982 produced the litter-mates Ch Karnak Blazing Star (sire of Ch Brandeswood Harrier), Karnak Melissa (one CC) and Karnak Golden Seal (two CCs). Karnak Rosemary (Ch Blazing Star's daughter), mated to Dk Ch Boxadan Junior Jumper, gave the kennel Ch Karnak Sassafras and Ch Karnak Damiana.

Kaskarak

My own kennel was founded in 1972 with the purchase of Nosilla I'm A Smartee, who was mainly from English breeding (Carloway and Horningsea lines), with the exception of one line back to Grandeur, via her grandsire Ch Horningsea Tiger's Eye. When mated to Ch Sacheverell Zukwala, she produced our first champion, Ch Kaskarak Khubara (Best Bitch Crufts 1979). A repeat of this mating produced Ch Montravia Kaskarak Hitari, the first Afghan ever to win BIS at Crufts (in 1983) and holder of the Breed CC Record (1984–1993). By modestly breeding within known family lines, five further champions were produced: Ch Kaskarak Gigolo and Ch Kaskarak Giselle in 1980, Ch Kaskarak Kochise in 1982, Ch Kaskarak Quincy Quartz in 1984

Ch Kaskarak Khobra.

and Ch Kaskarak Khobra in 1991. Other CC winners bred by the kennel were Kaskarak Clementine and Kaskarak Bethanny.

Also owned in the 1980s was Ch Barnesmore Imperial Wizard (Ch Moonswift Moonglade ex Ir Ch Pahari Chirkari of Barnesmore), who proved a prolific sire, with 16 champions to his credit. He was Dog World's Stud Dog of the Year in 1989 and 1990. His son, Ch Moonswift Medici, was our 'pick of litter' male from Ch Wizard's very last litter from one of Diana Bowdler-Townsend's few remaining Moonswift bitches, and he gained his title in 1995, becoming our ninth champion.

In 1985 we exported Kaskarak Best Of British (Ch Montravia Kaskark Hitari ex Kaskarak Coppelia) to Australia and, in 1993, we imported her daughter Calahorra Kasa Blanca at Kaskarak, by Aust Ch Calahorra Wherlwind, back into England in whelp to Aust Ch Khandhu Cracker Jack. Four puppies were born in quarantine, three of which have been retained by us to be incorporated gradually into our well-established bitch line. The fourth, Kaskarak Alice Springs, has already gained two CCs.

Katree

Les and Kathy Fulford's kennel started in 1975 with the acquisition of two bitches, Koolaba Jhalal and Mandy from Alyshan. Mated to Ch Karnak Shamrock in 1980, Jhalal produced Ch Katree Miss Schiapparelli, and a grandson of Jhalal, mated to Mandy, sired Ch Katree Miss Henna. Ch Schiapparelli's brother, mated to Miss Cleo at Katree, sired Ch Katree Miss Jhalal, who gained her title at less than two years of age, and litter brother Katree Lord Sanderman at Obadar (two CCs).

Ch Khamis Bhi-Candlelight, the youngest Afghan bitch to become a champion to date.

Khamis

June Leitch saw her first Afghan in 1966 outside the Glasgow School of Art, which she attended on Saturdays, being only 12 at the time. Now a talented artist, she is known throughout the world for her Afghan sculptures and models. Champions include Ch Deja-Vu of Khamis, Ch Khamis Zubedar and Ch Diaquiri of Khamis.

Gaining her title at $17^{1/2}$ months old, the home-bred Ch Khamis Bhi-Candlelight, co-owned with Mark Cocozza, is the youngest Afghan bitch on record to become a champion. She was also Top Puppy in the breed in 1995. Her brother, Khamis Bhi-Storm, won two RCCs before returning with his owners to the United States, where he is currently pointed towards his American title. Recently, Fabelhaft With All My Heat to Khamis (two RCCs) has been imported from the United States.

Kharakhan

Owned by Gloria North and established in the early 1960s, this kennel was founded with Ch Khanabad Honeydew and her half-sister Ch Khanabad Peach Blossom. Peach Blossom produced Gloria's first home-bred champion, Kharakhan Columbine, sired by Ch Khanabad White Warrior, and Kharakhan Coronette (one CC). Ch Columbine, when mated to Ch Koolaba Horningsea Eboni Earl, produced three champions; Ch Kharakhan Black Rose, Ch Kharakhan Lorah Rose and Ch Kharakhan Black Hussar.

Ch Lorah Rose produced Ch Lorah's Silver Winged Fantasy when mated to Ch Amudarya Shalar, and Ch Black Hussar went on to sire Tulak Gin Fizz of Kakara (one CC). A recent addition is Samanghan Desert Orchid of Kharakhan, who is of half American and half Khanabad breeding.

Kharisar

The Harcourt-Brown family's first home-bred champion, Ch Kharisar Karibh Khan (Alyshan Omahr Pasha of Kharisar ex Sharikhan Isakari of Kharisar), was born in 1973 and gained his title in 1976. He was the sire of seven champions, including Ch Lizzi of Kharisar, Ch Kharisar Nicomedes of Phinjani and Ch Kharisar Soloman of Sharikhan.

Ch Kharisar Zoe (Ch Khinjan Lorcah ex Kharisar Czarina) gained her title in 1979, but unfortunately never produced a litter. However, her bloodlines were preserved through her half-brother, Kharisar Mustapha Khan, who is behind their present-day stock.

Ch Kharisar Rhia at Cloudside. Photo: Michael M Trafford

Additionally, in 1984, Coastwind Apphia at Kharisar (one CC) (Am Ch Coastwind Jubilan Osiris ex Fermoy Holy Pilgrim) arrived from Richard Souza and Michael Dunham's kennels in America. Being the first American import in almost a decade, she introduced new bloodlines and, mated to Ch Lissue A Winters Tale, produced Kharisar Tobias (one CC) and Kharisar Tickety Boo of Sacheverell (one CC). Her second litter, to Ch Saxonmill Black Currant, produced Ch Kharisar Rhia at Cloudside. Another import, brought into the kennel from Canada, was Gypsy Steel Wheels to Kharisar (Am/Can Ch Jorogz Bluthara ex Am/Can Ch Gypsy Mood Indigo) who, when mated to Apphia, produced Can Ch Kharisar Elice.

Since 1977, the family has produced *The Afghan Hound Year Book*, an invaluable source of reference for all Afghan enthusiasts.

Khonistan

Roy Wilson and his late partner Wally Walker started in Afghans after seeing one in boarding kennels owned by Roy's father. Their first bitch, Barakzai Sta (Patrols Ali Khan ex Fiveways Araby), was purchased in 1946, and their affix, Barakzai, was registered with The Kennel Club at around the same time. Sta was mated to Rashnee of Closmidi and produced the CC and BOB winner Tamil Bey of Barakzai. Due to business commitments in the 1950s, the Barakzai affix was transferred into the ownership of Mr Ali Hupka, Roy and Wally re-starting in 1962 under their new affix – Khonistan.

Joining them in the partnership was their neighbour, Ian Hodgson, who became captivated with the breed while working in their boarding kennels. Ian now does most of the handling in the show ring. Ch Khonistan El-Cid (co-owned with Jackie Faith) gained his title at Blackpool in 1970, ironically exactly 20 years to the day and at the same place where Roy and Wally won their first CC with Tamil Bey of Barakzai. Another dog in partnership with Jackie Faith was Khonistan Bondor Kohendil Khan (litter brother to Ch Dera Ghazi Khan, Ch

Azim Khan and Ch Kumari Khanum) who unfortunately lacked showmanship, but proved his worth by siring Ch Khonistan Calypso and Ch Chayakhan Khamsin of Khonistan. His granddaughter, Ch Zoyford Christmas Carol at Khonistan, gained her title in 1988. Ch Calypso was retired to make way for a cream bitch, Ch Khanlidar Zuzini, their only champion unrelated to Kohendil Khan. Ch Zuzini produced a champion daughter, Khonistan Selina, when mated to Ch Khamsin. Also joining the kennel was Ch Lawkhan Kinkeesha of Khonistan (Ch Khinjan Lorcah ex Torikhan Demelza), who gained her title in 1976.

In 1993, Ch Anzani Silver Fox of Khonistan gained his title. He was mated to Ch Christmas Carol, and a bitch, Khonistan Misty Wych, was retained. Khonistan Eastern Mystic (two CCs) (Ch Asian Earl at Shalaszar ex Khonistan Misty Wych) is being successfuly campaigned at the present time.

Roy has been involved with the Northern Afghan Hound Society since 1947 and was Chairman from 1981–1998.

Mashour

In 1971, Jacquie Singleton acquired two bitches, one of which, Jahmeel Euragem, was mated to Dk Ch Kushra Ben Jashmal to produce Ch Mashour Kataghan Khan, who gained his title in 1980. Meanwhile, Jacquie obtained Kaskarak Georgia (RCC) (Ch Moonswift Moonglade ex Ch Kaskarak Khubara) and later Ch Kaskarak Kochise (Ch Barnesmore Imperial Wizard ex Ch Kaskarak Khubara), who gained his title in 1986. Ch Kochise produced four United kingdom champions and one Irish, including Jacquie's next champion, Tazkindi Pharoahs Gold. Ch Kochise also produced Mogell Memphis out of Landhavi Lafayette. Memphis gained one CC before becoming very ill as a result of a rare adverse reaction to sulphonomide (a form of antibiotic) whilst being treated for a cut pad, thus ending his show career. However, before his illness he sired Ch Melleck Impresario, Ch Kaskarak Khobra and Kaskarak Bethanny (one CC), the latter two co-owned with the author.

Mirsamir

Isobell Dyke's first introduction to Afghans was in 1965, but it was not until 1968 that she acquired her first, whom she registered as Crown Crest Samara (Hakim of Kethligarne ex Gigi of Veschambre). He gained his title in 1972 and this success was soon followed by Ch Pooghans Dalarna, who won her first CC in the same year but did not gain her title until 1979, after producing three litters. Ch Dalarna's second litter, to Ch Amudarya Shalar, produced Ch Mirsamir The Druid, co-owned with Jillian Knight-Messenger. Druid was Top Winning Afghan in 1979 and won his 16th CC in 1986, aged nine. In 1978, he was mated to Sundowner Fable, a Ch Horningsea Tiger's Eye daughter, and a bitch from the litter, Ch Sundowner The Witch from Mirsamir (co-owned with Mr and Mrs B Jones), gained her title in 1981.

In 1983, Isobell imported the Finnish litter-mates Tuohi-Tikan Luoti at Mirsamir and Tuohi-Tikan Loiske at Mirsamir, Loiske gaining her English title in 1984. More recently, she has successfully campaigned Ch Sashkan Eboni 'N' Ivory (co-owned with Mr and Mrs K Andrew) to his title.

Isobell is President and Secretary of the Afghan Hound Club of Wales.

Montravia

Peter and Pauline Gibbs owned their first Afghan in 1959, who was handled by Marita, their daughter, in the Junior Handling Classes when both were only two years old. Other breeding stock was acquired, mainly of Carloway and Khanabad lines. The first major success was in 1970 with Montravia Arabibi El Bazaz (sired by Ch Ranjitsinhji of Jagai), with whom Marita, then aged eleven, won their first CC and BOB.

Later, the Gibbs acquired Montravia Dun-Dun v Bornia State, imported from Holland, who became the first European import into Britain to gain his title. At about the same time they purchased a puppy, Montravia Kaskarak Hitari, from the author. Hitari had a spectacular career, being Top Afghan Dog in 1980 and Afghan of the Year in 1981, 1983 and 1984. He was also the first ever Afghan to win BIS at Crufts (in 1983) and, with 33 CCs, the Breed CC record holder for a number of years. Other successes followed with three home-bred champions: Ch Montravia Mazar Rozanna, Ch Montravia Holy Man and Ch Montravia Kazar Kaskade. With Marita now married, there has been a lull in breeding and exhibiting, although the family has achieved great success with Standard Poodles.

Palamedees

Angela Brown's kennel was founded in 1972 with two bitches: Ch Badakshan Pink Pearl, who gained her title in 1979, and Khanabad Winter Fashion. Winter Fashion was mated to Ch Karnak Shamrock, and the resulting litter included the sisters Ch Palamedees Anaja of Calamayor and Ch Palamedees Anishka of Desertwind. Another sister, Palamedees Ariana, when mated to Ch Jahadi Achill, produced Ch Palamedees Kallista. Ch Achill was also mated to a daughter of Ch Pink Pearl to produce Ch Jahadi Bosch at Wilbus.

Ratheeli

Pauline Mullins and Jill McBride's introduction to the breed was in 1968. Their foundation bitch, Kovalan Zilla, was mated to their own dog, Shah of Ilurose. This gave them their first champion, Ratheeli's Hooked Again, whose litter by Ch Balkasha Barabbas included the 1988 Crufts BOB, Ch Ratheeli Jadu. Ch Jadu's sister, Ratheeli Jarab, when mated to Ch Zendushkas Pekoe, produced a litter of two bitches, who became Ch Ratheeli Mahzuzh and Ch Ratheeli Murshadah.

Murshadah was never mated, but Mahzuzh was bred to two dogs, the first one being Ch Koolaba Alexander of Sacheverell, to whom she produced one puppy, Ch Ratheeli Zazzah. The second was to Ch Tianze Kalvados, this time producing two puppies, both dogs, one of which was Ratheeli Hajur (two CCs).

Sacheverell

This kennel was founded in 1962, based on Horningsea/Carloway/Tarril lines. Monica Booth-Thomson's foundation bitch, Zena of Sacheverell, when mated to Ch Horningsea Sheer Khan, produced the kennel's first champion: Ch Safiya of Sacheverell. Safiya was mated to Ch Ghurra Khan of Tarril to produce Ch Sacheverell Zukwala, who was for a time the breed CC record holder (27 CCs). Ch Zukwala sired seven champions, including Zensu Jacinth of Sacheverell and Koolaba Alexander of Sacheverell. Ch Zukwala's sister, Zelda, mated to Ch Koolaba Horningsea Eboni Earl, produced Ch Sacheverell Madam Zinnia, herself a Hound Group and BIS winner. A repeat of this mating was to produce Ch Sacheverell Kanika of Saxonmill, who became the foundation bitch for Roberta Hall. Other champions bred by the kennel include Ch Sacheverell Alexis and Ch Sacheverell Zorro of Zarzakos.

The kennel has won over 60 CCs and bred six champions from only nine litters of puppies.

Sadé

Chris and Julie Amoo acquired their first Afghan, Ashihna Raoul (Ch Oregano Tarragon of Karnak ex Ch Ashihna Charmayana) in 1979. Raoul, owned in partnership with his breeder, Meriel Hitchens, won 11 CCs (including BOB Crufts

Sacheverell Zelda (left) and her litter brother Ch Sacheverell Zukwala. Photo: Anne Roslin-Williams

Ch Sadé Sovereign.

1984 and BOB/Hound Group 1985) and sired the current CC record holder, Ch Solomon's Seal from Karnak.

Also owned by this kennel was Ashihna Charmaine who, when mated to Ch Sharazah Night Gambler, produced the 1987 Crufts BIS winner, Ch Viscount Grant. Along the way Gambler won many prestigious awards, including the Dog World/Spillers Pup of the Year Competition (1985) and Top Afghan 1986–1987. His champion progeny are Ch Sharazah Shannon and Ch Kulute Miles Ahead. In addition, frozen semen sent to Norway has produced a Norwegian champion. A repeat mating of Ch Viscount Grant produced Ch Sadé Solace, who gained her title at the age of two years and, when mated to Ch Sharazah Survivor, gave them a very successful litter that included Ch Sadé Hi Ranger to Sharazah (19 CCs), Ch Sadé Regina at Ifmaraf, Ch Sadé Sovereign, and Sadé Laeci (one CC). Laeci was mated to Ch Viscount Grant's grandson, Ch Karaburan Jelly Roll Morton, to produce Ch Sadé Beryk.

Sanstas

Sandra and Stuart Weston were both brought up with animals and started their kennel with the foundation bitch Gilzye Azuree, by Ch Amudarya The Pagan, in 1977.

Four years later they bought a puppy, Saxonmill Black Currant (Ch Karnak Shamrock ex Ch Sacheverell Kanika of Saxonmill), and in 1984 he gained his title, becoming their first champion. A prolific sire, Ch Black Currant produced winners when mated to bitches from many different lines, siring 13 champions in total. Four champions came just from his mating with Ch/Ir Ch Playfere's Petticoat Wag at Harlextan.

Ch Black Currant was mated to Azuree to produce the first home-bred

Ch Sanstas Rum Truffle (left) and Ch Saxonmill Black Currant.

champion: Ch Sanstas Rum Truffle. Presently being campaigned are Saxonmill Spitting Image and his daughter, Juzandia Ded Ringer at Sanstas, who carries lines on her dam's side to Boxadan, El Khyrias and Calahorra.

Sashkan

Bob and Ann Savage purchased their first Afghans in 1971, Sasha and Khan – hence their affix, Sashkan. But it was not until 1979 that their foundation bitch arrived, who was to become Ch Shechem Santinella, gaining her title in 1983.

In 1986 Dk Ch Boxadan Junior Jumper was imported in partnership with Jillian Knight-Messenger. Jumper sired Ch Sashkan Me And My Girl (17 CCs), Ch Sashkan Diamond Lil and Int Ch Sashkan Lilo Lil in his two litters to Ch Santinella. Ch Me And My Girl, when mated to Ch Karaburan Be Be King, produced Ch Sashkan Georgie Girl.

Sashkan Black Velvet (Dk Ch Boxadan Junior Jumper ex Bondor As You Like It) produced Ch Sashkan Miss Siagon at Karianca when mated to Ch Lissue A Winters Tale in 1990 and Ch Sashkan Eboni 'N' Ivory and Ch Sashkan Incognito when mated to Ch Karaburan Pretty Boy Floyd at Shirobana.

Saxonmill

Roberta Hall had an early interest in dogs. In 1965, while working for Monica Booth at her boarding kennel during the school holidays, she acquired her first Afghan. This was Shireen of Sacheverell, litter sister to Ch Safiya of Sacheverell. In 1969, when mated to Copper Coin of Davlen, Shireen produced Saxonmill Michaiah and Saxonmill Micah, who were both successfully campaigned. Unfortunately, neither was to produce puppies, so in 1974 Ch Sacheverell Kanika of Saxonmill (Ch Koolaba Horningsea Eboni Earl ex Sacheverell Zelda) joined the kennel. When mated to Ch Karnak Shamrock, Ch Kanika produced Ch Saxonmill Black Currant (Top Afghan Stud Dog 1991–1993) and Ch Saxonmill Black Iris. In 1985, a son of Ch Black Currant, Sanstas Liquorice of Saxonmill (one CC) joined the kennel and in 1988 a daughter, Ch Harlextan Piara at Saxonmill, who gained her title in 1992.

Ch Piara, mated to Ch Karaburan Pretty Boy Floyd, produced Saxonmill Currant Bun (two CCs), Spitting Image (six RCCs) and Lucy Locket (two CCs). When mated again to Ch Karaburan Jelly Roll Morton, she produced Ch Saxonmill Rum Tum Tigger, Ch Saxonmill Jennyanydots, Saxonmill Bustopher Jones (one CC) and Saxonmill Rumpleteazer (one CC). A mating between Ch Rum Tum Tigger and Ch Kharisar Rhia at Cloudside in 1995 produced the winning litter-mates Ch Cloudside The Ringmaster and Cloudside Black Marauder (one CC).

Severndene

Estelle and Godfrey Fryer established their kennel in 1970 with the acquisition of two bitches carrying Carloway bloodlines. One of these bitches, Meli of Index, produced Severndene Sensation who, when mated to Ch Moonswift Moonglade, produced Ch Severndene Marionette of Landhavi. In 1979, Horningsea Marisa, mated to Severndene Serpents Tooth, gave them Severndene Red Rooster (three RCCs). A repeat mating of Ch Marionette produced Severndene Spellbinder of Chardhuri, who in turn, mated to Ch Barnesmore The Baron of Landhavi, produced Ch Chardhuri Chianti for Drishaun and his sister, Chardhuri Pina Colada, dam of the litter-mates Ch Zareenas Firedragon at Severndene and Ch Zareenas Firecracker.

Ch Zareenas Firecracker, mated to Ch Dalparva Mr Bojangles, produced the CC-winning Zareenas Celeste, co-owned by Estelle with Joanne Smith.

Estelle is a Vice-President of the Afghan Hound Club of Wales.

Shanshu

Bettie and Bryan McClark owned their first Afghan in 1955 and in 1962 acquired Horningsea Mitanni, who was to become their first champion, from Marna Dods.

Later, the kennel achieved success with Shanshu Man At The Top (two CCs), Ch Gardwright Bibi at Shanshu and Ch Shanshu Casa Biere from Khados. In recent years Bettie has concentrated on her other breed, Tibetan Terriers, although the Shanshu lines are still continued through Ch Casa Biere's grandchildren.

Sharazah

Hazel Arris saw her first Afghan in 1956 but it was not until 1961 that, with her husband

Derek, she purchased Sheer Khan of Anzani. Later came Khinjan Angelique of Sharazah, born in 1970, who was to be their first champion. When mated to Ch Koolaba Horningsea Eboni Earl, Ch Angelique produced their first home-bred champion, Ch Sharazah Milwalki Stroller, who, mated to a daughter of Ch Khinjan Lorcah, gave the kennel another champion: Ch Maljan Golden Samarina from Sharazah (Top Brood Bitch 1989–1990).

Hazel and Derek also owned Ch Oregano Angellica of Sharazah (Top Winning Bitch 1977–1978) who, when mated to Ch Amudarya Shalar, gave them Ch Sharazah Blackberry Silk and Ch Sharazah Star Shooter. Ch Angellica's second litter, to Ch Stroller, produced Ch Sharazah Night Gambler (Top Afghan 1984), later to be exported to the Calahorra Kennels, where he quickly gained his Australian title. Prior to leaving for Australia, Gambler sired Crufts BIS winner Ch Viscount Grant and Ch Sadé Solace.

Ch Golden Samarina had two litters, her first, to Ch Viscount Grant, producing Ch Sharazah Shannon (Top Afghan 1990) and her second, to Ch Star Shooter, producing Ch Sharazah Sir Vivor (Top Afghan 1991 and Winner of The Pedigree Chum Veteran Stakes 1994). Ch Sir Vivor also sired five champions, including Sadé Hi Ranger, to Sharazah (Top Afghan 1993–1994).

Currently being campaigned is a daughter of Ch Sir Vivor, Ch Cotton Velvet to Sharazah, bringing the total of CCs won by this kennel to over 100.

Hazel is President of the Yorkshire Afghan Hound Society.

Weetoneon

Avril Lacey established this kennel in 1968 and has successfully bred not only Afghans but also Boxers and Hungarian Pulis. Her two Afghan foundation bitches were Chambleur Tamar (Ch Bondor Dera Ghazi Khan ex Zarakhan Soyala) and Pasharif Pukka Marharanee (Khinjan Banzai ex Pasharif Pandora).

Ch Weetoneon Dark Zaleta.

In 1985 Avril joined forces with Stan Szyczewski, owner of Ch Karnak Shamrock and also Shullimar Rainbow Warrior who, in their joint ownership, was to gain his title later in that year. Ch Karnak Shamrock sired 19 British champions and was Top Hound Stud Dog 1986–1987 and Top Afghan Stud Dog 1986–1988.

A bitch descending from Tamar, Weetoneon Mazelda (Koolaba Mazebon ex Weetoneon Honey Mink), mated to Ch Shamrock, produced their first home-bred champion, Weetoneon Dark Zaleta, who gained her title in 1988. A bitch descending from Marharanee, Weetoneon Witchcraft, mated to Ch Shullimar Rainbow Warrior, produced Weetoneon Dark

Warrior (two CCs), Weetoneon Dark Sapphire (one CC), and Weetoneon Dark 'N' Devoted, who in turn, when mated to a Ch Shamrock grandson, produced Ch Bellapais Touché Turtle. Also being campaigned are Weetoneon Dark Persuasion (one CC) and Weetoneon Fiddla on the Roof (one CC).

Wilbus

In 1970, Lesley and Alan Busby purchased their foundation bitch, Reina of Jagai. She was mated twice, and her granddaughter, Wilbus Emma Gee, produced Ch Ghinja La Peregrina and Ch Ghinja Popinjay.

Tatiana of Bowentree at Wilbus was added to the kennel and, when mated to Ch Gentleman Jim from Tazieff, produced Ch Wilbus Fleur De Lys of Bowentree. In 1982, Kanjanelli Ku-Mari (Kunte Kinte von Katwiga ex Pasharif Pepperpot) was also added and, when mated to Shullimar Super Trouper at Tazieff, became the dam of Ch Wilbus Hanukah.

Mated to Katree Lord Sanderman at Obadar, Ch Hanukah produced Ch Wilbus Kharjeem of Phinjani. In 1986, another puppy carrying German lines was purchased, who later became Ch Jahadi Bosch at Wilbus.

Zendushkas

Len and Norma Hitch's first Afghan was Zendushkas Wild Rose of Dywka, who was mated to a son of Ch Horningsea Sheer Khan in 1969. From the resulting litter, a bitch, Zendushkas Lady Zia, won her first CC at 19 months but lost a tooth in an unfortunate accident

Ch Zendushkas Pekoe. Photo: John M Hope

and had to be retired. Her brother, Zendushkas Desperado, became a Canadian champion and a sister, Zendushkas Dazla, when mated to Ch Bondor Azim Khan, gave them their first British champion, Zendushkas Dazravi. Dazla was then mated to Montravia Bondor Bolero, producing one male, Zendushkas Beau Dazla (two CCs).

Zendushkas Pandora, mated to Ch/Am Ch Huzzah Excelsis of Horningsea, produced Ch Zendushkas Pan-Celli, while a litter sister, Zendushkas Pansy, when mated to Beau Dazla, produced Ch Zendushkas Pekoe. Pekoe's daughter Firemont Azida was mated to Zendushkas Rubas, the litter including Ch Regal Lilly of Zendushkas, their first bitch champion. Ch Pekoe also sired Ch Ratheeli Mahzuzh and Ch Ratheeli Murshadah.

Zendushkas Blue Flint (one CC) was retained from a mating between Ch Bluestone Rocket of Zudiki to Tazieff Trinket at Zendushkas and his sister, Zendushkas Saphire, is behind Sparkling Soda of Zendushkas (one CC), currently being campaigned by the kennel.

Zharook

Pat and Robert Latimer started their kennel in the late 1960s. They acquired Sarik Sarawak from Zharook (RCC) (Ch Bondor Dera Ghazi Khan ex Rifka's Masindi) who, with his sister Sarik Shahara and another dog Moonswift Mozart (Ch Amudarya The Pagan ex M'sida of Moonswift), was the foundation of the kennel. In 1977, Sarik Shahara, mated to Moonswift Mozart, produced Ch Zharook Sugar 'N' Spice. In 1982, Zharook Airs 'N' Graces, mated to Ch Kaskarak Gigolo, produced Zharook High Society

Ch Zharook Hooked On Love.

(one CC). Ch Gigolo, used again in 1983 to Zharook Love In A Mist, produced SA Ch Zharook Love Is A Dream of Conde.

In 1985, Ayisha's Seductress from Zharook, mated to Ch Barnesmore Imperial Wizard, produced Ch Zharook Scarlet Flame, Ir Ch Zharook Scarlet Silk and Zharook Scarlet Pimpernel (*Our Dogs*/Pedigree Chum Top Sire 1994). Ch Kaskarak Kochise was mated to Seductress in 1987 and produced Zharook Heaven Sent (one CC). A litter brother, Zharook Heaven Help Us, when mated to Zharook Love Affair in 1990, produced Ch Zharook Hooked On Love, who in turn sired Zharook Heaven With Love (one CC). In 1991, when mated to Scarlet Pimpernel, Zharook Fancy Fashion produced Zharook Classic Fashion at Sherfiba (one CC) and Zharook Fashion Parade (one CC).

The Zharook dogs have been successfully raced, representing their teams at Intertrack, and Ch Hooked On Love sired the first British Afghan to gain the title of Lure Courser of Merit.

Ireland

Northern and Southern Ireland have different award systems. Northern Ireland (being part of Great Britain), adheres to The Kennel Club criteria, so CCs won in Northern Ireland count towards the Champion title in Great Britain. Southern Ireland adheres to the Irish Kennel Club criteria, their equivalent award system to CCs being Green Stars. These count towards the title of Irish Champion, which is calculated by a points system from the number of exhibits present, 40 points being required to gain an Irish title. The Irish Kennel Club is an Associate Member of the Fédération Cynologique Internationale (FCI), which does not

interfere with the Green Star system, but enables CACIBs (certificates counting towards the title International Champion) to be awarded at special shows.

Abberann
The Abberann kennels of Ann and Nicky White were founded on Ir Ch Braysheba and other Irish champions include Ir Ch Ayisha Shades of Topaz, Ir Ch Zharook Scarlet Silk and Ir Ch Abberann Star Wizard.

Arkenstone
Bob Margrain's Arkenstone kennel was founded in the late 1960s. The first Irish champion was Ir Ch Arkenstone Sherdil Bathsheba, who gained her title in 1967. Others were Arkenstone Mythwraith, Arkenstone Shadowfax, Arkenstone Apollo and Arkenstone Pink Panther. Bob is President of the Afghan Hound Society of Northern Ireland (AHSNI).

Barnesmore
The first Irish champion to be bred under the Barnesmore affix owned by Elizabeth Martin was Ir Ch Barnesmore Abdher Rahmann. Her next litter, from Ir Ch Pahari Chirkari of Barnesmore by Ch Moonswift Moonglade, was most successful, and included Ch Barnesmore The Baron at Landhavi and Ch Barnesmore Imperial Wizard, who were both influential stud dogs in Great Britain.

Khorlynton
The Khorlynton kennel of Paul and Lynn Johnston made up their first Irish champion in Ir Ch Barnesmore Abdher Rahmann. Their foundation bitch, Ir Ch Karima of Khamora, gained her title in 1975. Mated to Ch Khinjan Lorcah, she produced Ch/Ir Ch Khorlynton Kirjatharba, the first Irish home-bred United Kingdom and Irish champion since 1935. In 1979, Ch/Ir Ch Kirjatharba was mated to Ch Amudarya Shalar, producing Ir Ch Khorlynton Keltic Kestrel, Ch/Ir Ch Khorlynton Keltic Krusader and Ch Khorlynton Karibou. Mated to Ch Karnak Bay of Imrahn in 1982, Kirjatharba produced Ir Ch Khorlynton Kerdic Konsort and Ir Ch Khorlynton Kerdic Kara.

Metewand
The first champion for the Metewand kennels owned by Ann Mathers was Ir Ch Arkenstone Pink Panther. Other champions include Ir Ch Metewand Mississippi, Ir Ch Metewand Minnesota and Ir Ch Metewand Dashtikavir. In addition, Ir Ch Metewand Iezerai and Ir Ch Metewand Mimico both gained their United Kingdom titles.

Nilbud
Andrew and Berri Beare started their Nilbud kennels in 1966 with a bitch from Veldspringer and VdOM lines. Ir Ch Nilbud Polyzuu (Ir Ch Arkenstone Apollo ex Suzel of the Grove) was their first home-bred champion, and repeat matings produced Ir Ch Nilbud Star Sabu and Ir Ch Nilbud Iesha. Other champions include Ir Ch Tasia's Wunderbar of Nilbud, Ir Ch Nilbud Survivor, Ir Ch Yazdan Princess Daisy, Ir Ch Nilbud Roger The Dodger and Ir Ch Nilbud Florida Rose.
    Berri is President of the Afghan Hound Association of Ireland.

(Left to right) Ir Ch Yarabis Cu Buidhe, Ir Ch Yarabis Cu Ciara and Ir Ch Jhansi Armani.

Tejas

During the seven years that Ivor and Michele Keelan lived in Northern Ireland their American Tejas kennel was to have a huge impact on the show scene, both in Great Britain and Ireland. Bringing with them Am Ch Pahlavi Pandemonium, Am Ch Anasazi's Testarossa and Am Ch Anasazi's Maserati, their dogs quickly won their Irish titles, Pandemonium and Testarossa also becoming United Kingdom champions. Mated together, they produced Ch Tejas Sahuara and Ch Tejas Conquistador, the current United Kingdom Bitch CC record holder.

Yarabis

The Yarabis kennels of Brian and Zita Fogarty made up their first home-bred champion, Ir Ch Yarabis Tafna, in 1984, followed by Ir Ch Khorlynton Kerdic Kara in 1986. Their foundation bitch, Khorlynton Kampari, produced five Irish Champions, including Ir Ch Yarabis Cu Ciara. This bitch, mated to their own Ir Ch Jhansi Armani, gave them Ir Ch Yarabis Java (one CC), Yarabis Jeddah (one CC) and Ir Ch Yarabis Jali at Kazdanabad.

Yazdan

Marjorie and Colette Doody's Yazdan kennel was founded in 1968. Their first champion, from United Kingdom bloodlines, was Ir Ch Yazdan's Sweet Charity, followed by Ir Ch Yazdan's Princess Daisy and Ir Ch Yazdan Fire Spirit. The kennel also owned Ir Ch Jonitella Firedragon of Bacchante.

chapter four

Afghan Hounds world-wide

Australia
Contributed by Wendye Slatyer

The quality of Australian Afghan Hounds has long been recognised: many international breeders and judges have stated that they consider them the best in the world.

Home kennels

The major early kennels that still exert a strong influence are generally acknowledged to be Frank and Barbara Skilton's **el Tazzi**, Helen Furber's **Furbari**, David Roche's **Fermoy**, Lynette Schelling Watson's **Shaaltarah** and Stuart and Wendye Slatyer's **Calahorra**. Other early kennels who provided invaluable foundations that are still influential today were Lester and Joyce Davey's **Emir**, Vic and Eve Siebrecht's **Raushan**, Nina Luiken's **Jordaan**, George and Shirley Hansen's **Jallal** and Paula Lawes' **Ghurian**, Peter and Cathy Frost's **Dzum**, Colleen Khoury's **Quom**, and Paul and Pauline Hewitt's **Khandhu**. Each developed its own special blends from these basic genetics.

Equally successful, but with different genetic bases, are Stephen Wheeler and Harold Greensill's **Jacosta**, Birgit Jentsch Ferguson's **Tahkira**, Mary, Louise and Jim Hickie's **Gengala** and Don Day and Ross Sinclair's **Aboukir**. Each traces to one or more of those early sources, but all now involve current American lines via imports and frozen semen.

Aust Ch Calahorra Boccaccio: BIS at both Sydney and Brisbane Royal Shows, 1983.

Other notable kennels are: Terry and Ada Wilcox's **Alaqadar**, Ros Bacich's **Aviva**, Gary and Helen Elmer's **Karakush**, Colin and Helen Hamilton's **Kjavu**, Pam Bennett and Edwina Thomas' **Doyen**, John and Julie Janonis' **Ibadan**, Barry and Margaret Muir's **Jalalabad**, Molly Rule Steele's **Taejaan**, Arthur and Pat Batty's **Pierhelo**, Jean Duncan's **Hanrovia** and Marilyn Tonks' **Rajmal**.

Aust Ch Karakush Irresistable U.

Overseas influences

Great Britain initially had the most influence, because quarantine regulations for many years only permitted importation from or via there. However, many of the early imports also carried American bloodlines and, as an added bonus, some pedigrees also transported the influence of famous European and Scandinavian affixes. Later, American dogs were permitted to come directly into Australian quarantine.

Although many individual imported stud dogs have produced top winners, those generally acknowledged as having the most ongoing influence are:

From the United Kingdom: Ch/Aust Ch Mazari of Carloway, Ch/Aust Ch Waliwog of Carloway, Chandhara's Emir of Gray Dawn, Ch Furbari Kusan Kabul, Ch Chandhara Tarkhun Khan, Chandhara Talukdar and Ch/Aust Ch Sharazah Night Gambler.

From the USA: The Flying Dutchman of Isfahan, Ch Coastwind Holyman, Ch Furbari Foreign Affair and brother Ch Shaaltarah Black n Tantrum (via the United Kingdom), Ch Sanallah's Man of the Moment, Ch American Eagle at Calahorra, Ch Kabik's Limelite of Aries and Ch Kabik's the Candidate. The American influence is currently exerted mainly through frozen semen from, amongst others, Am Ch Pahlavi Puttin' on the Ritz, Can Ch Rhayder's the Right Stuff and Am Ch Qamari Rainbow Rider.

From Europe: Int/Nl/Aust Ch Badin vdOM, Int/Nl/Aust Ch Koem vdOM and Boxadan the Conqueror.

Imported bitches whose valuable contribution continues today are the three sisters Ch Khanabad Blue Frost, Ch Blue Mink and Blue Smoke, Ch Horningsea Kishta, Ch Ajman Shiramin and Rypunzel of Isfahan, all from the United Kingdom. From the United States there are Ch Cadburyhill Flash'n'Filigree and the champion Crown Crest sisters, Ch Miss Carousel and Ch Miss Capriole. Many significant bitches also left an important legacy in only one or two outstanding offspring.

Type

Type is very important to Australian breeders. On the whole, we want dogs representing the greatest possible number of hallmarks detailed in the Breed Standard, while very much retaining their breeder's mental picture of *type*. In other words, to their everlasting credit, our breeders have largely retained the great variation that is a natural inheritance of our breed because of the different regions in which it developed. Equating this to desert and mountain type would be an over simplification, but it is hard to describe in any other way the scope of Australian Afghan Hounds.

Much of the attraction of Afghan Hounds to so many people in so many countries is because of this conscious preservation and enhancement of variation within the breed. Unfortunately, influence is increasingly being exerted to have a particular 'look' considered more correct than others, and to promote the current trend throughout the world for show dogs rather than Afghan Hounds, the latter sometimes much more difficult to award highly, especially if they retain many of the original unique characteristics such as aloofness, dignity and independence.

Fortunately, judges still come here and steadfastly 'do their own thing', so we can but see what time will do to our breed. Undoubtedly now the emphasis is on glamour and show presentation, although fortunately a few kennels conscientiously strive to keep the Hound in the Afghan.

The Australian show scene

Afghan Hounds are enormously popular here as show dogs and probably win more In *Show* and In *Group* awards than any other breed, including at Best In Show and Best In Group level. In the 1970s and early 1980s our entries rose to around 300 at Royal shows and major all breeds championship events, and as high as 600 at Afghan Hound Club of New South Wales specialties. In 1997 a good specialty entry is around 150, at Royals and major all-breed events 90 or so, and at other all-breed shows very often 30 or lower.

Puppies are not easy to sell, but then they never were, largely because of the rising appeal of 'macho' breeds in Australia. Unfortunately, nowadays their great benefits as family companions are not promoted as they should be, so the wonderful support we had in the 1970s, when breed popularity was at its highest, has been lost. At that time a large number of people genuinely wanted to own an Afghan Hound as their family dog, and they did a marvellous job.

Fortunately, many still come back after they have lost their aged one. Often this is second generation or even younger 'because we remember the one that our grandparents loved so much' – a marvellous sign that our breed may be returning to general favour and not just sought after as a show animal.

Four Afghan Hound championship shows – we call them *specialties* – are held in Australia each year, two in New South Wales and one each in Victoria and Queensland. Every few years, one of these clubs gives up its regular specialty to host the national.

Despite the vast number of championship shows held throughout a country of this size, it is not all that easy to become a champion, because our top dogs compete for many years, and, as with the British system, all dogs remain in the classes – in other words, there is no *Specials* or *Champions* class. To win the points, rising stars have to beat established and often famous dogs. Of course, we have some dogs not worthy of their title, but so do other countries. What is important in the Australian system is that a quality dog will normally gain its title, and that enough opportunities to achieve this are provided to dedicated newcomers.

Many shows are held in and around the major capital cities, so it is not necessary to travel at all. On the other hand, many Australians exhibit at specialties, royals and other major events in different States, some involving long air flights or several days' travel. Also, our country show circuits are extremely popular as they are usually relaxed events, sometimes three or four in a 'cluster' with social gatherings as a bonus.

The average cost of entering a championship show in Australia ranges from as low as $5 (approximately £2.50 sterling) to around $15, with some of our specialties at $25. The entry fees are extremely low compared to other countries, and we fight to maintain these as they keep our shows within reach of the average family, ensuring that breeding pure-bred dogs remains an activity in which all members can participate.

We have both breed specialists and judges who officiate on many breeds, the latter being in the majority at championship shows. Where we differ – especially from the United Kingdom – is that Australian breed specialists very seldom judge at our own specialty shows, overseas breed judges usually being employed for these events.

Health
To my knowledge, there is no major illness affecting Afghan Hounds in Australia. They have always been an incredibly healthy breed genetically and hopefully will continue to be so, provided breeders act responsibly.

Austria
Contributed by Heinz Anschober

Home kennels
Afghan Hounds are not a popular show dog in Austria; indeed, there are only 250 sighthounds in total registered in the Austrian kennel book. During the last 25 years there have been just a handful of people who have bred maybe one litter a year, and these include **el Mashad**, **den Hertog**, **Ray-An-Wa-Sahir**, **Ras-el-tin's** and the better known **de Absorba** kennels, which disbanded two years ago. For the most part these kennels were founded on **vdOM** (see **The Netherlands**). The only kennel still breeding today is **Risa Chan,** which is based on **El Khyrias** stock and to date has produced over 20 champions.

Type
Type has never been important for most Austrian breeders, many of them choosing to exhibit stock from the latest winning dogs, irrespective of type. Glamour and presentation score a lot of points with many judges, although we do not have an extreme type of show dog with special American influence, so a good mixture of function and glamour can still be seen.

The show scene
In Austria there are 10 all-breed championship shows, 6 nationals and 5 international (CACIB) shows held each year. Most of the judges are all-rounders (FCI), with very few sighthound specialists. Entry fees range from 400 (£21 sterling) to 500 Austrian shillings.

The average Afghan entry would be 30–40, with Whippets being the most popular of the sighthound breeds.

Belgium
Contributed by Louis and Bernice Dehaes

Home kennels

Early 1970s kennels were Mrs Fossé's **de Pandjah** and Mr Sacco's **du Mocoloc**, which were both founded upon British breeding. Other breeders have continued with the vdOM lines of Eta Pauptit, the Von Katwiga lines of Erika Rödde and the El Kharaman lines of Mrs Grevelt-Kruize.

Kennels starting in the 1980s included Mrs Van Mechélen's **el Rachman**, Jan Jacob's **el Jafistan**, Dr Detaellenaere Johan's **el Champhyr** and Louis Dehaes **du Jegdalek**.

Type

There are two types of Afghans in Belgium. One of them is vdOM and the other from mainly British, American and Scandinavian bloodlines.

At present, most of the Belgian breeders continue to incorporate Scandinavian and American bloodlines into their breeding programmes to give the desired showmanship. Current winning dogs are Belg Ch Cartier Simply Irresistible, Belg Ch Cartier's Halston of Bonanza, Belg Ch Quanita du Jegdalek and Belg Ch Pahlavia du Jegdalek.

The show scene

Being situated in the middle of Europe, Belgian exhibitors can travel easily to shows in France, Luxembourg, Netherlands and Germany. We have nine international (CACIB), five national championship (CAC) plus one special sighthound championship (CAC) show each year. Championship shows are quite expensive to enter and range between £24 and £34 sterling, depending upon whether it is a national or international show.

At present, Afghans are not so popular in Belgium and a typical international show entry would be around 30 dogs. At national shows we average 10–25 dogs. Because there are so few breeders it is not particularly difficult to sell puppies, many purchasers being exhibitors and people who have owned an Afghan before. Good handling and presentation is important in Belgium. Most of our judges are sighthound specialists who understand the breed characteristics and appreciate correct conformation. The all-rounder judges seem to prefer a lot of glamour and showmanship.

Canada
Contributed by Vivienne Machen

Home kennels

Very few of the kennels that were actively breeding throughout the 1970s were still active in the breed by the end of the decade, so most of the influence from the incorporation of those early imports failed to be of any real subsequent significance.

The more predominant kennels of that period, whose foundation breeding is still represented in today's pedigrees and on the current show scene, are: Sandy and Archie Nagel's **Sanarr**, formerly of Ontario, Canada. They are still active in the breed and living in

California, and their bloodline remains successful in Canada through Peter and Vivienne Machens' **Gypsy** kennel affix. Other important kennels were Arthur and Inge James' **Spectrum**, Sherril Wallack's **Mijkehl** and June Beard's **Jenfield.**

Significant Canadian breeders whose home-bred Afghans made top honours in their day were: Patricia Murphy (formerly McCubbin) with Can Ch Blue Onyx of Norpatra, Chris and Linda Schotts with Am/Can Ch Aziz Lookin' Good Summerwind, Gerda Falcon with Can Ch Gertan's Stellar Liquidity, Nancy Boudreau's Can Ch Charon's Little Lucas and the Ternovatski's Can Ch Azaanta's Scorpio Rising.

Am/Can/Bda Ch Coastwind Mijkehl Niatron, Top Afghan in Canada 1987. Photo: Alex Smith

Other breeders who imported Afghans from the United States with considerable success at the time include the Nielson's **Jolterra** kennels and the Bajonas **Jagar** kennels.

Imports and their influence

It is extremely difficult to convey how much influence the original imports have had on the overall picture of the Afghan Hound in Canada at the present time, mainly because very few breeders throughout this whole period have really stuck with a continuous breeding programme. Even those that did have produced Afghans that have had little if any influence on the breed in Canada today, with the exception of those mentioned later on.

In the early-to-mid-1970s Canadian show ring was dominated by the *big red dog – big* body type compared to what we see today and *big* hair, mostly influenced by the British imports brought in by the Phillips (Kophi kennels) from Horningsea and Aryana bloodlines. There were also some British imports incorporating Bletchingley stock. Throughout the early 1970s almost 60% of Afghans in the show ring were either direct from the United Kingdom or first and second generations showing some British breeding, plus a little Scandinavian influence.

Around the mid-1970s, particularly after the introduction of the world-wide bi-monthly publication *The Afghan Review*, Canadian breeders began to look almost exclusively south of the border to the United States of America. There followed a major importation of numerous quite different looking dogs, predominantly influenced by the Holly Hill Afghans of the Kaufmans and Jay Ammon's Ammon Hall Nomad. These were soon followed by imports from the kennels of Akaba, Mecca, Coastwind and Sandina, bringing with them a whole host of colours. The *big red dog* dominance began to disappear from our rings.

Subsequent mid-1970s imports introduced Akaba, Coastwind, Jubilan, Mecca, Elmo, Sandina and Shangrila to the Canadian fancy, plus one very different looking navy blue dog that stood out like a sore thumb. He was the extremely powerful Mecca's Falstaff son, Cadburyhill Vida Blue, imported from the United States by Boggs and Livingstone.

The show scene

It is virtually impossible to top the standings in Afghan Hounds in Canada without the services of one of the well-known and well-advertised professional handlers. An expensive and extensive advertising and travel budget is the norm. Costs of campaigning an Afghan to the top at breed level alone can amount to many thousands of dollars which, combined with the numerous Group placement/BIS bonuses, can cause the cost to escalate beyond the reach of all but the most affluent fanciers.

Top Afghans in Canada from 1990 are Am/Can Ch Sandina Sunburst (1990–1991), Can Ch Azaanta's Scorpio Rising (1992), Am/Can Ch Sha Zahn Zekiel (1993), Am/Can Ch Paladin Fancy Pants Trinity (1994–1995) and Am/Can Ch Yours Truly of Grandeur (1996). Amongst the leaders in 1997 is Am/Can Ch Elmo's Don't Shake The Pyramids.

Denmark
Contributed by Gurli Christiansen and Birthe Rønnow Petersen

Kennels and influences

The Afghan Hound became popular in Denmark in the 1970s, the most famous kennel at the time being Stinne and Karin Fonsholm's **El Kama**. Their foundation bitch, Ch Horningsea Jamussah, was imported from England, and from this line came Dk Ch El Kamas Wladimir, Dk Ch El Kamas Memory of Wladimir and Dk Ch El Kamas Nahrimah, plus many others bearing the El Kamas affix. These dogs feature behind many of today's Danish and Scandinavian pedigrees, even though the kennel was disbanded in the mid-1980s.

In 1972, Hanne and Finn Lassen started breeding Afghans under the **Boxadan** affix, with their Finnish foundation bitch, Tuohi-Tikan Jumina and principal stud dog, Ch El Khyrias Drambuie. In 1975, Lotte and Ulf Jørgensen took over the Boxadan kennel and have since attained world-wide recognition for

Int/Dk Ch Dur-I-Durrans Masquerade (left) and Int Ch Dur-I-Durrans Gazebo. Photo: Willy

producing quality stock. The combination of Boxadan and **El Khyrias** (Sweden) bloodlines has been the basis upon which the breed has flourished in Denmark up to the present time. Many Boxadan champions have been produced, including the famous Int Ch Boxadan Xercise Makes Master, born in 1987, who was the sire of the A, C, D and E litters in the beginning of the 1990s, which included the top-winning Ch Boxadan Alexis The Bitch.

At the beginning of the 1980s, the **Dur-I-Durran** kennel owned by Oliver Hamilton was started. The kennel was extremely successful, with many champions bred and owned, although since 1990 the kennel has not been active. A further winning kennel started in the 1980s was Claus Hermansen's **Windsurf**, but this has now discontinued.

Birthe Rønnow Petersen started the **Lakshmi** kennel in 1991, based upon the Dur-I-Durran lines and also the French female Ch Evisa de la Chapelle Saint Blaise. Else Holmegaard's kennel **Exxos** is also founded upon Dur-I-Durran bred bitches

A recently-started kennel is Helle and Ivan Martini's **Abica**, home of Afghan Female of the Year 1996, Ch Boxadan Annie Get Your Gun. Other kennels started recently are Anne and Claus Mogensen's **Sheer Khan**, Anette and Søren Madsen's **New Vision**, Yvonne Graugaard's **Ninalli** and Marietta Foxmar's **Raquette**.

The show scene

Very few puppies are bred in Denmark as they are not easy to sell. Some go abroad, with the result that fewer Afghans are being exhibited (around 30 per show). Between 10 and 12 shows are held each year by the Danish Kennel Club and the Danish Afghan Hound Club. The average cost of entering a championship show is 220 kr (approx £22 sterling). Many judges officiate on a number of breeds, so the Afghan Club often combines its shows with those held by other clubs. To become a Danish champion, a dog must win three CACs from different judges, the final CAC being awarded after the dog is two years old.

Finland
Contributed by Helena Launonen and Terja Koivumaki

Home kennels

The major kennels in Finland (1970–1997) are Anna-Leena and Pirkko Konttinen's **Tuohi-Tikan**, Hilkka Nousiainen's **Kirman**, Aili Lindelöf and Mona Tukkimies' **el Miharaja**, Aulikki Norometsä-Malley's **del Flamante**, Marianne Karppinen's **Al-Faraz**, Raili Aurala's **Goldshadow**, and Ann-Marie Högström's **Tazi-Pa-Chenga**. Active from the late 1970s were Jaana Laatto-Huvinen's **Taikatassun**, Arja Kettunen's **Neliapilan**, Maija Arlander's **Choice** and Aino and Liisa Airas' **Scaramis**. Becoming active in the 1980s were Riitta Aho's **Punapaulan**, Maarit Tiainen's **Sonate's**, Eija Kontio's **Byblos**, Jaana Frondelius' **Sagoslottets** and Riikka Aro's **A'Rosafan**.

Foreign influences

The Finnish breeders started out with Swedish dogs in the late 1950s and, by exchanging material with Swedish and Danish breeders, have built the famous Scandinavian type. The most important influential kennels have been **Tuohi-Tikan** (Finland), **El Kamas** (Denmark), **el Khyrias** (Sweden), **Boxadan** (Denmark) and **Dur-I-Durrans** (Denmark).

Pedigrees in Finland, Sweden, Denmark and Norway are strongly influenced by certain

Scandinavian dogs, and a very good example of this is the world famous Swedish male Su Ch El Khyrias Hazztafer, who has a Finnish father, a Danish mother and was bred in Sweden. The El Khyrias influence is predominant in the whole of Scandinavia. In addition to the numerous imports from Scandinavia, we have had a few imports from other countries over the years, which have fitted very well into our lines, the most important and influential of them being Int Ch Panameric of Stormhill, who has over 40 champion offspring in Finland and the other Scandinavian countries. Although the Scandinavian type remains the most predominant, there are dogs to be seen that clearly display the influences of American, Australian and Continental lines.

Type

The great majority of our Afghans are show dogs and we want them to look as glamorous and well-presented as possible. However, we do not want to forget that under the coat there must be a functional dog with a structure that is appropriate for a sighthound. Some of the Finnish Afghans participate in racing and lure coursing and they are mainly the same dogs that go to the shows. In 1996, a male and female from the same Scaramis litter became the first 'triple' champions in show, racing and coursing.

The show scene

Afghans are very popular show dogs in Finland. At international all-breed shows it is common to have 60–100 Afghans entered and this figure increases to more than 150 dogs at our annual National Specialty Show. This is very good considering that only about 100 Afghans are registered each year. At many all-breed shows Afghans have the highest entries.

About 40 championship shows are held in Finland and 11 of these have international status. In addition we usually have six to eight specialty shows. The shows are spread evenly across Finland, so almost everyone can attend a show near home, travelling further if they so wish. Entry fees are 140–160 Finnish marks (£15–£19 sterling). Competition is tough because so many Afghans take part, making it quite difficult to become a champion.

At the shows we have breed specialists and all-round judges from all parts of the world, with many more foreign judges than Finnish judges officiating.

The leading Afghan male of the 1990s

Int Ch Scaramis Da Capo.

so far is Int Ch Scaramis Da Capo (Int Ch Boxadan Xercise Makes Master ex Ch Scaramis Carmina) and the leading Afghan bitch of the 1990s is Int Ch Neliapilan Superapila (Boxadan As You Like It ex Int Ch Neliapilan Onnenapila).

Health and welfare
Afghans are a healthy breed in Finland and we have perhaps a unique situation whereby 40% of our dogs have had their eyes checked during the past 20 years. Practically all of the dogs that have been used for breeding have been examined. According to the official statistics from 1967–1987, only 1% of our Afghans had juvenile cataract. Some of our dogs have been X-rayed and we have had no recorded cases of hip dysplasia.

Selling puppies is not too difficult and, with a few exceptions, we don't have abandoned Afghans and don't need rescue programmes.

France
Contributed by Bev Ward

Home kennels and foreign influences
Since the early 1970s the Afghan Hound in France has seen a meteoric rise in popularity, and an almost equal slide down the ranks in the late 1980s. At the present time 60–70 litters are registered each year. There appears to be no overall dominance of type or influential breed lines. Many imports have come from United States, Scandinavia, Australia and Great Britain. The only kennel with pre-1970 roots still in existence is the Bourcey's **Koulangar** kennels. The most consistent winners of the 1980s and 1990s have come from the Danel's **Tchekhana** kennels, based predominantly on the Kassan lines of the USA and the **Chapelle Saint Blaise** kennels, who had enormous success after leasing the Danish dog Ch Dur-I-Durran's Gazebo. At the present time, Martial Robin is consistently in the news with his **Le Menuel Galopin** Afghans, which are based on Chapelle Saint Blaise lines combined with the United States lines of the Pahlavi kennel.

The most influential lines to have contributed towards the winning kennels are from the United States. A consistent winner has been Marc Chevalier's Ch Adjar de Tchekhana, whose wins have included French, Spanish, International and European championships. Unfortunately he died young, leaving few progeny.

The show scene
When observing classes at the larger shows one notices the wide divergence in types and on looking at catalogues one is aware of the lack of true line breeding, possibly because of the great distances needed to travel to find the ideal male. This also affects entries at shows. Apart from the French National at Longchamp, which attracts about 7000 entries (all-breeds) and possibly 100 Afghans from all over Europe, and the breed national of FALAPA, with an entry of some 120 Afghans, other international shows may attract around 30 dogs and the others (with CACs) may have only 5–10 entries. Another contributing factor to the small show entry is the cost – between £20 and £30 per dog. You can only enter your dog in one class, judging is carried out in the morning and the dogs must remain in their cages until 6.00pm to be on view to the public.

To become a French champion a dog must win either a CAC or Excellent qualification at Longchamp or at FALAPA. Three additional CACs must also be won under three different judges within an 18-month period. Therefore, only four champions may gain their titles each year and, with the opposition coming from all over Europe, this is not very easy.

Racing and coursing are also taken very seriously and working classes are scheduled at all the shows. Only winners of the Open and Working classes are eligible to challenge for the CAC. As most judges in France would be classed as all-rounders or group specialists, few have ever owned an Afghan themselves.

Emphasis in the show ring is predominantly placed on glamour, both in coat and movement. Unfortunately, this has led to the abhorrent development of clipping and scissoring of saddles, necks and even faces on our 'natural' hounds. On the plus side, with the demand for an all-round Afghan, all dogs have to pass an aptitude test to prove that the Afghan is still first and foremost a sighthound, not just something to adorn the cover of a glossy magazine.

Germany
Contributed by Erika Rödde

Foreign influences

Germany has always attracted imports from other countries (but rarely exports), which is still the situation today. This changes constantly, depending upon the current vogue. Presently, American Afghans are the 'flavour of the month' and tend to win under judges from foreign countries. We have many Afghans with German/American bloodlines, some with German/English bloodlines and many are a mixture of all the blends. The current trend is for glamour and to win in the show ring.

Type

For many older German breeders, our heritage stems from the vdOM bloodlines of Eta Pauptit in Holland, whose kennel type originates from English and Irish stock. It is this 'true type' that has existed in Germany for over 50 years and which forms the backbone of our breed. Many of our top breeders have tried to maintain this type of Afghan, with the emphasis also on balance and strong movement. We have tried to eliminate only faults, without the sacrifice of true type. Our Afghans must be dignified, aloof and proud, showing that certain keen fierceness required by the standard, without any

A group of Erica Rödde's von Katwiga hounds.

tendency towards shyness or aggression. We require well built and well muscled hounds, essential for true Afghan movement.

The show scene

Our principal sighthound club, the German Sighthound Breeding and Racing Club (DWZRV) was established in 1892 and has about 5000 members. In 1988, the German Afghan Club (DAC) was founded, but this can only hold National Certificate Shows, at which CACs are given out under German Kennel Club (VDH) rules.

During 1996, some 75 shows were held, 10 of them with International status (giving out CACIBs and CACs), with the remainder open for sighthounds only. The main specialty show is the Club Winners Show (Verbandssieger-Schau), which is open for members of the DWZRV and for sighthounds solely bred in Germany and registered in the *German Sighthound Stud Book.* Held annually in July in Cologne, the show usually attracts an entry of around 500 sighthounds. In 1996, 114 Afghans were entered. During the month of May, the Europassieger Show, organised by the VDH, is held. The last title

Int Ch Wind Against Ace of Base,
Top Afghan in Germany and Switzerland 1996. Photo: Tell

show, the Bundesseiger Show (all-breed) is held annually in October, in Dortmund.

Every sighthound bred or in residence in Germany must be registered in the *German Sighthound Stud Book.* This includes all imports, 23 of which were registered last year.

In line with the world-wide decline, only 40 German Afghan litters (241 puppies) were born and registered during 1996 and, whilst finding good quality homes is difficult for lesser-known kennels, it presents no problem for the major ones. Entries at shows have fallen by 50% compared to what they were in the 1970s.

At present, some 32 German Judges are registered; most judge a variety of breeds, with some specialising in sighthounds only. All judges must adhere to the FCI Standard. During

1996, a total of 24 judges from other countries officiated at our shows. Our judges' main priority is for structure and movement, not forgetting that an Afghan must be able to function 'as nature intended' in its country of origin. To us, a truly functional hound with true breed type and Afghan character is far more important than glamour. Unlike the rest of the world, Germany has always placed 'type' before the emphasis on more and more coat.

To become a German champion, a dog must attain four CACs from three different judges, with more than 12 months elapsing between the first and last award. This is not difficult considering the number of shows that are held each year. Entry fees range from DM32 (£12 sterling) for CAC shows, to over DM80 for CACIB shows.

Other activities

Racing dogs, bred for speed as their main criteria, can also compete at conformation shows, although it is difficult to find a top quality dog in this category. Many racing enthusiasts therefore tend to adhere to racing and coursing events which can earn points towards a working title. However, many show enthusiasts love to take their dogs racing, not only for the exercise but to meet up with fellow exhibitors.

Hawaii
Contributed by Twylla-Dawn Steer

Although Hawaii is one of the United States of America, it has been decided to treat it as a separate country because it is so far away from the US mainland.

The breed in Hawaii owes much to Rudolph James Maffei, MD (Mafreeka Afghan Hounds), who helped guide the fledgling breed club as ambassador from the parent club, mediator, advisor and event host or coordinator. He encouraged novices starting in the breed, and is passionate about its welfare.

Afghans have not taken off in Hawaii as a premier canine companion or show dog. Their size, coat, an 120-day obligatory quarantine (since 1912), combined with the high cost of living, have kept both pet and show dogs to a bare minimum. A number of people have imported dogs from Australia (to avoid quarantine), while others have sought their show and/or breeding stock from mainland United States of America.

With only two Hawaiian Kennel Club Shows a year, making up champions was a slow process until April of 1975, when the Windward Hawaiian Dog Fanciers was licensed for all breed shows and obedience trials. To date, two Afghan Hounds have achieved all-breed BIS status in Hawaii: Rudolph Maffei MD and Joe Ricca's Am Ch Valymir Kristoffer Jokari and Twylla-Dawn and Bobbi Steer's Am Ch Camri's Res Judicata. Two island-breds are also Hound group winners: litter-mates Am Ch Inisfailte Archie Goodwin and Am Ch Inisfailte Tupenc Beresford, both owned by Twylla-Dawn and Bobbi Steer.

Due to the efforts of Rose Upper, Rudie Maffei and Virginia Phillips, the Afghan Hound Club of Hawaii Inc was formed, and a licence to hold championship specialties was granted by the American Kennel Club in 1976. At the height of its popularity, the breed club roster boasted over 40 members.

Hawaii's isolation has not been a total barrier to importations and the kennels who have contributed one or more dogs to Hawaii's rainbow are: Abergonny, Cadburyhill,

Calahorra, Camri, Carmel, Chordayer, Coastwind, Crown Crest, Cregdala, Druid Glen, El Sayyad, El Tazzi, Furbari, Kuhsan, Ronee, Scheherezade, Sforzy, Shaaltarrah, Shaadar, Stormhill, Tahkira, Vagabond, Valymir, Westwind, Yev'rah, Zafara, Zardonx and Zorro.

In 1991, Richard Brown and Barbara Benson began to import Afghans from Australia, bringing in seven from Calahorra and one from Tahkira. Five of their Australian imports gained their titles, along with a locally-bred dog.

Hawaii reduced its quarantine restriction in 1997, from 120 days to 30 days. However, dogs now have to be vaccinated, tested and micro-chipped before entry.

Italy
Contributed by Titti Padova

Home kennels

Major kennels are Paolo Simeoni's **Settebello**, Rosemma Aymaretti Barosso's **Gran Pamir**, Renata Stacchini's **Montecchio Della Val D'Era**, Cesare Padova's **Dei Kirghisi**, Lucia Migliorati's **Jestak**, Roberto Bongiovanni's **Xenos**, Daniela Sabato's **Del Sadani** and Fulvio D'Andrea's **Kouros**.

Foreign imports

In the 1970s the most influential imports into Italy came from Great Britain, Denmark, Spain and the United States of America. In the 1980s there was a predominance of Scandinavian lines and the 1990s saw imports from the United States increase. In the latter years dogs have also been brought in from Australia.

Int/Fr/World Ch Sanallah's Jerome, owned by the Xenos kennel. Photo: Visintini

The show scene

About 200–300 Afghans are registered annually. At an all-breed international show with a total entry of 1200–1300 dogs, one would expect to see 20–30 Afghans exhibited.

To become an Italian champion a dog must win two CACs at National Shows, two CACs at International Shows plus two CACs awarded at clubmatches (club meetings) with awards being won under five separate judges. During the year approximately 20 International Shows, 60 Nationals and 6 Clubmatches are held. Shows are held throughout the country, so making up a champion can involve travelling long distances. Entry fees are between Lit 35.000 (£13 sterling) and Lit 45.000. Our judges are mainly all-rounders, with just three or four breed specialists.

Other activities

Other sports such as racing are beginning to arouse interest, although with no official greyhound tracks in the country, fanciers are travelling to Switzerland, France and other European countries in order to obtain FCI international racing licences.

Japan
Contributed by Fukie Yoshimoto

Home kennels

The major early kennels from whom strong influence still continues are generally acknowledged as Ms Fukai's **Three F** (formerly **Jardin Petit**), Mr Seki's **Joy Bell's**, Ms Seki's **Sawa Barriea**, Mr Fujimoto's **Fujimoto**, Ms Iida's **Kohyokaland's** and Ms Yoshimoto's **Afghan Arg**.

Kennels that became established after 1970 were Mr Kobayashi's **Afghan Land**, Ms Fukai's **House Expo**, Mr Tanida's **Success Tanida**, Mr Tokui's **Shining Coast**, Mr Higuchi's **H Tolfan**, Mr Ishii's **Tip Top**, Mr Kamura's **Kennels Kamura**, Ms Suzuki's **Ever Bell's**, Mr Takeuchi's **Gran Rowa**, Ms Inaba's **Lyncrest**, Ms Yoshikawa's **Royal Dolls**, Mr Kuribayashi's **Rainbow Express**, Mr Inoue's **Twilight**

Ch/Am Ch Renwick's Color Me Badd, owned by Mr Yahiro of Japan.

Angels, Ms Saito's **Mountain Majesty**, Mr Yahiro's **Vis-A-Vis JP**, Ms Iidaka's **Royal Benelux**, Ms Matsuda's **La Fayette** and Ms Hosoi's **Sacrae JP**. (Names are in no particular order).

Foreign influence

The majority of Afghans are imported from the United States of America, although imports from Australia and Scandinavia are gradually increasing.

The show scene

It was in 1970 that Afghans began to make a real impact at Japanese dog shows. The after-effects of Tochiku (a company involved in the mass purchase and exportation to Japan of female puppies and champion males of all breeds) were gradually subsiding but, as a result of the bad press surrounding Tochiku's dog dealing exploits, British breeders were no longer willing to send out stock. Japanese enthusiasts, encouraged by the country's economic recovery, therefore looked to the United States of America to purchase dogs. Under such circumstances, it was sensational for a British import (from Carloway stock) to win BIS at the biggest show held by Japanese Kennel Club in 1970: Ch Askle Plos of Mirror Field, owned by Ms M Fukai. Unconnected to the Tochiku case, he had a great effect upon the increased popularity of the breed in Japan.

At the height of the Afghan Hound's popularity, there were 13 Breed Clubs in existence, but this amount has now decreased by half. Ironically, yearly Afghan registrations are today around the 550 mark, the same figure as they were in 1970, although they reached their highest in 1983, when 2088 Afghans were registered.

It is not particularly difficult to become a champion in Japan. Around 240 championship shows are held annually and a dog must win four CCs to gain its title. Entry fees range from 6000 yen (£28 sterling) to 8000 yen for a large FCI show. A catalogue and light lunch are included in the fee. Unique to Japanese custom, all exhibitors receive a small gift for participating, which is usually a T-shirt or bath towel. Most dogs are handled by professional handlers, who drive large customised vehicles and attend shows at different locations on Saturdays and Sundays. Ordinary exhibitors usually attend shows that are held locally. Nearly all judges are all-rounders, although clubs occasionally invite a breed specialist from overseas for their specialty show.

Afghan entries at shows are currently below the 100 mark. For example, at the biggest Japanese Kennel Club show held in 1996, in a total entry of 2268 dogs, there were 68 Afghan Hounds, 223 Golden Retrievers (the most of all), 130 Siberian Husky, 90 Miniature Long-haired Dachshunds, 71 German Shepherd Dogs and 70 Maltese.

Glamour and presentation are extremely important in the show ring and it would seem that more and more judges and owners have lost sight of the original purpose of the breed. Enthusiasts do not participate in other activities such as racing or coursing.

Puppies are easy to sell, but it is difficult to find suitable homes for them. Exhibitors are always eager to buy puppies from champion parents or from today's top dogs (usually imported) and one can only wonder how they estimate the value of the pedigree realistically.

The Netherlands
Contributed by
Ad van der Snee

The Netherlands has played a great part in the early history of the breed in Europe and the importance of Dutch Afghans in the period between the 1930s to the 1970s can still be seen in the offspring of exports to countries such as Germany, Sweden, Finland, Denmark and Australia.

Home kennels
Early renowned kennels were **Barukhzy**, owned by Mrs Jüngeling and her son Han and the world famous **van de Oranje Manege (vdOM)**, owned by Mrs Pauptit. Both kennels were founded on Ghazni stock and both maintained the original

A wonderful group of typical Jebel Musa hounds owned by Mrs Marten in the 1970s.

mountainhound type. Early imports with international influence were Mrs Jüngeling's Baber of Baberbagh and Shahib of Wasdarb (sired by Ch Sirdar of Ghazni).

In the 1970s, another kennel of note was Mrs Marten's **Jebel Musa** whose lines were a mixture of vdOM, English and German (see group photo) and typical of the type of dog to be seen in the country in this period. However, the last decades show a drastic decline in numbers, with less than 100 puppies registered in 1996 compared with 1300 in 1973.

The show scene
Around 16 championship shows are held each year, with top awards being won mainly by dogs from Germany and Belgium; one exception being Nl/Belgian/Dk/Int/W95 Ch Serra Parecis Fair Player (Ch Boxadan Xercise Makes Master ex El Minja's Midnight Sun) owned and bred by Mrs De Meijer and her daughter Kelly.

Because of the geographical size of the

Nl/Belg/Dk/Int/W95 Ch Serra Parecis Fair Play

country, we do not have to travel far to shows. Entry fees range from £20–£30 and, of the 15 judges in Holland, 9 are breed specialists.

New Zealand
Contributed by Brian Hobbs

The early 1970s saw a huge upsurge in Afghan ownership, which continued throughout the 1980s. The 1990s have seen the breed diminish at an alarming rate, with today only one or two litters born each year throughout the country. Most serious breeders/exhibitors are in the older age bracket and there are no younger members coming into the breed, which does not look good for the future of the breed in New Zealand.

There are three clubs: Dominion Afghan Club (north half of the North Island), Central Afghan Club (South of the North Island) and Canterbury Afghan Club (consisting mainly of members from the South Island). Membership at all the clubs averages around 40.

Home kennels
Active breeders who have bred a litter within the last five years are B and P Hobbs **(Koh-I-Baba)**, L and L Waugh **(Shahdazar)**, G and B Campbell **(Chakdarra)**, A and D Powell **(Juwain)**, A Gilchrist and W Hansen **(Jhanzi)**, J Howman **(Belladonna)** and G and M Herdman **(Tjibulan)**.

Foreign influence
From the outset, the Afghans imported into this country were mostly British dogs, either brought in directly or imported from Australia. Due to import restrictions it was many years before New Zealand was allowed access to Afghans from other countries. With the arrival of a free market economy and less restrictions over the last few years, the breeding scene has opened up, particularly with the advent of frozen semen. The country has always had a close association with Australia and the situation remains the same today, with the majority of imports coming from Australia. In the last three to four years the most prolific winner at All breed shows is the Australian import NZ Gr Ch Khandhu Moody Blue.

The show scene
Whilst the functional hound is at the back of most breeders' minds, with the limitation of only three specialist club shows, the general aim is to breed for an all-breed show dog – in other words, a glamorous dog that will win under all-breed judges who are not necessarily familiar with the breed. Because the judging educational system is based on a group system, most judges in New Zealand are group specialists.

Because the Afghan is no longer an overwhelmingly popular show dog or pet, entries at all-breed championship shows average 15 dogs. Entry fees are around $8 (£3.50 sterling) to $10. Puppies are extremely difficult to sell, which means that breeders only breed the occasional litter for themselves.

Norway
Contributed by Åge Gjetnes

As in most countries, the popularity of the Afghan Hound in Norway is dropping, although there are still enough breed enthusiasts to prevent the breed from going into decline.

Home kennels

The major kennel of the early 1970s was undoubtedly kennel **Nordkroken**, owned by Mossen Enger. Most of her breeding was based on Danish El Kama and Finnish Touhi-Tikan lines. Another kennel that started in the 1970s and is still active today is **Al-Dahna**, owned by Torill Knutsen. Her most important foundation bitch was Ch Nordkrokens Gentiana. **Unjan**, originally owned by Unni and Jan Tefke with the later addition of Sissel and Kjell Bøhaugen, is probably the most famous Norwegian Afghan Hound kennel, having produced several top winners and producers. Again, they also based their stock on the Nordkroken line, their foundation bitch being Nordkrokens Fonda and their foundation sire being Ch Nordkrokens Kim. Ch Unjan's Tino is from the breeding of Fonda and Kim, and Tino himself was used by many breeders, including the famous Swedish El Khyrias kennels of Christina Jernberg. Unjan also used the famous Ch El Khyrias Hazztafer to produce Ch Unjans Gjengis Khan, sire of the famous K-litter when mated to his half-sister. The top dog from the K-litter was undoubtedly Ch Unjans Kaztor Khan, winning 50 BOBs and himself a

Nor Ch Moving Mystic Love.

champion producer. His litter sister, Ch Unjans Kazzandra, was the dam of the last Unjan litter in the mid-1980s. In total, Unjan bred 16 litters, producing more than one champion per litter.

The **Oskani** kennel, owned by Berit and Trond Frøyland, also started with a bitch from Nordkroken, later adding several British dogs into their breeding. The **Skahera** kennel of Ragna Hegsvold and later also Ragnhild Raanes was started in the 1950s on old Norwegian **Khasru** lines and was active for some 30 years. Mrs Bjørg Foss of the **El Camici** kennel based most of her breeding on German dogs and produced a significant number of champions. Of all the above mentioned kennels, only **Al-Dahna** is still active.

Fortunately the breed has gained new enthusiasts who have been influential in producing good dogs and winning well in the show ring. The **Moving** kennel, belonging to Monica Huse Jacobsen, has produced nearly a dozen champions in a relatively short time span and is based on Swedish and Australian dogs, focusing on the American export to Australia, Ch Kabiks Limelite of Aries. Åge Gjetnes and Elsa Storesund started with two bitches from El Khyria in Sweden. The first, Ch El Khyrias K'Call Me What You Want, was of pure Scandinavian breeding. Ch El Khyrias Never The Less was half Scandinavian, half

Australian through her father, Ch Rahzmundah Psidium. These two bitches produced 13 champions between them. Dogs from the **Gjetnes and Storesund** partnership have won seven BOBs at the prestigious Skokloster show in Sweden, three of these being won by Ch Hunting High and Low. Their most famous sire is Ch Yesterday, Today and Tomorrow, a son of Am Ch Pahlavi Puttin' On The Ritz. After several years of breeding together, Gjetnes and Storesund no longer co-breed, but are still actively breeding in their own right, both having produced a number of champions.

Foreign influence
The most important imports to Norway have come from Sweden.

Health
It is hard to sell Afghans in Norway and because of this, breeders need to have facilities to keep puppies over a long period of time. This is a lot of work, as the climate in Norway can be very hard, and all dogs need to be kept in the house or in a heated kennel. There are no major illnesses within the breed, but all dogs and bitches used for breeding are required to have their eyes checked.

The show scene
Whilst Afghans are still popular show dogs, entries at general shows have fallen dramatically, with sometimes only five exhibited. Around 40 championship shows are held each year in Norway, spread throughout the country. There are 11 international shows each year, all arranged by the Norwegian Kennel Club. The entry fee is approx. £21. Because of the limited Afghan entry, the breed is all too often judged by all-breed judges. However, a breed specialist is always invited to judge the specialty. Entries at specialties sometimes number over 50.

With the advent of intrauterine insemination through the vagina, Norwegian breeders have had access to artificial insemination (AI) since the late 1970s, producing champions with semen imported from the United States, Australia and Great Britain. More recently, with the abolition of quarantine from Western Europe, it has become much easier to import breeding stock. With several recent imports and planned litters, the breed seems to be experiencing an upsurge in interest and popularity.

Poland
Contributed by Janusz Zielinski
The very first Afghan Hound registered with the Polish Kennel Club was Taban, whelped in 1960, breeder unknown. The dog was imported from Iran and his owner was Iran's Ambassador to Poland, residing in Warsaw. We do not know much about this dog, apart from the fact that he was the only specimen of the breed being shown in Poland at the time.

Political and economical changes in Poland influenced canine matters to a certain degree. After a slight increase in puppy registrations a sudden depression came and registrations dropped by half for several years. However, the situation has now improved and in 1996 there were 500 Afghans registered with the Polish Kennel Club.

Home kennels

Leading Polish kennels include **Kontrapunkt**, **Complement** and **Krist Will**, with **Clasic**, **Van Arden**, **Kristwil**, **Fortunatus**, **Sannatis**, **Z Przegoni** and **Z Plemienia Chayenów** featuring in many pedigrees. The first five Polish champions were; Ghanton Osiris (imported from Germany), Khonistan Aquarius (imported from Great Britain), Sherdil Sahara (imported from Great Britain), Khanikush Rajan Rashan (imported from Great Britain) and Sirokko von Katwiga (German born and owned). Top Winning Afghan ever is Multi-BIS Int/Polish/CR Ch Caiwana's Kingclasic (imported from Germany), the first import to be given the Int (FCI) title.

Foreign influence

From 1960–1996, there were 120 imports into Poland from 15 different countries, the first ones coming from Sweden, Great Britain and Israel. Looking back, the most dominant lines have been from Great Britain, Scandinavia, Germany and the United States.

In the 1970s, several *desert-type* or *Khalag* Afghans were imported into the country from Russia and Afghanistan, but they never found their place in breeders' hearts and went into obscurity.

Show scene

There are over 40 shows giving CACs in Poland and 11 giving CACIBs (FCI international title certificates). Afghans share just one club show with the rest of the sighthound breeds. Entries at championship shows range between 10 and 50

Portugal
Contributed by Patrenella Rylatt

Since Portugal's entry into the EEC, we have experienced a boom in cars and *caes* (the Portuguese word for dogs). The number of dog shows held each year is increasing dramatically and this is helped by the permitted movement of dogs between Portugal and other European countries.

The Afghan Hound is very popular with the Portuguese because of its glamour, but is still comparatively rare due mainly to the fact that people are predominantly flat-dwellers and their preference is for a smaller breed.

Home kennels

One of the few early breeders was the present re-appointed President of the Portuguese Kennel Club, Carla Molinari, whose **Vale Negro** kennel produced Afghans from 1965–1988. Carla bought her first Italian-bred Afghan in 1965 and has since imported dogs from Great Britain, the United States and Sweden. Altogether, over 50 champions were bred or owned by the Vale Negro kennel.

Apart from my own **Afeena** kennel, the only other one in operation is Mrs Louisa Ruffino's **Gallahad** kennel, which has been successful over the past 10 years in producing mainly Spanish/American type dogs. However, it is pleasing to see new Afghan breeders coming along and producing some interesting stock.

Ch El Dorado do Vale Negro

Foreign influences

At the moment there are very few Afghan breeders in Portugal and the entries at shows are augmented by dogs from countries such as France and Spain, the most influential being the Huilacos kennel of Mr Norman Huidobro Corbett (Spain).

The show scene

Due to the lack of numbers, there is only one Afghan breed show a year in Portugal and, generally speaking, it is easier to make up a champion here than it is in Great Britain. Having once achieved championship status, the dog is then obliged to challenge champions from other breeds in the groups - failing to do so would result in confiscation of the 'ticket'.

Whilst there are breed specialists in Portugal, they invariably judge all breeds. Since Portugal is smaller than Great Britain and many shows are held within reasonable distance of Lisbon, exhibitors do not have to travel too far. However, there is much visiting to and from neighbouring countries, which can increase travel considerably. Entry fees in Portugal are comparable to those in Great Britain.

Russia
Contributed by Natalia Gherasiova

Afghan history in Russia goes back to the 1960s when two were given to the Russian Premier, N Khruschev, by the King of Afghanistan. In the 1970s, several hounds were imported from the West and the East, thereby establishing two breed lines in the country. One line is founded on the Western type of 'civilised' Afghans (known in Russia as *decorative* – in other words, show dogs). The other line, *Bakhmulls*, (known in Russia as working/coursing *Tazi*), originates from the Royal kennel **Karizamir** in Afghanistan, from dogs brought back by Russian Army Officers before the 1978 *coup d'etat*.

Home kennels

The main public dog fanciers' associations since the 1970s have been: MGOLS, Fauna,

ARTA, Elita, Zoosphere, Zoopractica and Olf. The main kennels are; **Havas Purab** (Mrs Vetrova), **Al Zsharbua** (Muravieva), **Kai** (Kapralova), **Prioritet** (Mr Shipov), **Grand** (Kuksina), **Gerat** (Osipova), **Carmin** (Zshitkova), **Iv Zaraut** (Vodneva), **Contempory** (Dementieva), **Nigri's** (Grigorash). and **Djan** (formerly **Zahab al Tadj**) (Uvenalieva). For hunting dogs, the main ones are: **Dynamo**, Moscow and Military public associations and the kennel of **Blue Dale el Bark** (N Gherasiova).

Foreign influence
The foundation stock of 'decorative' Afghans in the former USSR from 1970–1980 came from Australia, Finland, Great Britain, Germany, Czechoslovakia and Poland.

Type
Russian dogs fall into three catagories; guard/search, hunting and decorative (companions), although owners prefer to think that all three can be companions. The 'decorative' Western type Afghan is considered a 'newly-made breed' that has existed for no longer than 50 years and is still under development according to the tastes of breeders and fashion trends. The aboriginal Afghan Hound (Bakhmull) originated in Northern India but was later cultivated in Afghanistan, and it is an ancient breed that Russian breeders do their best not to alter in proportions, bone structure, temperament, coat and coursing instincts.

Western 'show' Afghans in Russia and the world over are very impressive and beautiful because of their long, abundant coats, graceful movements and various colour combinations. Yet most of Russian decorative Afghans, according to judges, are skinny, badly muscled, have fragile bone structure, a narrow shallow chest and bad nervous systems. The proportions of the body parts have substantially changed. Decorative Afghans have lost their hunting function and obtained a new one; to move gracefully in the show ring to please the onlookers. An Afghan of today is a beauty created by a human, whereas the original Afghan Bakhmull is a beauty created by natural evolution. Russian breeders try their best to improve the exterior of Afghans.

The oriental type of hound Bakhmull is harmonically built, has a natural (not trimmed) saddle, broad and deep chest, always broad back, high withers and pretty abundant but not so long, silky coat. The front of the fore and hind feet (pasterns and ankles) must be short coated as well as the muzzle and the saddle. The loin and first thigh must be long for speedier galloping. They also have substantial flesh, well developed muscles, firm bone structure and good nerves. They are always of light colours – fawn or white, never black or brindle.

The distinctions between the types of Afghans were officially fixed in the 1980s when decorative Afghans failed the field tests. They refused to chase game (a hare in the field) and the owners were asked to quit from hunting clubs and join 'decorative' clubs instead. In 1985, the National Standard for the aboriginal Afghan Hound (a hunting dog), was officially developed. The model for this Standard was Ch Rad-o-Bark (son of the original King of Karizamir, imported from Afghanistan in 1974). For the Western 'decorative' type, the English Standard was applied and later the FCI Standard. The two types of hounds were thereafter shown in different rings.

Aboriginal Afghan Hounds 'Bakhmulls' Ch Rad-o-Bark and his son Ch David el Bark (standing) with their quarry, a wild hare.

According to old Russian traditions, every Afghan is predestined to work in field, their working characteristics being checked by field experts and evaluated. They are awarded field diplomas on a wild hare or fox which are graded 111, 11 and 1, experts being convinced that the exterior of a hound is connected with its working characteristics and cannot be separated.

Show scene
Top winning decorative Afghans are Nechaeva's San Darii (dog) and Solovieva's Ch Samanta Gerat (bitch). Top winning aboriginal Afghan Hound Bakhmull is Ch Rad-o-Bark (two field diplomas 111gr), his son Ch David el Bark (two field diplomas 111,11 gr), owned by Natalia Gherasiova, Nironova's Ch Guldara el Bark (bitch), Fausek's Gardes el Bark (bitch) and Privalovskii's Virsavia el Bark (bitch).

South Africa
Contributed by Milan Anteglievic
In South Africa, Afghan Hounds and all other recognised breeds of dogs are judged to British Breed Standards and, because of this, top quality, well-bred hounds from

established lines in Great Britain are highly prized. At present, South Africa must be one of the last outposts of the true British Afghan and the majority of our breeders stick rigidly to tried and tested British lines.

In a numerically small country such as ours, the influence of famous sires and dams in the breed is perhaps easier to follow than in countries with much larger numbers of Afghans. Also, because of our limited gene pool, careful consideration is given when planning a mating.

Home kennels
In 1972 our breed in South Africa was greatly influenced with the arrival from Great Britain of Bondor Talk Of The Town (Ch Bondor Dera Ghazi Khan ex Bondor Cinnamon), imported by Milan and Anka Anteglievic, **Nas Dom**. Other influential dogs imported from Great Britain by this kennel, were Landhavi Mr Shoestring at Nas Dom and SA Ch Jhansi Royal Performance, winner of numerous Hound Groups and BISs. Over a 45-year period the Nas Dom Kennel has produced 87 champions, including the multi-BIS-winning SA Ch Nas Dom Batu Khan.

Other influential kennels include Barbara Longworth's **Sarkari**, James and Carol Marwick's **Kenwick**, Angus Peden and Peter Dye's **Lakemere**, Gael Morison's **Atlantis**, Pat and Dave McCann's **Whodeanie**, Jill Dunckley's **Eglinton**, Sue Mitchell's **Konpara**, Carolyn Blair's **Kohinoor** and Pat and Jackie Kelly's **Mistral**.

Foreign influence
Presently there are about 20 breeders countrywide and 80% of these keep the British type, either purchasing locally or importing from Great Britain. The remaining 20% import from the United States of America and adhere to the American lines. Apart from one or two attempts, there is virtually no interbreeding between British and American lines.

The show scene
The show scene in South Africa is mainly centered on three regions: Johannesburg and its neighbouring reef towns, Durban and Cape Town. Approximately 45 championship shows are held annually and a dog must win five CCs under five different judges to become a champion. The highest entry to date was 105 (in 1978), although the number of entries at present is about 40. Entry fees range from R15 (£2 sterling) to R25 per dog.

Spain
Contributed by David Allan
The Afghan Hound is not a popular breed in Spain and most breeders find great difficulty in placing their litters, preferring generally only to breed when they need to carry on the line. This does not mean that the average dog lover does not appreciate the breed – you should hear the 'Oohs!' and 'Aahs!' as the BOB comes into the Group ring. It's just that most people know their limit regarding the amount of work that is involved. However, the breed over here on the Continent enjoys a great number of Group and BIS wins, and is probably the most frequent winner in the sighthound group.

Home kennels

The two oldest remaining kennels on the scene today are Norman Huidobro's **Huilacos** and David Allan and Javier Blanco's **Shikarah**.

Other successful kennels of the past and present include Cynthia Madigan's **Branwen**, Andrea Meyer's **Saidias**, Andres Garcia's **Kalikos**, Ignacia Vidorreta's **Sumavas**, Iñigo Garcia's **Akras** and the **el Corregidor** kennels, which were based in Cadiz. A relatively new kennel is **Rayma**, owned by Cristobal Ramos.

Foreign influence

In years gone by most imported dogs were from the United States, from kennels such as Akabas, Crown Crest and Coastwind, but more recently the Scandinavian dogs have played an important role in the breeding programmes of a few of the remaining kennels. Some of the winning imports include Ch Huilacos Antar Rakashi (Mexico), Ch Zanavars Kochis at Shikarah (Great Britain), Ch Shikaris Moro of Sotogrande (United States), Ch/Am Ch Sandinas Satellite (United States), Ch/Am Ch A Kais K'nypton (United States), Dk Ch Dur-I-Durrans Music Man (Denmark), Ch Dur-I-Durrans Unique (Denmark), Ch Afgandens Buffolo Bill (Denmark) and Ch Dur-I-Durrans Wine and Roses (Denmark).

World Ch Dur-I-Durrans Unique. Photo: Willy

Top Afghan 1996 was another import, Ch Kabiks In The Nick Of Time (United States), handled by Philip Gallard.

Show scene

We only seem to get a breed specialist judge (if we are lucky) for the Club show and usually have all-rounder judges for general championship shows. Many of the all-rounders do not have a good understanding of true Afghan Type and tend to put up the showy, extrovert dog, thinking only of the dog's opportunity in the Group. Unfortunately, many breeders are guided by this kind of judging and tend to breed for the flashy type and forget the functional side of the hound.

Int Ch Xciting Bullet The Blue Sky. Photo: Ingrid

Spain is a large country and travelling distances to shows can be great – up to a 10-hour drive. Add to this the expense of a hotel and costs begin to escalate. Entry fees range between £16–£18 sterling.

We get an average of 25–30 Afghans entered at the show and that or less doubles at the Club show or the Madrid show. I would imagine that if Spain were smaller then we would get better entries as the distances would be much reduced.

Sweden

Contributed by Ingrid Moholm

Home kennels

The top kennel in Sweden is **El Khyrias**, owned by Christina Jernberg, with over 75 champions being produced since the 1960s. The latest is Int Ch El Khyrias Zon of the Master, Afghan of the Year 1995 both in Sweden and Denmark. Other very well known Afghans bred by Christina were Int Ch El Khyrias Never Say Never Again (Top Afghan 1991) and Int Ch El Khyrias Never The Less, Top Afghan Bitch 1990 in Sweden and Norway.

Other top winning kennels in the 1990s are Yvonne Ljungkvist and Tommy Carlssons' **Alphaville's**, Christina Aldrin's **Khaos**, Lilian Söderman's **Mandrill's**, Eva Hildorsson's **Syringa**, Gunilla Holmgren's **Kingsleah**, Britt-Marie and Carina Ekwall's **Xciting** and Louise Le Pluart's **Tash-Kurgan**. Many of these kennels have incorporated Australian and American bloodlines into their breeding programmes with great success. The **New Fashion** kennel of Ingrid Moholm is based on Australian and, more recently, Nordic lines.

Additionally, successful kennels who have stayed mainly within Nordic lines are Eva and Ulla Jonssons' **El Shahzade**, Inger Andersson's **Shahnadir** and Anette Stone's **Khalibadh**.

Foreign influence

In Sweden we have many active breeders who will breed one or two litters a year. Some breed every second or third year. We have many different bloodlines in our country and very few breeders base their programmes solely on Scandinavian lines. Imports from Australia have had the most influence in the 1980s and 1990s. Type is important to many of our breeders.

Show scene
In the north of Sweden you can normally see around 20 Afghans at the shows, in the middle and south 20–70 and at the large Skokloster show around 100 Afghans are exhibited, but many of these come from other countries. Annual registration of Afghans in Sweden is 150–170, with Whippets, Irish Wolfhounds and Greyhounds above them in the sighthound registration table. Puppies are not easy to sell in Sweden and many breeders have to hold on to their puppies until they are five or six months of age before finding them good homes.

We have about 35 international and national shows and about 15 sighthound specialty shows each year. There are also five Afghan specialties. To become a Swedish champion, three CACs are required and the dog must be two years of age to get the title. For the international title, four CACIBs must be won in three different countries under three different judges. It must be one year between the first and last CACIB. A dog under 15 months of age cannot win a CACIB. Entry fees are around £17 sterling.

Top Afghan in 1990 and 1996 was Multi-SBIS and BIS Ch Yesterday, Today and Tomorrow, bred by Åge Gjetnes and Elsa Storesund and owned by Elisabet Levén and Sven Westerblad.

(Above) Am Ch Kabik's The Challenger.
Photo: Fox & Cook
(Below) Am Ch Stormhill's Who's Zoomin' Who.
Photo: Missy Yuhl

United States of America
Contributed by Sandy Frei
Home kennels
The foundation stock of the major kennels in the United States today is mainly (with the exception of Grandeur, a closed kennel that does not allow outside breeders to use its stock) a combination of the successful kennels of the 1950s to the early 1970s – **Akaba**, **ben ghaZi**, **Crown Crest**, **Dureigh**, **Grandeur**, **Holly Hill**, **Majara**, **Mecca**, **Moornistan**, **Scheherezade**, **Stormhill** and **Tajmir**. The last influential import was Ophaal (from the vdOM kennel of Eta Pauptit), imported into the United States by Kay Finch of Crown Crest in 1954.

Two very popular and prolific stud dogs in the 1970s were Ch Coastwind Abraxas and Ch Mecca's Falstaff. Of those two, the one whose significance is still seen today is Falstaff, who is behind Am Ch Pahlavi Puttin' on the Ritz, Am Ch Elmo's Tutankammun and Am Ch Genesis Red

Cloud – three of the most influential sires in this country in the late 1980s and 1990s.

In the 1980s the **Kabik** kennels, owned by Chris and Marguerite Terrell, dominated the scene first with Ch Kabik's The Challenger (a grandson of both Abraxas and Falstaff) and later with his son Ch Kabik's The Frontrunner. Currently, the all-time top-winning dog and bitch at all-breed level belong to the **Grandeur** kennel. They are Am Ch Triumph of Grandeur and his daughter Am Ch Tryst of Grandeur. The all-time top-winning specialty Afghan and all-time top sire is Am Ch Pahlavi Puttin' on the Ritz, owned by Karen Wagner. 'Taco' has sired over 70 champions in the United States to date as well as many champions internationally. He is the sire of Am Ch

Am Ch Casbar Sugar-n-Spice. Photo: Booth

Stormhill's Who's Zoomin Who, owned and bred by Dave and Sandy Frei, who retired as the all-time top-winning bitch in the history of the breed. Taco is also the sire of the all-time top-winning specialty bitch in this country, Am Ch Casbar's Sugar N' Spice, owned by Jerry Bazar and Kevin and Barbara Cassidy. The all-time producing bitch with 20 champions to her credit is Cypress Slightly Kaotic, owned by Jia Miller. Currently, Am Ch Tifarah's Hi-Flying Victory, owned and bred by Janis Reital, is the number one Afghan Hound in the United States.

Show scene

Afghans were a popular show dog back in the 1970s, when entries were amongst the largest at any given show. However, since that time their popularity has waned and, at most all-breed shows, their numbers can vary between 10–30. Specialties remain popular, especially in the more populated areas. Increasing costs have caused exhibitors to become more selective about where and to whom they will show. The National tends to hold a fairly steady entry of around 300 dogs, although this number may vary depending on where it is held and who is judging.

Approximately 1300 America Kennel Club conformation championship shows are held each year, including one Afghan Hound Club of America (AHCA) National Specialty and

Am Ch Tifarah's Hi-Flying Victory. Photo: Kohler

over 40 regional specialties. Whilst not a championship show, the AHCA Breeder's Cup is held annually in Spring and rotated around the country. To win this, the breeder pays a fee to nominate a litter and the pups are entered at a later date prior to the show. The National is always held in the fall and is also rotated around the country. Both the National and regional specialties hold sweepstakes classes for dogs of 6–18 months. Winners receive only money for their wins, not points towards their championship. However, during the regular classes it is possible for puppies to be awarded 'Winners' and receive points towards their championship.

Achieving championship status is not easy. To become an official American Kennel Club champion of record, a dog must earn 15 points. Essentially, these points are based upon the number of dogs in actual competition – the more dogs, the more points. However, the number of dogs required for points varies with the breed, sex and the geographical location of the show in accordance with a schedule set up by the American Kennel Club to help equalise competition from breed to breed and area to area.

A dog can earn 1–5 points at a show. Wins of 3–5 points are termed 'majors'. The 15 points required for championship must be won under at least three different judges, and must include two majors won under different judges.

Exhibitors living in the West have to travel much further than those living on the East Coast or Midwest, where several shows may be held within easy driving distance on any given weekend. There are also 'cluster shows', where exhibitors can attend a number of shows (organised by different kennel clubs) on consecutive days in the same location. Sometimes specialties are linked with these cluster shows.

Entry fees range from $16–25 US dollars (£10-£16 sterling). Sometimes clubs will offer reduced rates for puppies and/or the 'bred by exhibitor' class.

There are both breed specialists and judges who officiate on many breeds, the latter being in the majority at general championship shows. Specialty shows are usually judged by breed specialists. Judges are generally selected by a vote of the general membership of the specialty-giving club.

Other activities

Other Afghan Hound activities in America include obedience, coursing and agility.

Health and welfare

Regarding puppy sales, the market is somewhat limited because Afghans are not the breed for everyone. Responsible breeders work hard to educate prospective puppy buyers and find the best homes are usually with return buyers and people who have owned the breed before. Maintenance is a key factor. In America, leisure time is at a premium – most people have to work and therefore grooming time is limited. Also, property is at a premium in many areas and many people are moving to apartments, townhouses or condominiums which aren't suitable for a large breed such as an Afghan.

In the past few years, the Afghan Hound Club of America and the regional Afghan Hound clubs have become quite involved in rescue. Unfortunately, some individuals within the breed have neglected their dogs and the rescue groups have stepped in to find suitable homes for them to live out their lives. In some cases this has involved nursing them back into good health and condition prior to being placed into a new home.

Glamour and presentation are very important factors in the show ring and there are various kennel types, resulting in many different 'looks'. The current trend of breeding for a longer back (to increase side gait) is resulting in topline problems and subsequently, basic shape (squareness) is being lost. Sickle hocks (inability to straighten the hock joint on the back reach of the hind leg) are also cropping up and tail problems (too short, too curly, too straight or carried to the side) are appearing within some lines.

All Afghans should be checked for hip dysplasia, eye problems and thyroid before they are bred. Other problems that have cropped up in American-bred Afghans include heart disorders such as cardiomyopathy, skin complaints, immune problems, bloat and chylothorax.

chapter five
The Breed Standard

The first detailed description of an Afghan Hound

The first detailed description of an Afghan Hound, 'Zardin', appeared in the *Indian Kennel Gazette* in October 1906. Used as a model for future breed standards, this standard was adopted by the first Afghan Hound Club in 1925, revised by the newly-formed Afghan Hound Association in 1927 and revised by them again in 1946. In 1987, The Kennel Club slightly rearranged the Standard, without altering its interpretation.

'Zardin' is a light-coloured hound, almost white, with a black muzzle. He has a very long, punishing jaw of peculiar power and level mouth; his head resembles that of a Deerhound, but with skull oval and prominent occiput, surmounted by a top-knot; ears fairly large, well feathered, and hanging to the side of the head more than carried in front.

He has a keen, dark eye, and little or no stop. A long, strong, clean neck, fairly well arched, running in a nice curve to shoulder, which is long and sloping and well laid back; his back is strong, loin powerful and slightly arched.

He, as well as all this class of hound, falls away towards the stern

Zardin, owned by Captain John Barff.
Photo courtesy AHA.

(tail), which is set on low, almost destitute of hair, and usually carried low. He is well ribbed, tucked up under the loin; forelegs straight and strong and covered with hair; great length between elbow (which is straight) and ankle.

The forefeet are long, fairly broad and covered with long hair. Not too narrow in brisket, which is deep, with good girth of chest. Hind quarters very powerful, furnished with plenty of muscle; great length between hip and hock, which is long and strong, a fair bend of stifle, hind feet not so long as forefeet, but fairly wide and well protected with hair.

The hind quarters, flanks, ribs and forequarters are well clothed with protective hair, thick and fine in texture, showing some undercoat. The coat on the back is shorter.

Note: Zardin's owner, Mr John Barff thought him to be *at least 26in at the shoulder.*

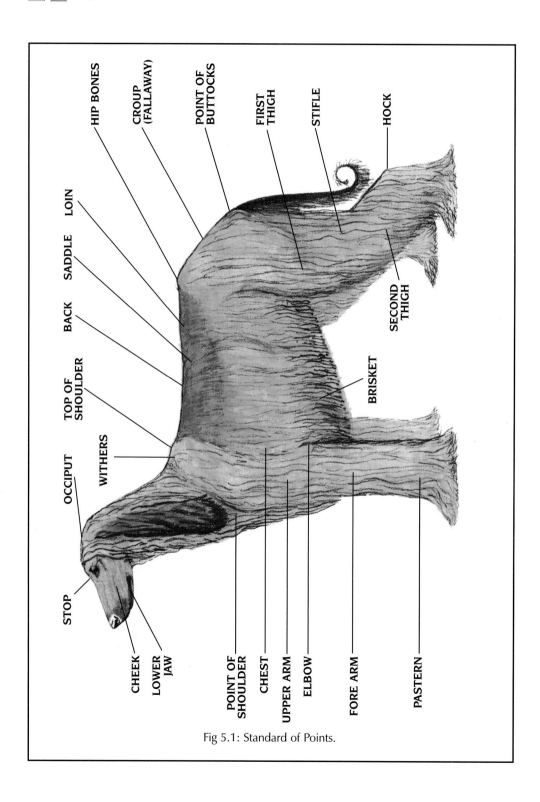

Fig 5.1: Standard of Points.

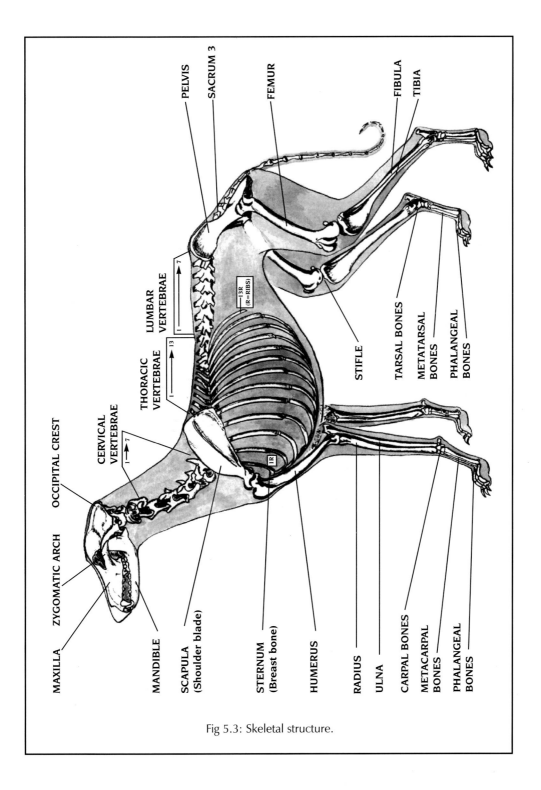

Fig 5.3: Skeletal structure.

The Afghan Hound Breed Standard
Kennel Club and Fédération Cynologique Internationale (FCI)
(Reproduced by courtesy of The Kennel Club. The pre-1987 wording is used in Australasia.)

General Appearance: Gives the impression of strength and dignity, combining speed and power. Head held proudly.

Characteristics: Eastern or Oriental expression is typical of the breed. The Afghan looks at and through one.

Temperament: Dignified and aloof, with a certain keen fierceness.

Head and Skull: Skull long, not too narrow with prominent occiput. Foreface long with punishing jaws and slight stop. Skull well balanced and mounted by a long "top-knot". Nose preferably black, liver permissible in light coloured dogs.

Eyes: Dark for preference, but golden colour not debarred. Nearly triangular, slanting slightly upwards from inner corner to outer.

Ears: Set low and well back, carried close to head. Covered with long silky hair.

Mouth: Jaws strong, with a perfect, regular and complete scissor bite, ie the upper teeth closely overlapping the lower teeth and set square to the jaws. Level bite tolerated.

Neck: Long, strong with proud carriage of head.

Forequarters: Shoulders long and sloping, well set back, well muscled and strong without being loaded. Forelegs straight and well boned, straight with shoulder, elbows close to rib cage, not turning in or out.

Body: Back level, moderate length, well muscled, back falling slightly away to stern. Loin straight, broad and rather short. Hipbones rather prominent and wide apart. A fair spring of ribs and good depth of chest.

Hindquarters: Powerful, well bent and well turned stifles. Great length between hip and hock with comparatively short distance between hock and foot. Dew claws may be removed.

Feet: Forefeet strong and very large both in length and breadth, and covered with long, thick hair, toes arched. Pasterns long and springy, pads well down on ground. Hindfeet long, but not quite as broad as forefeet; covered with long thick hair.

Tail: Not too short. Set on low with ring at end. Raised when in action. Sparsely feathered.

Gait/Movement: Smooth and springy with a style of high order.

Coat: Long and very fine texture on ribs, fore and hindquarters and flanks. In mature dogs from shoulder backwards and along the saddle, hair short and close. Hair long from forehead backwards, with a distinct silky 'top-knot'. On foreface hair short. Ears and legs well coated. Pasterns can be bare. Coat must develop naturally.

Colour: All colours acceptable.

Size: Ideal height: dogs 68–74cm (27–29in); bitches 63–69cm (25–27in).

Faults: Any departure from the foregoing points should be considered a fault and the seriousness with which the fault should be regarded should be in exact proportion to its degree.

Note: Male animals should have two apparently normal testicles fully descended into the scrotum.

Explanation of the Breed Standard

I shall now give my personal interpretation of how our dogs relate to the Afghan Hound Breed Standard, based on my own experience of breeding and showing over the past 26 years.

General appearance

The Afghan Hound is a long-legged hunting dog developed from an original greyhound type to meet and withstand the differing types of terrain in Afghanistan. It is muscular, fast and versatile with flexible joints, which would have enabled it to chase and catch small prey. Its body is balanced in proportion to its legs, its neck is comparatively long and it holds its head high.

Sp Ch Indira of Shikarah (aged 11), displaying correct conformation not hidden by coat.

Characteristics

Whilst the Standard mentions only the expression as a characteristic of the Afghan Hound, a question regularly posed to examinees at judging examinations is, 'Can you name the characteristics of the Afghan Hound which set it apart from any other breed?' Examinees would be falling short if they only mentioned the expression. The originality of the coat pattern, the large forefeet and long hindfeet, the prominent hip bones, ring tail and distinctive springy gait are undoubtedly among the answers that an examiner would be looking for. Regarding expression, I can think of no other breed that would look at you with such indifference whilst mentally banishing you from their mind.

Temperament

Afghans view approaching strangers warily, especially on their own territory. Whilst they will not attack, they will probably bark, keeping the unfamiliar visitor at a distance. This natural suspicion should not be mistaken for excessive nervousness or a wicked temper, both of which are undesirable traits.

Head and skull

The foreface (nose to stop) is approximately the same length as the skull (stop to occiput). The stop is a point between the eyes, which the standard calls for to be *slight* and is a fault if too deep as in a Setter or totally filled in as in a Borzoi. The foreface must have strength, yet show refinement and be neither too thick nor too weak and snipy. The top of the foreface leads into a very slight prominence of the nasal bone structure, causing a slightly

Roman appearance, and should not be dish-faced or overly convex, which are both faults. The nasal bones and blood vessels are quite visible, much desired and referred to as *chiselling*. Flews (upper lips) should be clean and neat and not held loosely. The nose should be black with a lighter brown colour allowed in light coloured dogs. Some black-nosed dogs experience a seasonal colour fade to liver. This is known as *winter nose* and is not a fault.

The skull should be slightly domed from ear to ear, not flat as in a greyhound, with an accentuated ridge of bone (the occiput) giving height at the back of the skull before sloping downwards towards the base of the skull. The width of the skull is determined by the shape of the *zygomatic arch* or side bones, which can be felt at the upper corner of the eye broadening slightly outwards towards the ear. Too wide a curve to this bone gives a coarse, broad skull shape and a straighter, flatter bone gives a narrow skull, both of which are incorrect.

Head study: Ch Saxonmill Rum Tum Tigger.
Photo: David Paton

The upright part of the lower jawbone slots under the zygomatic arch and eye socket, and attaches to chewing muscles which provide power to the *punishing jaw*.

Bitches should be finer in head than dogs, the definition being *demonstrative of its sex and in relative proportion to the body*.

Eyes

The Afghan Hound is far-sighted and displays a distant and haughty expression when looking at close objects.

Eyes should be set slightly to the side of the head following the line of the side bones. They are almost triangular in shape, slanting slightly upwards from the inner corner to the outer, giving the Oriental or Eastern expression so typical of the breed. They must not be large, bulging or round. A dark brown or dark hazel colour is preferred; they should not be yellow. Rims are dark in colour and the lower lid must not sag. An unpigmented third eyelid (inner membrane) will detract from the true expression and should not be encouraged.

Ears

Should be set on low, level with the outer corner of the eyes and lying close to the side of the head. High set ears with short leathers are a fault.

Mouth

The Afghan Hound should have 42 teeth (20 on the top and 22 on the bottom) and, although judges do not count teeth in Great Britain, it is important that all the incisors and premolars are present.

The correct bite is the *scissor bite*, best described as when the upper incisors fit closely over the lower incisors and the upper canines fit behind the lower canines. A *level bite* is when the upper incisors meet the lower incisors edge to edge. While it is acceptable in the show ring, most breeders and judges would agree that the scissor bite is the more suitable. Faults of bite arise when the lower jaw grows too short or too long. (See fig 5.4: Faults of bite.)

Many young dogs have a tendency to be overshot, as the lower jaw tends to grow on after the top, but this often corrects itself as the puppy grows. However, a level bite in a puppy should be closely watched as there is a possibility of this becoming undershot.

Discoloured or broken teeth that are clearly the result of an accident should not count against the dog.

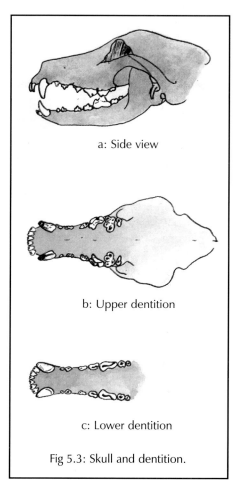

a: Side view

b: Upper dentition

c: Lower dentition

Fig 5.3: Skull and dentition.

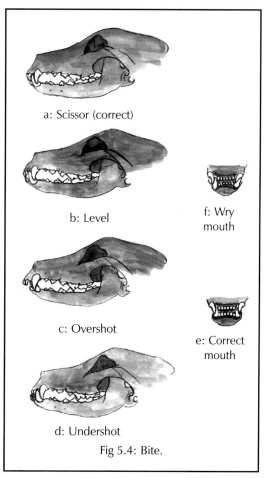

a: Scissor (correct)

b: Level

c: Overshot

d: Undershot

f: Wry mouth

e: Correct mouth

Fig 5.4: Bite.

Neck, forequarters and chest

Any fault in the construction of the forequarters contributes towards incorrect movement and this area must be assessed in conjunction with the chest and rib cage as all are inter-relating. The neck and shoulders should be evaluated together, as the conformation of the shoulders determines the visual length of the neck, which should be strong and slightly arched. It is also important to mention here that the angulation of the forequarters and hindquarters should totally balance with and complement each other, enabling the hound to cover sufficient ground and produce the characteristic gait.

The shoulder blade (scapula) should be long and well laid back with the upper arm (humerus) set at such an angle as to place the forelegs and elbows well under the body. The shoulder blade and upper arm should be of equal length. The shoulder blades are anchored to the first five ribs by sheet muscles and if there is lack of depth to the rib cage or it is narrow or barrelled, the blades will not lie cleanly.

A well laid back shoulder with a corresponding short upper arm will give the exaggerated thrust of a hackney type of action and, whilst this may look showy in the ring, it is incorrect as the dog will be unable to reach forward sufficiently to give good ground coverage.

A short, straight shoulder blade with a correctly angulated upper arm is often difficult to assess as the dog will appear to have sufficient forward reach. However, the top edge of the blade will fall short of the spine, with the neck set on in too upright a position.

The best way to understand these points is to run your hands over your dog, tell yourself what you can feel and compare with skeletal diagrams. Pose the following questions:

- Do the shoulders feel too wide and lumpy and, if so, is this because the chest is too barrelled? (Ideally, there should be the width of three fingers between the top points of the shoulder blades.)
- From the front, can the correct width of chest be felt with ease between the front legs, or is the chest too narrow, with elbows held too close together? (Depending on the size of the dog, correct width is usually a hand's breadth between the elbows.)
- Is the chest too shallow in depth? (Ideally, the deepest part is in line with the elbow, decreasing gradually towards the tuck-up of the loin.)

Remember that all problems are inter-relating and the pieces either fit together and work very well or they just don't; your hands and eyes will tell you.

The forelegs are straight when viewed from the front, with the feet pointing forwards. Pasterns are sloping to counterbalance the angle of the upper arm, absorb impact and make a vital contribution towards the typical springy Afghan movement. *Forelegs straight with shoulder* is wording that has always been controversial and should not be mistaken for a short, straight upper arm, as this will give less freedom of stride, resulting in a terrier type of action.

Forefeet are large both in length and breadth, with toes well arched.

Body

The body should be muscular but not fat. The topline is level from the shoulders to the loin but rises very slightly over the broad, powerful loin before falling away towards the stern.

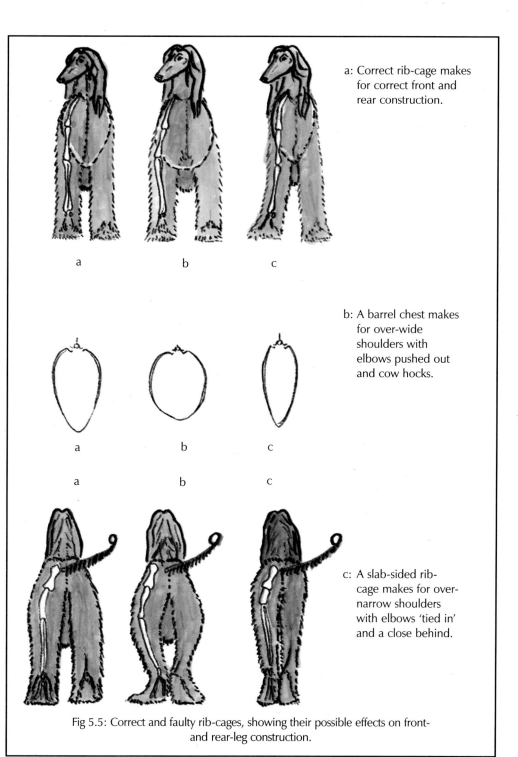

a: Correct rib-cage makes for correct front and rear construction.

b: A barrel chest makes for over-wide shoulders with elbows pushed out and cow hocks.

c: A slab-sided rib-cage makes for over-narrow shoulders with elbows 'tied in' and a close behind.

Fig 5.5: Correct and faulty rib-cages, showing their possible effects on front- and rear-leg construction.

a: Back too short, unbalanced. Probable movement – back legs will interfere with front.

b: Back too long, unbalanced. Tail too straight. Probable movement – will give the appearance of extended side gait. Could break in topline.

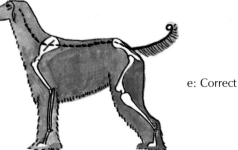

c: Unbalanced front and rear angulation, excessive lay-back of shoulder blade, short upper arm. Straight pasterns, long hocks. 'Teapot-handle' tail. Possible movement – uneven gait, will lack forward extension. Topline will rise, due to excessive rear angulation.

d: Lacks front and rear angulation. Short, straight pasterns. Long-backed (hollow). Tail set too high. Possible movement – will lack reach, drive and spring.

e: Correct

Fig 5.6: Conformation.

Hip bones are pronounced. The body is balanced: the height at the top of the shoulder is equal to the distance from the point of the shoulder to the point of the buttocks.

The rib cage is deep and approximately pear-shaped, providing plenty of heart room, with a flatness where the forequarters lay against it. Just after the elbows the ribs show a gradual widening or *spring*. A narrow, *slab-sided* (flat-sided) chest, lacking in depth of brisket, gives the impression of forelegs coming out of one hole whereas, if the rib cage is barrelled, the shoulder does not lie clean and the elbows are thrown outwards.

The loin (or coupling) is approximately one third of the length of the back and allows for freedom of movement and length of stride. It is strong, well muscled, almost square and must never roach. Too long a coupling indicates structural weakness and too short a coupling inhibits movement, particularly if combined with a short back.

The fallaway or croup (pelvic bone) is wedge-shaped and slopes downwards from the hip-bones to the buttocks, with the tail vertebrae set on approximately two-thirds of the way down. The angle of the fallaway is important, as it affects the tail set and the scope of the hind movement. If the angle is too steep the tail will be carried very low and hindleg backward extension will be restricted. An insufficient angle would create a tail set on too high and there would be no limit to how far the hindlegs could extend backwards, giving a high 'kick-back' movement that would be incapable of balancing with front extension.

Hindquarters

These are powerful, with angulation in balance with correct front assembly.

The standard calls for *great length between hip and hock* and *well bent and well turned stifles*. The long thighbone (femur) is attached to the pelvis by a ball and socket joint and connects with the second thigh (tibia and fibula) at the knee joint (stifle). The power to drive forward is determined by the angle at which the hindlegs are attached to the pelvis, coupled with the degree of angulation at the stifle joint. The bend of stifle is very noticeable when the Afghan is standing naturally with weight distributed evenly on all four legs.

If any part of the hindlegs is lacking in length, the stifle joint will be straight. There will be no strength from the pelvis to the thighbone and movement will be restricted, as the dog will be unable to place its feet sufficiently underneath the body to give the necessary forward propulsion.

If the hindlegs are too long with the dog over-angulated at the stifle, weakness in the hock will result. When moving away, the back pasterns will be close together with the stifle bending outwards to compensate.

The hock joint is low-set and extends downward to the rear pastern which, unlike the sloping front pastern, is vertical. Strong hocks make a great contribution towards the leverage system in hind movement. When viewed from behind the hocks and feet should turn neither in nor out. Hindfeet are slightly narrower than front feet, toes arched.

Tail

The tail is set two-thirds down the croup, has light feathering on the underside and a distinctive ring on the end. At its full length it reaches to the hock joint, although it is more important that its length balances the overall picture of the dog. When raised on the move it is carried at an angle of approximately 45° and completes the balance of the dog.

High-set tails carried over the body, double-ringed tails and completely straight tails are all faults.

Coat

In adults the coat is long and silky on the hindquarters, forequarters, ribs, ears and feet, and short and close on the face, pasterns and saddle (so-called because its natural shape along the sides of the body resembles a rider's saddle). On the top of the

The show trot.

head the 'top-knot' hair grows long and silky. The short hair on the saddle and pasterns can sometimes be covered in a heavily-coated dog but the primary pattern must still be found underneath, or the coat is incorrect.

The Afghan is born smooth-coated and slowly develops a coat of rather woolly texture all over its body. Puppy whiskers appear on the face and these are cast off as the adult coat approaches. The coat continues to grow thickly and begins to change during adolescence which, depending on the dog, can occur between the ages of nine and eighteen months. At this time the woolly hair growing through the saddle and on the upper side of the tail begins to fall, exposing the coarser, shorter hair that has been developing underneath. Long silky hair grows over the rest of the body.

On occasions you will see dogs carrying the old-fashioned coat pattern with deep, smooth saddles, pasterns, hocks and receding topknots. These are traits usually accompanied by a sparse coat of cotton wool texture which is difficult to grow and tends not to retain length. Unfortunately, these dogs have had a pretty poor deal in the ring as the trend over the years has been towards glamour.

Colour

Many wonderful colour combinations are found and basically anything goes. However, a white flash down the face, although not a fault, is not particularly desirable.

Size

If the dog is perceived as a good example of the breed and can be easily distinguished by its sex (masculine dog or feminine bitch) a little leeway on size is permitted.

Note

Male animals should have two apparently normal testicles fully descended into the scrotum, but in Great Britain a male may be shown without testicles if they have been removed for a good veterinary reason.

Gait/movement

When viewed from the side the Afghan appears balanced, free-flowing and well coordinated. Front and rear legs reach well forward and extend well back, achieving long, free strides. We have discussed the importance of good angulation earlier, in that it provides power of movement both upward and forward in the hindquarters and spring, reach and flexibility in the forequarters. Poor angulation throughout will mean the dog taking shorter steps and the resulting action will be choppy and bouncing rather than smooth and graceful.

The head is carried proudly and counter-balanced by the raised tail. The topline appears level and must not roach or dip in the middle.

Afghans are shown moving in the *show trot*, a coordinated *trot in two-time*, whereby the hind foot falls simultaneously into the footprint vacated by the front foot (on the same side). When moving towards or away the legs should turn neither in nor out. Feet must always point forward and should not cross or interfere with one another.

Pacing (when the hind and forelegs on the same side move forward together), rolling, shuffling, crabbing (moving with body at an angle to the line of travel) and favouring a leg all detract from the *style of high order* and should be penalised.

The American Breed Standard
By courtesy of the American Kennel Club

General Appearance – The Afghan Hound is an aristocrat; his whole appearance one of dignity and aloofness with no trace of plainness or coarseness. He has a straight front, proudly carried head, eyes gazing into the distance as if in memory of ages past. The striking characteristics of the breed – exotic, or 'Eastern,' expression, long silky topknot, peculiar coat pattern, very prominent hipbones, large feet, and the impression of a somewhat exaggerated bend in the stifle due to profuse trouserings – stand out clearly, giving the Afghan Hound the appearance of what he is, a king of dogs, that has held true to tradition throughout the ages.

Head – The head is of good length, showing much refinement, the skull evenly balanced with the foreface. There is a slight prominence of the nasal bone structure causing a slightly Roman appearance, the center line running up over the foreface with little or no stop, falling away in front of the eyes so there is an absolutely clear outlook with no interference; the underjaw showing great strength, the jaws long and punishing; the mouth level, meaning that the teeth from the upper jaw and lower jaw match evenly, neither overshot nor undershot. This is a difficult mouth to breed. A scissors bite is even more punishing and can be more easily bred into a dog than a level mouth, and a dog having a scissors bite, where the lower teeth slip inside and rest against the teeth of the upper jaw, should not be penalized. The occipital bone is very prominent. The head is surmounted by a topknot of long silky hair. **Ears** – The ears are long, set approximately on level with outer corners of the eyes, the leather of the ear reaching nearly to the end of the dog's nose, and covered with long silky hair. **Eyes** – The eyes are almond-shaped (almost triangular), never full or bulgy, and are dark in color. **Nose** – Nose is of good size, black in color. **Faults** – coarseness; snipiness; overshot or undershot; eyes round or bulgy or light in color; exaggerated Roman nose; head not surmounted with topknot.

Neck – The neck is of good length, strong and arched, running in a curve to the shoulders which are long and sloping and well laid back. *Faults* – Neck too short or too thick; a ewe neck; a goose neck; a neck lacking in substance.

Body – The back line appearing practically level from the shoulders to the loin. Strong and powerful loin and slightly arched, falling away to the stern, with the hipbones very pronounced; well ribbed and tucked up in flanks. The height at the shoulders equals the distance from the chest to the buttocks; the brisket well let down, and of medium width. *Faults* – Roach back, swayback, goose rump, slack loin; lack of prominence of hipbones; too much width of brisket, causing interference with elbows.

Tail – Tail set not too high on the body, having a ring, or a curve on the end; should never be curled over, or rest on the back, or be carried sideways; and should never be bushy.

Legs – Forelegs are straight and strong with great length between elbow and pastern; elbows well held in; forefeet large in both length and width; toes well arched; feet covered with long thick hair; fine in texture; pasterns long and straight; pads of feet unusually large and well down on the ground. Shoulders have plenty of angulation so that the legs are well set underneath the dog. Too much straightness of shoulder causes the dog to break down in the pasterns, and this is a serious fault. All four feet of the Afghan Hound are in line with the body, turning neither in nor out. The hind feet are broad and of good length; the toes arched, and covered with long thick hair; hindquarters powerful and well muscled, with great length between hip and hock; hocks are well let down; good angulation of both stifle and hock; slightly bowed from hock to crotch. *Faults* – Front or back feet thrown outward or inward; pads of feet not thick enough; or feet too small; or any other evidence of weakness in feet; weak or broken down pasterns; too straight in stifle; too long in hock.

Coat – Hindquarters, flanks, ribs, forequarters, and legs well covered with thick, silky hair, very fine in texture; ears and all four feet well feathered; from in front of the shoulders; and also backwards from the shoulders along the saddle from the flanks and the ribs upwards, the hair is short and close, forming a smooth back in mature dogs – this is a traditional characteristic of the Afghan Hound. The Afghan Hound should be shown in its natural state; the coat is not clipped or trimmed; the head is surmounted (in the full sense of the word) with a topknot of long, silky hair – that is also an outstanding characteristic of the Afghan Hound. Showing of short hair on cuffs on either front or back legs is permissible. *Fault* – Lack of shorthaired saddle in mature dogs.

Height – Dogs, 27in, plus or minus one inch; bitches, 25in, plus or minus one inch.

Weight – Dogs, about 60lb; bitches, about 50lb.

Color – All colors are permissible, but color or color combinations are pleasing; white markings, especially on the head, are undesirable.

Gait – When running free, the Afghan Hound moves at a gallop, showing great elasticity and spring in his smooth, powerful stride. When on a loose lead, the Afghan can trot at a fast pace; stepping along, he has the appearance of placing the hind feet directly in the foot prints of the front feet, both thrown straight ahead. Moving with head and tail high, the whole appearance of the Afghan Hound is one of great style and beauty.

Temperament – Aloof and dignified, yet gay.   **Faults** – Sharpness or shyness.

Differences between the American and Kennel Club/FCI Standards

	AMERICAN	KENNEL CLUB/FCI
Nose	Black	Preferably black, liver permissible in light coloured dogs
	Slightly Roman appearance	*Roman appearance* not mentioned
Head	Little or no stop	Slight stop
Bite	Level, scissor bite allowed	Complete scissor, level bite tolerated
Eyes	Dark	Dark for preference, golden allowed
Neck	Arched	*Arched* not mentioned
Ears	Long, set approx. on level with outer corners of eyes	Set low and well back
Body	Length and height in equal proportion	Moderate length
Loin	Loin slightly arched	*Arched* not mentioned
Hips	Hipbones very pronounced	Hipbones rather prominent
Tail	Ring or curve	Ring
Coat	Thick and fine	Long and fine
Height	Males 26–28in (66–71cm)	Males 68–74cm (27–29in)
Gait	Trots at a fast pace	*Speed* mentioned under *General Appearance* but not under *Gait*.

Judging

In Great Britain, if you are a successful exhibitor in the show ring or the breeder of several winning dogs, a natural progression is to be invited to judge. The advice in this chapter is particularly aimed at the Afghan enthusiast who has owned the breed for a few years and would like to enter the arena as a judge.

You will probably start by being invited by a canine society to judge a few (five or less) classes at an open show, your name being proposed for the appointment by a committee member who sees you as up-and-coming and sure to bring in a good entry. If this initial experience proves enjoyable and you feel competent in applying your knowledge impartially, you may well have aspirations of going further and judging on a regular basis, maybe eventually at a breed club show. To do this it will be necessary to attend educational seminars and take part in the Junior Judges Training Scheme to meet the judging criteria laid down by your breed club. All breed clubs are required by The Kennel Club to have their

The author judging in Australia, with Aust Ch Khandhu Cracker Jack and Aust Ch Karakush Irresistable U.

own Lists of Approved Judges and it is from such a list that canine societies with six or more Afghan classes scheduled will be required to select a judge. In 1997 The Kennel Club Judges Working Party reviewed current practices for the training, assessment and approval of judges. Following its report, changes embracing may aspects of the show scene came into force in July 1998.

Breed clubs organise training days whereby an experienced lecturer (a championship show judge who has already awarded at least five CCs in the breed) gives an informative talk on the Breed Standard, followed by a practical session where individual hands-on tuition is received from a championship show judge. Students who wish to proceed and take an examination are required to attend three of these sessions over a two-year period.

The examination takes the format of candidates examining and placing in order of merit at least five Afghan Hounds, giving a verbal appraisal of each dog and answering questions about their placings put to them by the assessors. There are no trick questions and no pre-determined placings and I have sat on panels where five candidates have placed the same dogs differently and have all passed, because they expressed a personal preference while explaining their placings with both logic and knowledge, spotting obvious faults and weighing up shortcomings.

It takes a lot of courage willingly to yield to the trauma of taking an examination and, if you fail, the assessors (who will identify with your disappointment) will point out clearly the areas where they feel you will benefit from more experience and tuition. In the past, successful enthusiasts have tried to by-pass the system by not taking an examination, and this has only led to disappointment if they are turned down for a championship appointment by The Kennel Club. Unfortunately, the longer and more successful you have been in the breed, the more daunting the prospect of taking an examination, so when you feel you are competent, do get it over with and save yourself disappointment in the future.

After passing the examination, candidates are eligible to apply for inclusion within Breed Club Judging Lists. It should be mentioned many experienced people who breed and show wonderful dogs decline appointments because they know in their 'heart of hearts' that judging is just not for them. Doing what they do best, these people are to be admired for their honesty.

I do not want to spend much time in this chapter discussing the mechanics of how you judge and what you wear, as it is more important from the exhibitors point of view that you know what you are looking for and have the courage to abide by it. However, do dress neatly and wear comfortable shoes, arrive in plenty of time to check your judging book and meet with your stewards to discuss the organisation of your ring. If you then quietly and confidently take charge of your ring, are courteous to your exhibitors and judge impartially and decisively, a happy atmosphere around your ring will prevail.

At the start of judging, when your steward has reported all the exhibits present, walk around the class to make initial observations and then move the dogs all together in a large circle, giving them a chance to loosen up and settle down. Call each dog out for individual evaluation, standing well back to appraise from the front, the side and the rear, noting outline and balance and general appearance. It must be borne in mind that the owner will have stacked the dog to look aesthetically pleasing, with its front feet pointing forwards, head pulled up high and hindquarters pulled back. Don't be afraid to re-position the legs in a more natural stance if you feel the dog has been over-stretched, always keeping in mind the Breed Standard throughout your appraisal.

Approach from the front or side to examine the head, but do make sure that the dog has seen you; it may be startled and back away if its attention was elsewhere and it suddenly finds your hands in its mouth. Go on to examine the neck, shoulder placement, forequarters, body, hindquarters, testicles and tail-set. Check also that front and rear angulation complement one another, appreciating the whole picture as opposed to seeking to find faults.

Ask the owner to move the dog away from and then towards you in a straight line to assess soundness and alignment of front and hind action. Move the dog again in a triangle or circle to assess side movement, finally pausing it in front of you in a natural stance. Make your final selection from the standing position, but move the exhibits as many times as you consider necessary At the end of the class dictate or write a rough but thorough critique on your first and second placings which can be tidied later before sending to the canine press.

A word about ethics: in your very first class of puppies you will be confronted with exhibitors who are friends and there will also be Miss Well-Known Face, a Mrs Very-Well-Known Face and a Mr He-Gave-Me-A-CC-Last-Month Face, which can all be quite daunting to the novice judge. You will only get into a terrible mess and create ill-feeling if you yield to such pressure or are side-tracked by personal ambition. If you start as you mean to go on and put the best dog up irrespective of its owner, the rest is easy. Unless you're judging a junior handling class there is no reason for you to take your eyes off the dog and look up the lead.

Do not take your judging lightly; in future years, when you judge at championship level, your judging will influence the breed. Always remember that, as well as judging, you will be judged!

chapter six
Starting Out

Character

Afghan Hounds have an independence of mind which sets them apart from any other breed and I truly believe that you need to be of a certain temperament to share your life with one successfully. They are slow to mature and their wonderful sense of humour and clown-like antics will stay with them long past adolescence. Since they are sighthounds, it is their natural instinct to chase and hunt and within each and every one is the call of the wild, which can never be taken away. They love to run free and ignore all pleas to return when in pursuit of self enjoyment. While they can be taught to chase a ball and return it on the understanding that it will be again thrown for them to chase, they will never greet you with your slippers in their mouth or carry your newspaper when out for a walk.

Neither can they be relied upon to accept that 'No' means 'No'. If chastised whilst in the process of destroying something that you hold dear, they will return to complete the destruction long after you have forgotten about it. Allegiance is offered on their terms only but, once it is given, the deep relationship will be binding and your rewards manifold upon realisation that this basically wild and free animal chooses to be with you when so many other exciting things beckon. An Afghan can never be 'owned' in the true sense of the word. It is by nature a pack animal and prefers the company of other dogs and people to a solitary existence. If left alone with only toys for companionship it will quickly tire of them and move on to other things much more interesting, particularly if forbidden or dangerous. Although a very independent creature, it also loves to interact and, once you take on the responsibility of pack leader, will live quite happily with you, although it may not always obey you.

Teaching a young Afghan matters of respect takes longer than for most other breeds. This is not because the Afghan is incapable of learning – more that its self will takes over if it sees no reason or instant reward. Now teach it something where there is a reward – for instance, to give a paw for a biscuit – and not only will the trick will be perfected in under an hour but any future mention of the word 'biscuit' will cause its ears to prick and its eyes to become fixed to the cupboard in which they are kept.

Because this concept of dog ownership will never appeal to the majority, it is absolutely vital that you are realistic and examine thoroughly all the pros and cons with regard to character and temperament, before deciding that an Afghan is for you and your family.

Not to mention grooming! How well I appreciate your attraction to this glamorous and eye-catching breed, but careful consideration must be given to the hard work and dedication required to keep it physically fit as well as looking smart and knot-free. The Afghan requires a lot of exercise and must have purpose in life; otherwise it will become bored, frustrated and destructive. Afghans do not experience hair loss as such, but a bitch usually drops her short saddle coat a couple of months after a season. Neither is there the doggy smell associated with many breeds, although Afghans do get pretty bedraggled if caught in the rain when out for a walk.

Group of puppies aged five weeks (golds and black-and-tans). Photo: David Paton

True Afghan enthusiasts regard their hounds as intelligent companions and feel a great sense of overwhelming pride in mutual achievements. They have a great deal of respect for their Afghan's independent attitude, love its comical antics and accept its total disregard for what doesn't interest it. Undoubtedly, they will have friends in other breeds who take a totally different view of their lifestyle (which is dominated by walking and bathing) and who fail to understand how the merits gained can possibly justify all the hard work involved. I can only repeat: do be realistic and don't let the glamour cloud your judgment. Owning an Afghan means taking on an enormous responsibility and additional expense for the next 10–15 years of your life and should not be undertaken lightly. There are several other engaging long-legged sighthound breeds that have coats much easier to manage and do not demand quite as much tolerance.

Afghans on their own territory are possessive rather than aggressive and will often view those unknown to them with caution, not recognising their scent. They have an acute sense of hearing and unfamiliar sounds, sights and smells will cause them to bark rather than growl, quickly alerting the household of approaching strangers. An elderly friend who lives alone above her shop premises recently telephoned to tell of her great pride when her Afghan leapt from his rug at the foot of her bed, barking, at two o'clock in the morning, raced downstairs (with her in pursuit), to find a hand halfway through her ground floor window, stealing merchandise. What is quite amazing is that, during the day, this particular dog is accustomed to strangers and regularly greets, with wagging tail, all the customers entering his owner's shop. However, instinct told him that intruders were not welcome in the middle of the night.

Security

A major prerequisite is that the perimeter of your property is secure, particularly if visitors or children are around. A gate accidentally left open is an accident waiting to happen, as an Afghan will chase anything moving that catches its eye, unaware of the dangers that a busy road can present. You may believe that you have instilled in your Afghan that it is wrong to venture outside your garden but, on the one occasion when your mind is elsewhere, its instincts will take over and it will be gone, which could result in dire consequences. If it is impractical to fence around all of your garden, an enclosed exercise/play area with a paved or concrete floor can be constructed, where your Afghan will be safe when out of your sight. When we acquired our first Afghan, we were unfortunate to live next door to neighbours who owned and housed pet rabbits in a hutch in their garden. Afghans can fall into three categories: jumpers, diggers and climbers. Since Cassie was a climber, the six-foot chain-link fencing proved no problem whatsoever to her. We dutifully raised the fencing by a further two feet with a degree of incline to make the task more difficult for her, but the neighbours complained that our Colditz actions were very anti-social (I must admit, it did look a mess) so we decided it was time to relocate to more rural surroundings.

Expenses

The cost of food is not the only expense to be offset against the weekly housekeeping account. Veterinary treatment is not cheap and, whilst insurance can be taken out to cover for illness and accidents, it will not cover preventative treatments such as annual booster vaccinations, spaying/neutering, worming preparations, ear cleaners and anti-parasite sprays. Additional money is required for collars, leads, beds, brushes, shampoo and conditioner. As previously mentioned, the adult coat requires considerable attention. It is hoped that you will be able to groom the dog yourself (which will mean investing at the least in a professional dog dryer) but otherwise prepare to budget for regular professional coat care.

Finding a breeder

Whether you want an Afghan for a pet or a show dog, you are advised to start with the best stock available. If you do not know of an Afghan enthusiast in your area who can tell you the name of your local breed club secretary, contact The Kennel Club, which will have this information to hand. If you are looking for a show puppy then do not buy the first one that you hear of, but do some ground work first and visit shows where Afghans are scheduled. By talking to as many breeders and exhibitors as you possibly can, you will discover the type of Afghan you would like to own and hopefully pick up valuable tips along the way. Enthusiasts usually know of other specialists who have litters planned and can point you in the right direction. You will quickly learn that the show scene is one large grapevine and what one enthusiast knows, the others soon will!

At all costs, be prepared to wait, as breeders of today do not have puppies ready and waiting for potential owners to arrive on their doorstep. There just isn't the large pet market for Afghans that there used to be and therefore enthusiasts will generally only breed when wanting something for themselves. Believe me, your patience will be rewarded when you take home the puppy of your dreams.

Dog or bitch?

Both sexes have proved excellent family pets, although bitches can be tiresome in that they regularly come into season. If you have no intentions of breeding and would find her seasons problematic, spaying would end her reproductive life without detriment to her character. Dogs can be more of a handful, being larger and stronger, but the pet owner need only consider castration if the dog is particularly dominant or over-sexed. Personally, I find my dogs more responsive and affectionate than my bitches, but my husband finds that the boys never do a thing he says and feels much more affinity with the girls.

If you get bitten by the show bug and own a bitch who makes a name for herself in the ring, you can mate her to a suitable dog and keep her best puppy for yourself. On the other hand, if you start out with a dog, the progress of your kennel depends upon him winning and being sought

Gold male puppy aged approximately seven weeks.

for use at stud, in which case the owner of his puppies will usually want to keep the best for themselves. It all depends how quickly you want to progress in the breed, but do not 'over-dog' yourself, as collecting too many in a short space of time can only lead to disaster. Careful forethought and planning will give you happy dogs and, more importantly, the time to spend with them.

Visiting the litter

Puppies are born smooth-coated and will be around six to eight weeks of age when you are invited to view the litter. If you can take along a friend who has practical knowledge of the breed, all the better. Common sense will prevail in that you would expect the premises to be clean, with the mother looking fit and reasonably tidy, bearing in mind that she has just finished maternal duties. She will probably bark warily at you as she is protecting her offspring, but be concerned if she dives out of the way and appears nervous. Correctly reared puppies will have well-covered ribs and plenty of substance about them. If they look thin and stark it will be apparent that they haven't had a good start in life, which unfortunately can never be regained.

Two domino puppies aged approximately nine weeks.
Photo: Michael John.

It is difficult to assess the coat texture at this early age, but ask to see photographs of Mum before she had the litter and also of Dad, in full coat. Avoid the puppy with the very deep, shiny saddle and sparse leg coat, as it could have inherited the old-fashioned heavily-patterned coat, which is fine for the experienced exhibitor but inadvisable for the newcomer, who at first may be a little heavy-handed with the brush.

Puppies that have been reared in the house are generally accustomed to visitors and should be outgoing and responsive to your admiration. The order of dominance will be setting in and it is usually the largest male who is the bullyboy or, in the case of an all-girl litter, the female who is the most verbal.

Temperament is now being established and this is a major learning period. If you collect your puppy when it is eight weeks old you will find it very responsive to basic training and it will relish the individual attention. Puppies are very susceptible to environmental influences between the ages of eight and sixteen weeks, and this is when a puppy needs as much socialising and worldly experience as it can get. Puppies left with their mother and litter-mates after this time can become dependent upon each other, the bold ones becoming more unruly and the shy ones retreating more into their shells.

As you watch the puppies at play with their litter-mates you can learn a great deal about their construction, movement and attitude. Look for a springy, cocky little movement rather than one which is crouched and unstylish. By process of elimination, reduce your choice down to the two or three who really appeal before attempting to stand the little wrigglers in show pose to feel for finer detail.

The breeder will always have the advantage in selecting their choice from a home-bred litter because they know what they are looking for from their own lines. They have been able to observe the puppies from birth and obviously had their reasons for arranging the mating in the first place (refer to the chapter 10).

Choosing a show puppy

You have chosen to exhibit a breed that is very strong numerically in the ring. If you can start with a first-class animal your show career should begin with everything in your favour.

However, I can only advise you very broadly what to look for in a show puppy, as this is merely the beginning. Correct feeding, mental awareness and good coat presentation also play major roles. It is to your advantage that you have chosen a breed in which a novice exhibitor with a good dog will never be overlooked; if you have the best dog on the day, you will win. Many Afghan champions have been made up by newcomers to the breed, often with their first dog.

The guide I am giving relates to puppies between eight and fourteen weeks of age. After this time you will find their hindquarters begin to straighten and rumps begin to rise as they shoot up on their legs. Your pedigree puppy for a while takes on the awkward appearance of young colt, all legs and fluff, bearing little resemblance to the gracious animal it will become. Choosing a puppy at this age is a gamble in any breed, but it should look balanced. If it is long in the loin with bad front and rear angulation, these faults will not alter. While it is worth reading the chapter on the Breed Standard, interpretation of many of the points will be difficult to relate to a puppy.

Head

The head is the most difficult to assess, as the squat muzzle bears little resemblance to the long foreface to come. As you look down on the skull it should be oval in shape, domed on top as opposed to flat, not too wide between the eyes and with a slight stop. The muzzle should not be snipy or mousey. Young puppies with the slightly Roman finish usually have good length and strength of muzzle to come. If choosing a dog puppy, look for depth of head and a good strength of underjaw, as a weak underjaw often results in a bite that is overshot. For comparison, look at all the heads in the litter and decide if they are representative of their sex. If the dog you have your eye on has a finer head than all the bitches, or vice versa, then they may finish too fine or too heavy for their sex.

Eyes should be small, triangular, dark and set to the side, although young puppies' eyes take on a bluish hue that may have disappeared by the time you view. Avoid a very light eye and unpigmented third eyelids if possible, as these can detract from the desired expression.

Ears should be set on low and lay close to the side of the head. Young puppies tend to carry their ears high, and this can be checked by feeling that the cartilage at the top of the flap does not overly protrude. High set ears will be shorter in length.

To summarise: you are looking for an oval-shaped head with prominent occiput, dark triangular

Head study of a puppy aged approximately 12 weeks (pale gold with shaded mask).

eyes set slightly to the side, slight stop and ears set fairly low, as opposed to a round apple head with large round eyes set to the front, deep stop, thin, pointed nose and high set ears.

Bite

The bite should be scissor or slightly overshot at this stage. If it is level, the chances of it turning out correct are 50:50, but if it happens to be on the puppy of your choice, you could consider asking the breeder to hold on to it for another couple of weeks and then view it again. Alternatively, if you take the gamble, give plenty of hard bones and chew sticks to encourage the baby teeth to loosen as quickly as possible. If it is undershot now, the chances are that it will worsen with age. Incorrect mouths are not generally prevalent within the breed, as enthusiasts tend to by-pass breeding from such animals, knowing the fault to be genetic. However, they do still occasionally crop up.

Front

Lay of shoulder should be clean, with no protruding tell-tale bumps at the top. If the angulation is correct, the desired length of neck will follow. The angulation of the upper arm will correspond to that of the shoulder blade, enabling the front legs to be placed well underneath the body with elbows on a line with top of shoulder. Front legs should be straight with elbows held in.

The chest should be deep and pear-shaped, reaching approximately to the elbows. An incorrect, narrow, shallow chest can be easily spotted at this age and, when you view it from the front, you will see the elbows tied closely together with little room between, causing the feet to turn outwards slightly.

Balance

The puppy should appear balanced, with the length of the back neither too long nor too short in relation to the length of the legs.

Hindquarters

The angulation of the hindquarters is now apparent, but it will tend to straighten slightly before reappearing at 10–14 months of age. Look for good length to the second thigh; if this is short to start with, the adult dog will probably lack the desired ground coverage. At this stage, the puppy will not have any muscle on its hindlegs and so may appear a bit unsteady.

Front and rear angulation will be seen to complement each other at this age

Tail

Puppies tend to carry their tails high, but look for some length to the fallaway, although the angle of fallaway will not yet be apparent. Avoid a high set tail carried well over the back, which can be spotted when the puppy is on the move. The tail should show some indication of curving at the end, but the ring does not generally form completely until the puppy is four to six months old.

Entirety

It is very difficult to tell whether the male puppy will be entire as testicles are not fully descended at this age. As you feel gently when the pup is relaxed or asleep on its back, two tiny peas near the base of the penis will be apparent but, if there is any doubt, ask the breeder to have the dog checked by a vet before you purchase.

Movement

Movement is not too difficult to assess and I would sooner pick a puppy on its movement than have it standing for ages on a table and deliberating over the finer points.

Colour

If choice of colour is a priority there are several breeders you can contact who own lines that will produce your favoured colour, whether it be black, gold, brindle or cream. Once again, contact your local breed club secretary, who can put you in touch with a breeder noted for producing a certain colour.

To summarise...

If push comes to shove and you have to make the decision between the happy, cocky pup whose conformation may be a little lacking in comparison to the beautifully constructed pup with the shy temperament, pick the happy one with which to make your debut into the ring. Hopefully, your puppy will have it all but, at the end of the day, the object is to have fun and make friends, and this is difficult to achieve if you are miserable because your Afghan hates the show ring.

Breeding terms

There are alternatives to buying a puppy outright, and another way of starting out is to buy a puppy on breeding terms, although this is not a common practice with Afghan Hounds. If a breeder has a promising bitch puppy that they do not wish to sell outright, they may offer her for sale at a reduced price on the condition that you exhibit her and/or breed a litter from her, with them taking back one or more puppies to complete the payment for the bitch. This can be advantageous to the novice exhibitor in that they are able to obtain the quality puppy they would otherwise not have been allowed and, at the same time, receive knowledgeable advice from the breeder.

The main disadvantages are that you may have to pay the stud fee *and* absorb all expenses incurred during the rearing of the subsequent litter. The breeder will also decide the choice of stud dog and request a number of puppies from the litter, which will probably mean that your favourite puppy does not stay with you.

These agreements entail a great deal of trust on both sides and are more common between people who know each other well than between complete strangers. In any event, such arrangements should be set out formally in writing and signed by both parties. The Kennel Club has introduced a form for this purpose which can be lodged with them on completion.

Choosing a pet puppy

If you are choosing a puppy for a pet with no aspirations of joining the show world, your primary concern is that it is healthy and has a good temperament.

Adopting a rescue dog

Sometimes it is much less disrupting to choose a mature dog past the naughty stage, and I know of many people, some quite elderly in years but young in mind, who have had an Afghan in their household for many years and would never be without one. Taking on a puppy is rather too much for them, so they choose to 'adopt'.

Dogs find themselves homeless for a variety of reasons. Their former owners may have died, emigrated, split up or simply found themselves unable to cope any more, leaving the dog in need of another home. If you feel that you would like to give an unfortunate dog a good home for the rest of its life, contact your local breed club secretary, who will be pleased to deal with your enquiry and put you in touch with the rescue coordinator. To ensure that the transfer is trouble-free, dogs are normally matched to the individual as closely as possible, with the dog's previous circumstances taken into consideration. For example, it is not a good idea to introduce an older dog who has lived with an elderly owner into a home full of children.

These dogs normally come without papers and are not to be bred from or used at stud. Those known to have bitten or be aggressive are not considered suitable. Afghans adapt very well to their new homes and quickly realise that their new life is good, but do be prepared for some gruelling questions from the coordinator, who will want to ensure that you are in a position to provide a permanent, caring home.

The rescue situation has eased somewhat over the years and, at the time of writing, there are more people wanting to adopt than dogs for adoption, so you may have to go on a waiting list. However, adopting a rescue should never be considered a cheap option and you should be prepared to give a realistic donation so that this essential work can be continued.

Official paperwork

The breeder will forward the Kennel Club registration certificate to you, having first signed it on the reverse side, so that ownership can then be transferred into your name. This must then be returned to The Kennel Club with the appropriate fee, so that official records can be altered on the computerised system. Should you decide to enter the puppy for a show whilst the transfer is in progress, (*Transfer Applied For*) must be added after your puppy's name on the entry form until you have received official notification that the transfer has taken place.

If the puppy has already received its first vaccinations, the certificate stating what vaccines have been given should be taken to the veterinary surgeon when the second inoculations are due. It should then be kept in a safe place, with a reminder written on your calendar of the date when annual boosters are to be given.

Insurance

If the breeder has taken out cover, the puppy will be insured for the first six weeks in its new home. The insurance company will write to you with the option of renewing for a further year and I would advise you to take this up as puppies can get themselves into all sorts of mischief. Most policies dictate that you pay the first £30 of any claim but, with the costs of veterinary treatment escalating, it is a safeguard worth having. Remember, however, that routine treatments such as vaccinations and worming are not covered.

Taking your puppy home

Everything that happens from this moment onwards will make some impression upon the future disposition of your puppy, so it is up to you to ensure that all its first encounters and experiences are pleasurable. A feeling of security now will pay off time and again in future years.

Start by taking someone with you when collecting your puppy, as it will be unaccustomed to travel and will benefit from the reassurance of being nursed on the journey. I make no excuse for repeating that first experiences stick in a puppy's mind for a long time and, if its first long journey is experienced huddled in a crate in the back of a car, it will probably shake with insecurity, dribble or be sick. This will lead to aversion to car travel, with obvious problems in the future, especially if you intend to show, which will entail travelling hundreds of miles up and down the country.

Settling in

Everything must be done to help your puppy settle happily into your home. Confidence, once destroyed, takes a long time to re-establish. Introduce your pup with some sensitivity to other members of your family, especially other dogs, who may overpower it with their inquisitive attentions.

When you arrive home, greet your other dogs first. They will no doubt be delighted to see you and be especially interested in the new puppy smells you have on you. Once this is over, introduce the puppy to them individually, preferably in the garden rather than the house; you will be asking for trouble by plunging the new pup into your other dogs' home territory. If your own dogs are of a pleasant disposition the introduction should pose no problem.

If your dogs sleep in the house there is no reason why the puppy cannot join them; the pup for one will enjoy the companionship. If you own or can borrow a medium-sized dog cage for the first couple of nights, where the pup can see the other dogs but not climb upon them, all the better – you will be assured of a trouble-free, peaceful night. On the other hand, if you are introducing a single puppy to a dog-free household, be prepared for a sleepless night. The puppy will undoubtedly cry when left alone in unfamiliar surroundings. Here you can consider doing one of two things: leave the puppy on its own with a radio playing, with the knowledge that the noise will only last for a couple of nights, or allow it into the bedroom where it can curl up on your bed and not make a murmur. I admit to being guilty of the second consideration but, once accustomed to the daily routine of the household, the pup quickly adapts, with no further expectations of sleeping with you.

There are obviously going to be times when you have to go out and cannot take the puppy with you. Brief absences on your part now will enable your puppy to come to terms with being left on its own for short periods. On such occasions you will need to ensure that it does not wreck your home or cry loudly enough to disturb your neighbours. Suitable attractions such as rawhide chews should be provided, and the puppy will be more inclined to sleep through your absence if you have spent time playing with it beforehand. Often a radio or television left on will give it the sense of people being around. It is not wise to leave your pup with the run of the house, and it will be safer left in the kitchen or elsewhere in the home where it can cause only minimal damage while unsupervised. Spread newspapers on the kitchen floor in case of accidents and do not scold the pup on your return for using such facilities; just be thankful that it has. Let it out into the garden and praise it if it relieves itself there.

Even when you are at home, there are certain times when it may be inconvenient to let the puppy have the run of the house, and here a baby-gate can be invaluable in confining it to a particular room while still allowing it to see other people

House training

House training a puppy entails considerable patience and perseverance on your part and, if approached in the right way, should present no difficulty. There is not much damage to be done if the puppy makes a mistake at this age when the puddles are only small but, in six months' time, if this area of training has been neglected you will have made a rod for your own back. The younger your puppy, the longer it will be before it is completely reliable day and night, mainly because it is not mature enough physically to control its bowel and bladder. Eventually, the training sinks in and the pup understands. (See also chapter 7.)

It is scarcely ever necessary or even wise to smack an Afghan. It will know at once from the angry tone of your voice that you are displeased and begin to reason why.

As puppies cannot be expected to be clean for long periods of time, arrangements must be made for during the night or, if you have to leave them unattended for any length of time, for during the day.

Feeding your puppy

The breeder will have given you a diet sheet and it is best to feed the same food that has been provided for at least a week after you get him home, to avoid an upset tummy. It is then largely a matter of choice whether you decide to continue with the existing diet or seek an alternative feeding method. (See chapter 7.)

It is important that the puppy should receive four meals a day, with regular feeding times adhered to. Suggested times are: 8.00 am, 12.00 noon, 4.00 pm and 9.00 pm. Puppies love milk, and goat's milk is a wonderful replacement for their mother's milk, but giving too much milk and sloppy foods can lead to loose motions.

If you decide to feed your puppy on a complete food, the amount to be given per kilogram of body weight will be advised by the manufacturer. Whatever your choice, common sense is essential. If the puppy cleans the dish, looks no fatter and is sniffing around hoping for more, increase the quantity. Some people get very worried because they think their puppy is not eating enough, while others go to extremes and overfeed. Keep an eye on general body condition. An Afghan puppy should be well covered, with the flesh over the ribs soft and pliable. An over-thin puppy will have nothing in storage should it succumb to a setback such as illness.

Some owners, anxious to give their dogs the best of everything, overdo it by giving calcium supplements, tonics and all manner of proprietary conditioners. Such things are unnecessary unless you are acting upon the guidance of a vet.

As the puppy gets older, it will dictate its needs, and more food will be required at less frequent intervals. At around 12 weeks, adjust the timetable by combining tea-time and supper-time meal into one. At around six months, the meals can be reduced to two a day. Once it is established, do try to keep to your chosen diet and not give too many titbits or scraps from the table. Bonios and Biscrok treats always go down well, but chocolate and over-sweet treats are best avoided.

Teething

By 16 weeks your puppy will have started to lose its needle-sharp baby teeth and replace them with the permanent set. The first ones lost will be the incisors (see diagram of skull and dentition in Chapter 5), which are the six top and bottom teeth between the four large corner canines. Next to go are the canines and, should one of the baby canines be retained as the new one grows alongside it, try giving your puppy a rawhide chew to loosen it

Two black-and-tan youngsters aged approximately 12 months. Photo: Diane Pearce

before consulting your vet about pulling it out. If the baby teeth do not loosen, causing the adult teeth to come in at an angle, they will require surgical extraction. The pre-molars and molars grow in last and, since the last molar will not come in until the pup is almost six months old, a little weight loss may be experienced until the teething process is complete.

Your puppy's gums will be sore for several weeks while it is cutting its teeth and there is an old wives' tale that the ring will not completely set in the tail until teething is completed.

Joining a breed club

If you are new to the breed, joining your local breed club will keep you informed of forthcoming events and social functions happening in your area. There are 12 Afghan Hound breed clubs in Great Britain, a list of which can be found in **Useful Addresses**.

chapter seven

Care and Basic Training

Diet

Everyone has his or her own view on how Afghans should be fed, and most dogs will eat quite happily the food you provide. The adult dog requires only one meal a day, and this can be given in the morning, afternoon or evening. But do remember that your dog's mealtime will be regarded as one of the highlights of the day. For this reason, when a routine has been established, it is important that it is adhered to. There are no hard and fast rules about exact quantities and you should be guided by physical appearance rather than the written word, the aim being to feed your dog the correct quantity of food each day for it to remain firm and well-covered for its size, never fat. Whichever feeding method you choose, whether it be complete, canned, fresh, or a mixture of all three, never make sudden changes to the diet. Different foods should be introduced gradually; otherwise an upset stomach and loose motions may result.

At mealtimes, it is always advisable to pop a snood over your hound's head and ears to ensure that the ear fringes are kept out of the feeding dish and mouth.

A snood is essential at meal times! Photo: David Paton

Types of diet

Dry (complete) feeding: There are many dry (complete) foods on the market today, which contain all the essential additives to keep your dog in peak condition. Manufactured by reputable companies to a high standard, they take the guesswork out of successful rearing. Growing puppies require more calories, protein, vitamins and minerals than adult dogs, and the safest way to ensure their correct feeding is to leave it to the experts. Manufacturers such as Pedigree Chum, Hill's and Eukanuba all produce different diets to suit your dog, depending on its age and lifestyle. Also, because proteins have been broken down during the manufacturing process, the food is more digestible, with the result that the dog produces less waste matter.

Wet feeding: Canned food is probably the most popular method of wet feeding, the more expensive brands having a higher meat content than the cheaper ones, which usually contain more cereal. Canned food contains all the correct vitamins and minerals needed to sustain a healthy diet and does not require supplementation. It is usually mixed with a wholemeal biscuit to make the meal complete.

Fresh feeding: This type of feeding includes fresh meat, frozen meat or tripe, although the advent of BSE has stopped the availability of many types of offal. Whilst feeding fresh meat is still the preferred method of many breeders, supplementation will be required, as meat does not contain calcium, which is essential for growth.

Drinking requirements

Fresh drinking water should be freely available. Afghans also enjoy the occasional drink of milk, but some are unable to digest it properly because of a lactose intolerance, which causes them to have diarrhoea.

Metal non-tip stands that hold the drinking bowl 50cm above floor level will prevent ear fringes from becoming wet and messy. Alternatively, a 'water-well' (a plastic bowl with a hole in the centre) serves the same purpose. Being non-spill, this type of bowl is also useful when you are travelling with your dog.

The use of supplements

Many complete vitamin and mineral supplements are available on the market today, the contents of which have been formulated by nutritional experts. Examples are Canovel and SA–37. These supplements are extremely beneficial to

Dog eating from a bowl on a raised stand.
Photo: David Paton

growing puppies, older dogs, pregnant bitches and dogs recovering from illness, particularly after the use of antibiotics, but are not considered necessary for the healthy adult dog who is receiving a normal nutritional diet. Reputable brands of canned and complete foods contain all the nutrients necessary to keep a dog in good condition, the balance of which would be upset by additional supplements.

Alternative supplements such as bone meal and calcium to aid bone growth, cod liver oil for vitamin D, brewers yeast for the vitamin B group, and seaweed for minerals and iodine can individually benefit a particular need, but should only be given after consultation with your vet, as excessive dosing can do more harm than good.

Garlic is advocated by many as an internal disinfectant for the prevention of worms, fleas and other external parasites, and cannot cause any harm.

Feeding problems

Some Afghans can be particularly finicky eaters and just will not eat the food you are offering, no matter how beneficial its properties. They simply are not interested and will merely sniff at their food before walking away. This can be so frustrating, especially if it happens to a dog that you need to keep at an ideal weight for showing.

In theory, the recommended procedure is to take the food away and wait until the next day before offering it again, repeating the act until the dog is so hungry it is forced to eat. But this doesn't happen in practice and, while you are awaiting the progress of the accepted 'cure', the dog will be getting thinner and thinner.

Poor appetite can be attributed to health problems or a worm infestation, so it is worth visiting the vet for a check-up to eliminate other possibilities. Whilst a painfully thin Afghan is not necessarily unhealthy, it will not be showable and, if the show ring is your goal, you must do everything in your power to get the weight on. Contradictory as this may seem, try not to let the dog know that you are over concerned; the more you fuss, the less inclined it will be to eat a normal diet, preferring the gourmet foods it knows will be offered.

Afghans are great thieves and you can use your guile by tempting them with strategically placed tasty morsels around the kitchen, letting them believe they are stealing while your back is

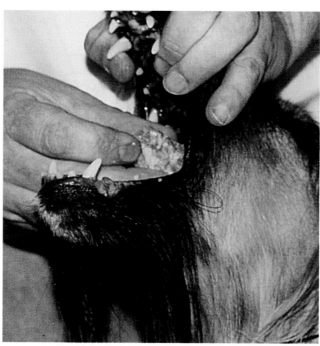

As a last resort, force feeding may be necessary.

turned. An Afghan is a large dog, so will not thrive on such a feeding method and will certainly require vitamin/mineral supplementation, but it just may be the kick-start that the dog needs. An Afghan will always think that your food is better than its own, so let it think that's what it is getting.

If your hound is competitive, try feeding it alongside a dog with a good appetite, supervising throughout. It is quite possible that your dog just does not like dog food in general, whether it be canned or complete, and would rather starve than eat something it does not like. If you do not want to stand by and watch your dog lose condition, you will have to experiment with other fresh foods. Appetite is stimulated by smell, so do not give food straight from the fridge – warm it first. Tempt your Afghan with chicken, liver and cheaper cuts of meat, baked or roasted in the oven as opposed to boiled or cooked in a pressure-cooker. Offer wholemeal rice or pasta shells instead of biscuit, to which has been added a little concentrated juice from the roasted meat. If you shop carefully, these foods need not wreak havoc with the family budget and cost only marginally more than proprietary dog food.

Various supplements and tonics are reputed to promote appetite, but avoid the ones that have to be sprinkled on to food, as they will be rejected anyway. Talk to your vet about giving a course of Vitamin B12 injections or try Vi-Sorbin Vitamin – Iron Preparation with Sorbitol, also available from the vet. Cytacon, made by Glaxo, is also recognised as an appetite stimulant and obtainable from the chemist. Homeopathic remedies can also be beneficial and, if you know of a homeopathic vet, it may be well worth consulting him or her.

Milk, white fish and scrambled eggs are usually good options, although rather bland in flavour. Canned tuna fish in oil or brine may arouse your dog's taste-buds. Green tripe is inexpensive and wonderfully smelly.

Force feeding should be attempted purely as a last resort and only for a couple of weeks at a time, or the dog will become accustomed to the routine as the accepted method of feeding. This is best performed using a complete, nutritionally-balanced food that has been thoroughly soaked and then molded into small, manageable quantities. If you add a little dry Ready Brek, the food will bind together more easily. Open the dog's mouth, with one hand over the muzzle, whilst literally pushing the food down the throat with the other.

Obesity
Our Breed Standard does not specify an ideal weight, and rightly so, as weight must be in proportion to the frame of the dog and bone substance. When an Afghan becomes overweight the breadth of loin becomes indistinguishable from the ribs and it takes on an unbalanced appearance. The last three ribs should be easy to feel and the loin easily distinguishable.

Obesity occurs when the intake of carbohydrates and fats exceed the body's energy requirements. It therefore makes sense to feed a diet that is lower in calories, yet still balanced in essential nutrients. Many reputable manufacturers produce suitable light diets containing balanced levels of protein, minerals and vitamins, but with an increased fibre content to keep the dog feeling full and therefore reduce hunger. Increasing exercise will also help to burn up the carbohydrates.

Obese dogs are more prone to health problems, in particular heart disease and diabetes. Also, their life expectancy is shorter than that of a dog of normal weight. Once your dog has reached its target weight, aim to maintain it by monitoring its food intake on a permanent basis and limiting all treats and titbits.

Training

Being pack hounds, Afghans are not as easily trained as breeds that have been bred to work closely with people, but that does not mean that they are untrainable – they just take a little longer than most! Any Afghan owner who has successfully trained a hound will tell you that there is nothing more rewarding than being able to let the dog off the lead in a danger-free environment, knowing that it can be relied upon to return when called. It is an accepted fact that not all Afghans can be relied upon 100% but, if you can achieve this one basic feat above all others, you have gone a long way towards ensuring the hound's safety and make life much easier for yourself. You will also feel an overwhelming pride in succeeding where many have failed.

Contrary to popular belief, Afghans are not stupid; they are naturally suspicious. Their high level of intelligence prevents them from being lap dogs who instantly act upon command. Everything has first to be weighed up, and you can virtually see them thinking, 'Should I, shouldn't I?'

The secret of training Afghans successfully is to begin when they are young and open to suggestion, and most definitely before sexual maturity. It has to be said that there is a greater chance of success with an individual puppy in the household than with one that is a member of the household pack. Many owners seem to find time to train their first puppy to behave in an acceptable manner, but tend not to be as enthusiastic as numbers increase. If we read books on dog psychology or indeed observe dogs in the wild, we find there is always a pack leader or *alpha dog* and, without going into a subject that is a book in itself, it cannot be stressed strongly enough that you must establish yourself in this role from day one. Once a puppy becomes established as part of the household pack it is very difficult for it to ignore its natural instincts and depend solely upon its owner. I can think of nothing worse than an unruly, untrained Afghan who overrules everything in the household, including you – and relishes the fact!

'No!'

Basic training should begin the moment that your puppy arrives home, with *little and often* as the motto. Say your puppy's name every time you ask it to do something and praise it when it responds. As you talk to your dog you will be surprised how quickly it comes to understand many of your words and enjoys having its brain exercised. Tone of voice is important in the training repertoire and it is vital that the youngster learns and understands the word 'No!'. This word is also important in teaching what is to be your dog's and what is yours, which is your dog's bed and which is yours, and so on. You are establishing a bond, not putting the fear of God into him, so training sessions should always be approached in the context of 'play learning'.

In all training exercises you will notice that the commands are simple. Keep your commands short and you will be surprised how quickly your dog will learn.

House training

All puppies will relieve themselves upon waking and after a meal so, with this in mind, ensure that the puppy has access to its designated spot out of doors. Puppies relieve themselves more frequently than adults and it will be helpful if the task can be associated with words of encouragement such as 'Good boy/girl', 'Hurry up!'. That way, the pup will learn to perform when you are away from home, in a strange place or at a show. When it finishes, let the pup know that it has pleased you by showering it with praise.

Accidents in the early days will happen and, if the puppy does relieve itself indoors, mop the puddle up with absorbent paper and put this outside in the garden so that, when the puppy goes outside, it will smell its own scent and relieve itself on the same spot. There is no point in yelling and shouting at the puppy after an accident or rubbing its nose in the spot; its memory at this age is short and it will not know what it has done wrong. Scolding your pup only confuses it and weakens the bond between you. Try to be more vigilant, bearing in mind that dogs do not always urinate and defecate at the same time.

As dogs become sexually mature, they show a desire to mark their own territory, and adult dogs will cock their legs to leave their scent. Should this happen in the home, remind the dog that you are pack leader and that such behaviour will not be tolerated.

Socialising

Once the puppy has had all its vaccinations it is important for its future self-confidence that it meets as many different people as possible. Allow the pup to be fussed by the milkman, the postman and even the refuse collector – they all have different smells and make different noises when visiting your home. Take your puppy wherever it will be happily accepted and always reassure it during these exercises

Join a training class that welcomes puppies and let your young Afghan mix with the other dogs. Free play with four-legged friends is absolutely essential for its mental health. When out for a walk you will undoubtedly meet other dogs and, unless the encounter shows signs of becoming aggressive, it should be allowed to follow its natural progression. Dominant dogs, usually entire males, prefer not to have strange dogs on their territory and often chase away an intruder, returning to the spot to urinate and reinforce territorial claim. Fights usually only result when both dogs respond in an identical manner and neither is prepared to back down.

Lead training

From day one your puppy should be encouraged to follow you around and gradually become accustomed to wearing a soft leather or nylon collar. A nylon lead can be introduced and connected to its collar during play and it should be allowed to roam around, under supervision, with the lead attached. If the pup decides it wants to play tug o' war, say 'No!' sharply and remove the lead until later.

When your puppy has become used to this extension of its collar, stand with the dog on your left side, holding the lead in your right hand across your legs, left hand free. Say 'Heel!' firmly and set off, left leg first, which puts a slight pressure on the dog to proceed forward without pulling. Pat your left thigh with your left hand and encourage your puppy to walk with you. Encourage constantly. If the dog holds back and pulls at the lead, bend down and call it to you. Do not pull, but encourage the dog to come to you. If it takes off in front of you, give the full length of the lead before pulling the dog back sharply, saying 'No!' Repeat the 'Heel!' command and set off again. If your dog walks wide of you, position it between yourself and a wall or a hedge until it is comfortable walking with you. Above all, be patient and consistent in your commands. If you have had a bad day at work and are feeling less than patient, do not attempt to train your puppy, as it will pick up on your tension. It is much better to take a day off than confuse the pup. A month's work can be destroyed with a minute's lack of patience.

'Sit!'

This is the easiest of all the commands to teach, and a good, non-confrontational way of teaching is to watch your dog carefully and, as it sits naturally, give the command 'Sit!', praising it when it has done so.

To get your puppy to sit at your request, raise its chin with one hand while running your other hand down its back, applying gentle pressure over the hips. Do not press down and always praise when your pup complies. You can also do this at mealtimes, which helps to introduce hand signals; the correct one for this exercise being arm outstretched, palm upwards. Holding the underneath of your dog's food bowl, raise it above your dog's head and, as it sits, give the command 'Sit'! As it is looking up at you, the first thing it will see is the back of your hand and, if you always raise your hand in this fashion when giving the command 'Sit!', it will come to understand visual as well as vocal commands.

For an older, more recalcitrant dog, begin the exercise with the dog on a lead and, on the command of 'Sit!', raise the lead with your right hand while bending at the knees and running your left hand firmly down his back.

'Down!'

'Down!'

The 'Down' is an extension of the 'Sit'. Use the puppy's natural behaviour as before by watching it and, when it goes to lie down, give the command 'Down!'. The hand signal for this exercise is to hold out your arm, palm facing downwards, and move your arm in a downwards motion, as if pushing the dog down. As before, lots of praise is in order.

Another way of teaching the 'Down' position is to start with 'Sit' and then go down onto the floor yourself and, with a treat or toy in your hand, encourage your dog to lie down by gently extending its front paws forward. Reward your dog with praise and the treat. As it lies down, give the command 'Down!' in a firm voice. With an older or more stubborn dog the following method may be more effective. Starting in the 'Sit' position, place the lead under your

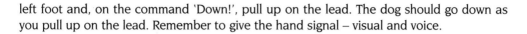

left foot and, on the command 'Down!', pull up on the lead. The dog should go down as you pull up on the lead. Remember to give the hand signal – visual and voice.

'Come' (Recall)

This is definitely the most important command you will ever teach your Afghan, and should be instilled into it from day one. Start as soon as you get your pup home by making sure that every time it comes to you it is rewarded by a small treat and lots of praise. Many owners have found using a whistle helpful in this exercise. Begin at mealtimes by calling the puppy's name and then piping the whistle several times, so that the puppy associates the whistle with food. If possible, have someone hold the puppy at the other end of the room, so that when you blow the whistle the pup is actually coming towards you. Reward your pup with its food. In the early stages, only use its mealtime food on the recall exercise and, when it has perfected it, you can practise during the day by calling the puppy to you at different times and from room to room, rewarding with a treat.

Outside, stand in an enclosed area with the puppy on a long line, calling its name first, followed by the command 'Come!', followed by the whistle. If ignored, slowly reel the puppy in, calling it in a bright and lively voice. Never scold a dog that is coming towards you and remember that you must be interesting enough to come back to. Kneel down, open your arms wide, smile, and let it know you love it to come back.

'Stay!'

Start in an enclosed area with the puppy on a lead and in the sitting position on your left. Firmly give the command 'Stay!' while raising your right hand, palm down, over its head. Slowly take two steps forward and face the pup, repeating the command 'Stay!'. Praise the pup as you return. If it moves during the exercise, return to its side and repeat. Patience and consistency is the key to this movement, so do not lose your temper if your puppy takes some time to get the hang of it. Move on to something else that it can do and return to it later. Always finish any training exercise on a good note. It is important during this exercise not to call it by name or wave your arms about.

You can then move on to *Sit Stays*, then *Down Stays* and finally *Stand Stays*.

'Stand!'

Even if you have no intention of showing your puppy, the Stand is very useful for grooming purposes and especially for visits to the vet, who will be most appreciative if he or she can examine your dog without it collapsing.

The easiest way of teaching the *Stand* is to start with your dog walking on your left side, stop, and give the command 'Stand!'. Gently support your pup under its tummy to prevent it from sitting and praise it. Repeat until it understands and is happy with the command 'Stand!'. Again, never rush it with any of these commands, *little and often* being the key words.

'Play'

After any training session it is important to have a release command that lets your puppy know that the training session is over and it is time to play. Use the word 'Play!' when you are having fun with your puppy.

'No!'/'Leave!'/'Off'

Afghans are extremely wilful and there will be many a time when your dog decides that it wants to play with or destroy something of yours. When this happens you need to be very careful how you handle the situation. For instance, if it decides that chewing your slippers is more fun than playing with its toys, never engage in a tug o' war. Take it by the collar with one hand and the object in question in the other and firmly say 'No!'. If it refuses to leave the object a gentle shake of the collar should induce it to let go. Then praise your dog and give it one of its own toys – fair exchange.

Should your dog decide that the sofa is more comfortable than its own bed, the command is 'Off!' – not 'Down!', as it will probably be lying down already. Be firm but kind.

Leaving your food alone is another lesson that must be learnt at an early age; otherwise when your hound grows taller, it will be on the kitchen work surfaces the minute your back's turned. When it tries to take food from your plate or steal any of your food, firmly say 'No!' and offer it its own food dish. If you stick to your guns and repeat this exercise whenever the dog approaches your plate, it will eventually accept that plates are taboo. I realise that this exercise completely contradicts my advice on dealing with a finicky eater; that is a totally different matter, and one where you will need to exercise your own judgment.

If your hound pulls towards anything when out on the lead, a sharp tug accompanied by a firm 'Leave!' should distract it. Make yourself more interesting than the object.

Off the lead

When you are sufficiently confident that your dog will stay with you, training off the lead can begin in an enclosed area. Whilst still attached to the lead, go through all the exercises, *Sit*, *Down*, *Heel* and *Stay*, and slowly release the lead for a couple of minutes at a time. With time, practice and unending patience you will progress to working without the lead.

Holidays

Going on holiday can present problems to the Afghan Hound owner, particularly if their hound is a show dog in full coat. A few years ago, we visited Australia for five weeks, and the organisation of the dogs seemed to take longer than the organisation of the holiday. Our show dogs were distributed amongst friends around the country who we knew could be trusted to look after them well and care for their coats, while the oldies stayed at home with a home-sitter.

Many caravan enthusiasts combine their holidays with the summer championship shows, all of which provide excellent camping facilities in close proximity to the show ground. When the day's competition is over, they get together on the campsite for parties and barbeques, knowing that the dogs are close by and safely contained behind windbreaks and awnings. In Great Britain, Kelso, Blackpool, Paignton, Windsor, Bournemouth and Wales feature among the favourite shows to which exhibitors can take their caravans, as there are many places of interest to visit in the area on the days when the breed is not scheduled..

Some hotels and guest houses in this country welcome dogs but, if you are going abroad, you will need to make suitable arrangements for the care of your dog well in advance of your holiday dates. Having a neighbour pop in a couple of times a day to check that your dog is all right and feed it may be acceptable for the odd night, but any longer and the dog will become bored and likely to cause damage. A friend or relative who will house-sit for you is the ideal solution, especially if you have more than one dog. Alternatively there are special pet-sitting agencies who will provide a resident dog-sitter. It is advisable to select a reputable agency rather than a local one that has recently set up in business to earn a bit of pin-money, and it is absolutely vital to take up references.

Choosing a boarding kennel

For the owner of a pet Afghan, this will be a matter of finding a good boarding establishment in their area to care for their dog while they are away and, unless you have a number of dogs, this method will be less expensive than employing a dog-sitter.

However, it has to be said that it is not the usual chosen option for the show exhibitor, concerned about the care of their dog's coat. There are a handful of boarding kennels around the country whose owners successfully exhibit Afghan Hounds themselves and who can be trusted to look after a show coat, and these people are well worth seeking out. Additionally, owners of boarding kennels who exhibit a similar long-haired breed will appreciate only too well the damage that two weeks without a brush can cause and should prove supportive to your grooming requirements. Boarding establishments are extremely busy places during the summer months and they have their work cut out just looking after the dogs in their care, never mind having any spare time for bathing and grooming – properly. Some kennels incorporate a grooming parlour and these would obviously be the better choice if you were going away for any length of time.

The best way of choosing a good kennel is by recommendation, either from your dog-owning friends or your vet. Your local council's Animal Health Inspector is always worth contacting, as he or she must make a yearly inspection of all kennels in the area before issuing a renewal licence and will know the good ones from the bad ones. Prior to 1998, regulations in respect of boarding kennels were not so stringent, but since the introduction of the revised Animal Boarding Establishments Act, existing establishments must either be brought up to the required specifications or be closed down. All councils employ an Animal Health Inspector who, if carrying out his or her duties properly, will not issue a licence unless the revised regulations are fully complied with.

Always telephone the kennel and arrange to visit prior to boarding and, if this is too much trouble for them, find another kennel. Choose a kennel where your dog has its own individual accommodation with an attached run, which should be of adequate size and covered if possible. If you have two dogs, it is usual to kennel them together, so check that the accommodation is large enough for the pair.

Ensure that your dog's vaccinations are up-to-date. In all boarding kennels there is a slight risk that your dog could contact the respiratory infection known as kennel cough which, although rarely life-threatening, can cause considerable discomfort to your pet (see chapter 12). Some of the more reputable establishments will not accept a dog for boarding unless it has been vaccinated against this illness, and advice on this should be sought from your vet well in advance of your holiday. Always leave the name and telephone number of your vet and a contact number in case of an emergency.

Having fun on the beach.

If you have a bitch and expect her to come in season whilst you are away, pre-warn the proprietor so that her accommodation can be planned to give the least disruption to male dogs that are boarded. Alternatively, you may wish to speak to your vet about the possibility of deferring this, by either injection or a course of tablets.

Travelling around
Touring with your dog can be great fun. Afghans love new experiences and you will find it rewarding and enjoyable to share all your dog's new encounters. However, while you will meet people on your travels who will gasp in sheer delight upon seeing your Afghan, there are others who will not appreciate the presence of a large dog.

Playing in the snow.

Some local authorities have introduced by-laws banning dogs from beaches, parks and gardens during certain months of the year, and it would be wise to check out the situation in advance of visiting your chosen resort. The local Environmental Health Officer will be able to provide you with this information.

Under no circumstances should your dog be left alone in the car when the weather is hot. You may think that you have left it snoozing in the car in a shady spot while you go into a restaurant for lunch but, because the sun moves around very quickly, you could return to find it in a state of collapse. Leaving windows open is not the answer, as no amount of through air will prevent the dog 'cooking' to death. A much better solution is to take a large umbrella with you and picnic in the shelter, out of the sun.

Whilst my own dogs love the beach, it wreaks havoc with their coats. They enjoy splashing around at the water's edge on a long lead, but I prefer not to let them go into the sea alone for fear of being swept away by strong currents. Sea water is not particularly good for an Afghan's coat, and sand can irritate the skin, so if your Afghan does get wet and sandy it will need to be rinsed off and brushed through at the earliest possible opportunity. If the beach is quiet and your dog is trustworthy enough to be let off the lead, this is fine, but always be aware that the minute it spies a seagull or a small dog it could be off. It is an Afghan!

Festive Periods

Festive periods are meant to be enjoyed by all members of the family, and that includes your Afghan, who would hate to be left out of the proceedings. With the exception of Bonfire Night, it will want to be in the midst of the fun, and a little advance planning and a watchful eye on potential hazards will ensure that happy occasions will remain just that.

We have enjoyed many barbeques with doggy friends who do not mind the odd nose creeping onto the table while we are eating but, if your visitors are of the non-doggy type, it would be best to keep your dog indoors to prevent uneasiness. Take care that no scraps of food are left where your dog can steal them and get burnt as a result. Broken glass is another hazard associated with outdoor occasions and, to prevent dogs from slicing their paws on a sharp sliver, it would be better to exercise them away from the party area until you have had time to check around thoroughly in the daylight.

Christmas can be chaotic, especially if you are entertaining. Christmas Day is the only time when my own dogs are completely banished from the kitchen, as our Christmas turkey was severely mauled one year while I was otherwise engaged in the dining room, and this presented an embarrassing situation that I would not wish to have repeated. Christmas food is extremely rich and, if given the chance, Afghans devour cake and mince pies without a thought that it may lead to tummy upsets or, even worse, a trip to the vet.

Unless you are having a quiet Christmas on your own, this is definitely not a good time to introduce a new puppy to the household. A reputable breeder would never sell a puppy knowing it to be a surprise gift, as they are well aware that in all probability it would be returned to them by the New Year. Afghan ownership and the subsequent work involved must be a commitment carefully thought out beforehand by the recipient. They should never be given as an unexpected present.

The Christmas tree, whilst fascinating, can also be quite hazardous. Fallen needles, if not swept up, can penetrate your dog's feet, and may then actually track up the leg like grass seeds, causing infection. Decorations are another irresistible attraction to youngsters, who will frequently attempt to remove them from the branches and, in so doing, pull the entire tree down on top of them. Be mindful of broken glass baubles, which may result in nasty cuts. Your Afghan will love to receive Christmas presents but, to avoid temptation, these and other presents and chocolate gifts should be kept away from the base of the tree until the last possible moment.

Opening presents with an inquisitive Afghan on Christmas morning will be enjoyable bedlam. However, in our excitement, we tend to become forgetful, and children in particular should be reminded to keep new toys away from the dog lest they get chewed.

chapter eight
Grooming

Careful coat management can have startling results!

Your decision to own an Afghan Hound must have been influenced partly by the magnificence of their long, silky, flowing coats, and by now you will have discovered that having an Afghan of your own involves a fair amount of work. Afghans can be likened to small children dressed up in their Sunday clothes – by the time Sunday evening arrives they are hopelessly dishevelled! If your Afghan Hound is to maintain a presentable appearance, yet remain functional, you must be prepared to devote a certain amount of time to the care of its coat. The critical period is from twelve months to two years of age, when the coat is changing from puppy (woolly) to adult (silky) and, because the two different coat textures tend to interact with each other, felts and tangles are inevitable. However, life becomes easier once all traces of the puppy coat have disappeared, and it is by adopting a gentle regime of grooming that you will pave the way towards the luxurious coat that is to come.

Coat texture is often associated with colour – the darker the coat the heavier it is in texture – and I have found the stronger, heavier textured coats associated with dark golds and reds among the easiest to keep tangle-free. Black-and-tans, golds and creams, when closely related to reds, have the same strong, straight, light-reflecting texture, while black-and-creams and pale golds have a lighter, finer texture and are inclined to kink at the first sign of dampness or humidity. Brindle coats, being made up of various colours and therefore several hair textures, can also prove difficult to maintain, as the incompatibility of the different textures when heavy hair is lying alongside light hair causes friction and inevitable tangles.

Static electricity caused by dryness and movement seems to be more of a problem in the whites, pale creams and pale golds, which have a tendency to be of a lighter texture. The movement of individual hairs against each other encourages the coat to become 'fly-away', whereas darker coloured dogs with a heavier texture do not appear to suffer with the problem to the same degree.

Kennel Club Regulations state quite clearly that *no substance which alters the natural colour, texture or body of the coat may be used in the preparation of a dog for exhibition either before or at the show. Any other substance (other than water) which may be used in the preparation for a dog for exhibition must not be allowed to remain in the coat of a dog at the time of exhibition.*

Unfortunately, water encourages static electricity in a fine coat, and matters are only made worse by spraying with water and subsequently brushing until dry with a nylon/bristle brush. In the past, the problem has been overcome by using anti-static products or simply by spraying with a solution of diluted conditioner and water (one teaspoonful of conditioner to one litre of water) to add weight to a dry, fly-away coat. Nylon dog coats worn to ensure that the dog is clean on arrival at a show can also encourage friction between hair and coat fabric, and I have found heavier cotton coats more suitable for this purpose.

Most colours are inclined to darken slightly with age, and it is not until around four years that the true colour finally

(Top to bottom) Mason Pearson nylon and bristle brush, pin brush and comb.

emerges. Brindles eventually darken to the more dominant colour in the coat, which may be grey or red/brown, whilst blacks, which absorb the heat more than other colours, often take on a brownish tinge if exposed to the sun.

Whilst the Breed Standard calls for coat to develop naturally, removing the dead hair from a saddle or cleaning the face of stray facial growth does not constitute changing the natural coat pattern. These areas are required to be *short* and, if a tidy appearance is to be maintained, a little work will occasionally be necessary.

The puppy coat

If you are starting out with a puppy it must become accustomed to the regular grooming routine that will be an essential part of its growing years. Whilst a puppy coat does not require much attention until around the age of six months old, the pup will need to be taught to stand still while being brushed all over with a soft bristle brush. If it hates this now and you do not persevere, I assure you matters will only get worse. It need only take a couple of minutes each day as you play and talk encouragingly to your puppy. If it objects and tries to bite the brush, tell it 'No!' and repeat this exercise for a short period the next day and every other day until it readily accepts the brush. Give it a reward and tell it what a good pup it is. How well I remember buying my very first Afghan at 10 weeks old from an all-breed puppy farm and being sold a six-inch-square slicker brush at the same time to groom her with. The brush was almost as big as the puppy and it took me a while to understand why she hated it. Apart from being totally unsuitable, it was lethal and would never have been recommended had I bought her from a well established enthusiast of the breed.

Afghans do not have the doggy smell associated with many breeds but they get very muddy in the garden or during road-walking, so it's in everyone's interest that they learn to accept regular bathing. We will discuss bathing further in this chapter in the section about preparing your dog for a show, and the initial bathing of your puppy is just a scaled-down version of this. Teach your puppy to accept standing still as the warm water shower is passed over it, avoiding the eyes, and gently shampoo with a regular or insecticidal shampoo, rinse off, towel dry, big hug and finish off with a small hand dryer on a low heat setting. Always make bath-time enjoyable, talk to your pup: 'Lift this leg – Good boy! – Now turn around – Good boy!' Give your puppy confidence, praising it and never becoming impatient or losing your temper.

Get your puppy accustomed to having its teeth inspected (you'll probably be doing this anyway to see how the adult teeth are coming through) and also inspect its ears for dirt, soreness or smelly brown wax that may indicate the presence of ear mites.

The most common complaint I hear from the owners of tatty, knotty Afghans is, 'He hates being bathed and groomed'. What they probably mean is, 'I can't be bothered to bath and groom him regularly.' If you want an Afghan, it's up to you to teach it while it's young, and that way you'll learn together. It doesn't have to be perfect grooming as long as the dog is knot-free and comfortable.

The junior coat

From the age of around six months, as the coat begins to thicken and lengthen, you will find knots and felts that need to be attended to as they occur. These are usually found behind the ears, between the front legs, under the chest and tummy and on the back legs, and you will find it a bonus if your training can be extended to the dog standing still on a grooming table. There are some excellent products on the market that can be sprayed directly onto the felt to allow it to be gently teased

Well presented junior coat (brindle):
Aust Ch Karakush Saint She Aint.

apart with fingers and a small pin brush. But remember – the longer the felt is left, the longer it takes to get out, and the greater the discomfort experienced by the dog.

From around the age of nine months the woolly puppy coat will begin to fall from the top of the back as the characteristic short saddle hair begins to emerge. To prevent felting where it falls into the longer body coat, regular, gentle brushing will be required.

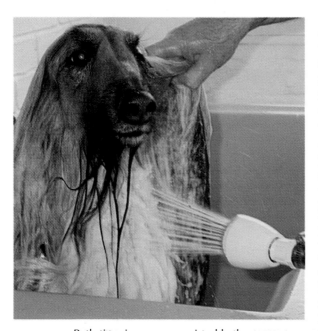

Bath-time in a power-assisted bath.

The show coat

Attending to a show coat requires total dedication, and seasoned exhibitors all have their own methods of preparing their dogs for the ring. Top winning exhibitors may have a few tips tucked under their belts but I assure you there is no magic cure, preparation or substitute for getting down to basics and thereby turning out a clean, shiny, knot-free exhibit. You need never be let down by poor presentation. Depending upon the type and amount of coat carried, a show dog in full adult coat will require bathing and grooming on a frequency of between 5–10 days. Exhibitors who make the time to bath and groom every five days will never lose coat of any consequence and the whole process from start to finish should only take a couple of hours. However, this frequency is determined mainly upon where and how the dog is exercised and whether it can be dry-brushed between baths. If you are fortunate to have a covered exercise area or large areas of short grass, your dog will not become as dirty as those walked on roads and farm pathways. I am always reluctant to put the brush through the dry, dirty and sticky coat of a dog I am campaigning as it tends to drag it out at the roots, resulting in loss of density, so would only groom when the dog is wet following its bath. Bitches tend to keep cleaner than dogs, but still get sticky on their hocks and trousers during exercise.

My own dogs are used to being groomed whilst standing on a table and will jump up quite happily, although I know of many exhibitors who prefer to groom their dog with it laying on its side on either the table or the floor. Basically, do whatever is comfortable for you so long as the dog is relaxed and will stay still.

Most exhibitors bath their dogs in a conventional bath, using either a separate overhead shower or one that can be attached to the taps. Buying a second-hand bath and plumbing it into the garage or utility room saves a lot of mess to the walls and carpet of the family bathroom, caused by wet and shaking dogs. Cleaning up the bathroom isn't a favourite job at the best of times, especially with the prospect of an early morning start the next day to drive a couple of hundred miles to a show. Always use a non-slip mat in the bath to prevent the dog from sliding around.

Power-assisted, purpose-made dog baths are an excellent idea and take away the labour of actually bathing your dog as the powerful spray enables the shampoo and conditioner to penetrate the coat with very little effort on your part. They are widely used overseas and are gaining popularity in Great Britain.

Prior to bathing you will need to plug your dog's ears with cotton wool to avoid water going inside them, and remove any twigs or leaves from the coat. Explained below is my own method of bathing:

Stage 1: If the coat is very dirty When using a conventional bath run about 15cm of warm water and add a squirt of good quality, mild washing-up liquid (the type that is *kind to hands* is ideal). Lift your dog into the bath and, using a plastic jug, ladle the soapy water over the coat until it is

thoroughly saturated. If the dog will sit or lie down in the water, all the better. Particularly dirty and sticky areas such as hocks, feet and ear fringes can be washed with neat washing-up liquid at this point. Empty the bath and rinse the dog thoroughly. You will now have removed most of the initial dirt and have a good base for subsequent shampooing and conditioning. Continue with Stage 2.

Stage 2 - begin here if the coat is not particularly dirty Apply shampoo from a squeezy type of applicator, such as an old

(Top) Start from the feet and work upwards.
(Centre left) Wet dog being groomed.
(Bottom) Arriving clean and dry in a raincoat.
Photo: David Paton

washing-up bottle, directing it on to all areas of the coat. It is important to use downward motions with your palms and fingers to massage in the shampoo to avoid tangling the coat. *Do not rub.* Most types of shampoo can be used, doggy or human and, as with your own hair, the better quality the product, the better the result. As with people, what suits one type of hair will give dreadful results to another, so in this respect it's a case of trial and error. If your dog has a scurfy saddle, apply an anti-dandruff shampoo to that area first and leave it on while applying a cream shampoo to the rest of the coat, always avoiding the eyes. To eliminate the possibility of scurf it is most important that all traces of shampoo are rinsed well away until the water runs clear.

Next, apply diluted conditioner all over with your squeezy applicator until all the coat is penetrated, applying it neat with your hands to longer-coated areas such as ear fringes, body coat, leg coat and hocks, massaging well in. At this point, using a pin-brush, brush the conditioner downwards through the hair. Do this one lock at a time, supporting the coat between thumb and fore-finger with one hand and brushing downwards on to your hand (*not* the dog's skin) with the other. If there are any felts they can be soaked with conditioner and broken down at this stage. Some exhibitors at this point prefer to leave in a small amount of conditioner in the hope that it will add weight to a lighter textured coat or assist in calming down a heavy coat, but this often conceals the natural light-reflecting properties and leaves the coat looking dull. Therefore, I prefer to rinse off all traces of conditioner, before squeezing out excess water from legs, body and ears and soaking up the remaining water from the coat with dry towels. Never rub the coat vigorously with a towel as this will cause tangles, but you can rub the face – your dog will love it!

Transfer the dog to a grooming table in a warm place and begin brushing with a nylon/bristle or pin brush, starting at the feet and working your way up the legs. Butterfly clips are useful to keep ungroomed hair pinned up out of the way, enabling the hair below to be worked on easily. Keep releasing layers of hair from the clip as you work your way up. If the dog is still particularly knotty at this stage, apply a tangle-removing preparation to help tease out the remaining felts. However, should a great deal of this be required on the main body of the coat and legs when the dog is to be exhibited the next day, I'm afraid it's back into the bath to rinse out the sticky residue, if the desired finish is to be achieved.

When the dog is thoroughly groomed with no knots, transfer it to the utility room or garage for drying, as this is the stage when the hair really starts flying and gets absolutely everywhere. Using butterfly clips again, start at the bottom, letting layers down as you brush and dry at the same time. Ensure that the dryer is blowing downwards onto the coat, not upwards and into it, as that would create tangles. If the dog has kinky areas to its ears or legs, gently pull the coat straight with the brush, hold, and dry thoroughly. If the hair is left damp the kinks will reappear very quickly.

If it is to be exhibited the following day the last thing you or your dog need after all this hard work is to go out and get wet, so Afghan exhibitors have invented all sorts of waterproof leggings and coats to keep their dogs clean and dry until they get to the show. Variations on these can be bought from pet shops and at shows.

You will know when the perfect finish has been achieved because the clean, shiny, reflective, silky qualities of the coat will resemble a sheet of glass. Unfortunately, with one shake, the illusion will be shattered!

Maintenance of a show coat

There is no point in having a beautifully tended coat if your dog is lacking in fitness, resulting in poor muscle tone and body condition. That extra bloom will only come from complete inner health so, to maintain an alert and happy show dog, there is no substitute for correct feeding, exercise and health care.

Protective 'clothing'

To keep ear fringes long, always use a snood at mealtimes and raise water bowls 45cm off the ground. Alternatively, fringes can be permanently tied up by taking a 25cm x 20cm (10in x 8in) piece of strong polythene and wrapping it around the length of the ear fringe, being very careful to avoid the actual ear flap. You then fold the packet upwards in half, then in half again, securing tightly with a strong rubber band. Poke a hole between the bottom fold and thread through a fine choke chain, securing both ends with a lead clip. The ears will be held close to the neck and unable to be dunked into

Male Afghan coat protector.

anything wet or smelly. The packets must be unwrapped and fringes groomed through every two to three days to avoid felting and to retain length.

Male dogs are notorious for squirting up their own front legs when spending a penny, depending upon which way the wind is blowing at the time. Urine will rot, break and discolour coat, especially on a white or cream, if not attended to fairly quickly, and ingenious exhibitors have designed exercise coats to protect the belly and front legs from discolouration. Alternatively, towelling bands can be wrapped pony-tail fashion around the long body and leg coat that is deemed to be in the line of fire.

All too much trouble you may think but, with show entry fees edging towards £20 per dog and petrol approaching £3 a gallon, attending a show is an expensive business. If you have prepared your dog to the best of your ability and it is physically and mentally on form, you can blame only the judge if you do not win.

Judicious trimming and stripping

We are frequently told by foreign Afghan enthusiasts visiting our shows that British dogs have too much coat as, in their countries, they do not interpret the requirement that *coat must develop naturally* quite as literally as the British. However, the world is getting smaller and British enthusiasts are travelling to shows abroad and seeing for themselves the type of presentation that can be achieved with a little help from the stripping stone and thinning scissors. Added to this, nearly all the overseas judges we have had officiating in this country opt for the dog with a clean outline as opposed to our hairy-backed, hairy-necked and hairy-tailed British dogs, whose coats literally have been *allowed to develop naturally*.

Correct presentation should highlight the distinctive breed hallmarks, and all the breed standards are quite explicit when referring to coat. The four most important requirements (and often the most misunderstood) are the following:

- *...on foreface hair short.*
- *...in mature dogs from shoulder backwards and along the saddle hair short and close...*
- *...tail...sparsely feathered.*
- *...coat must develop naturally.*

Much emphasis has been placed on the last statement. No coat on a show dog in the ring today has been allowed to *develop naturally*. Weekly bathing, de-matting, wrapping ears, and in fact general grooming and brushing are all artificial procedures that interfere with so-called natural development of coat. The other three statements quoted are all breed requirements, and a little judicious trimming and 'cleaning up' of the coat to allow these features to be easily seen is quite permissible. If you tidy up the coat in a subtle way, making it look as natural as possible, you will never be penalised by a competent judge; rather your dog be rewarded for having the aforesaid essential and unique breed features.

Before embarking on a make-over of your dog you must be aware of its faults and virtues and realise that the object of the exercise is to minimise the former and accentuate the latter. Study your dog before you start, proceed very carefully and have a mental picture of how you want it to look. At all times such preparation should be discreet, and judges are well within their rights to penalise dogs they feel have been incorrectly prepared.

There are various grooming tools to assist you in the preparation of your dog. These include a chiropody sponge (stone), a suitable stripping knife (one which does not cut the hair but merely grabs the fluff to help pull it out) and spiky rubber thimblettes (purchased from stationers) to help with hand plucking. The particular tool you use depends on the amount of coat you have to remove and whether it is the first time or a subsequent tidying up. Generally speaking, a knife is good for grown in saddles where the fluff is still quite short, a stone for longer, denser hair that may then need to be finished with a knife, and the rubber thimblettes for the face or side of the neck. Thinning scissors (46 teeth) can also be used with great care to remove hair from the sides of the tail, as the dog will usually object to this being pulled out.

If you have a dog that you do not show, it is a good idea to practise first until you are confident about using the scissors, knife and stone. That way your mistakes stay at home!

Starting with the face, long cheek furnishings and 'puppy fluff' can be removed with finger and thumb stripping, working from the muzzle back to the ears and downwards to the throat. The long hairs are grasped between finger and thumb, a very few at a time, and simply pulled out. The shape of the dog's head will determine how much you take out, although the Mandarin beard under the chin on a dog should be left.

A clean saddle can be achieved by removing the long, fine, fluffy hair, leaving only the shorter, coarser, closer-lying saddle hair, which is often of a darker shade in lighter-coloured dogs. It is a severe fault if saddle-textured coat is not present and, while you may expect the judge to prod and poke through the coat to discover whether or not the correct coat is present, precious time is wasted by this. No amount of stripping will create saddle hair if it is not already there, so there is no deception. Start in the middle of the back, just behind the shoulders. Hold the skin with one hand at the top of the dog's shoulders, usually the left if you are right-handed, or vice versa. With long, firm strokes, using the stone held with only a corner in contact with the skin, stroke the long hair out and regularly brush away the fallen hair to assess your progress. This is very time-consuming and must be done a little at a time, as the dog will soon become bored. The easiest way to do this is with the dog standing on the ground, you sitting in a chair and the dog's hindquarters almost on your knee. It is important to keep the dog 'straight', so it must be standing in a straight line. A second person may be useful to hold its head or you can tie its lead to an immovable object.

The same principles apply to the knife and the finger and thumb. Take out only a little hair at a time and continually review the overall picture. Try to keep both sides even and move around the area to avoid making bare spots in any particular place. Care must be taken around the bony parts such as the hip bones and spine; you may need to pull the skin gently in different directions to remove the hair from around these areas. Proceed along the back and croup to the tail.

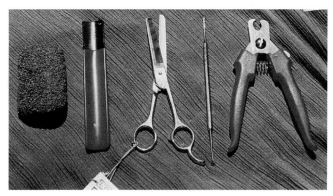

Equipment for show preparation: (left to right) stripping stone, stripping knife, thinning scissors, tooth descaler and nail clippers.

The requirement for the tail to be *sparsely feathered* should initially be bred for but, with the increasing demand for big heavy coats in the show ring, tails have naturally become more heavily furnished as well. Hair can be removed from the top and sides of the tail, leaving the feathering underneath, which can be further thinned if it is still too profuse.

Using the knife, gently stroke it along the top of the tail, taking out as much fluff as possible. Repeat this along each side right to the end, including the ringed part. Leave the long hair on the tip of the tail as this helps complete the ring – the crowning glory of a perfect Afghan Hound tail. If the dog objects strongly to this hair being pulled out or the hair is particularly stubborn, careful use of thinning scissors laid flat to the tail (straight blade in to the coat and pointing lengthwise from the tip of the tail to the base) may solve the problem. Make only one cut at a time and, after each cut, brush out the hair and hold up the tail to assess your progress. If the remaining feathering on the underside still looks too heavy, carefully thin and trim with thinning scissors.

To give definition to the outline and provide detail, neck patches can also receive attention. The texture on the neck patches will be similar to that on the saddle, and all sorts of illusions can be created by 'drawing in' the line of the shoulder with cleverly-placed patches. These are easiest dealt with using the stone. Look for where the coat texture changes under the long coat and stroke the area with the stone or pluck with finger and thumb. Once again, this will be impossible if the correctly-textured coat is not already present. If the overlying neck (hood) hair is very long, this can also be trimmed to a suitable length to expose and enhance the patches.

The maintenance coat

It may be that your Afghan is a much-loved family pet whom you just like to keep looking smart while still resembling an Afghan. In this case, your grooming time can be considerably shortened ('Thank God!' I hear you cry) by trimming the hair short under the armpits, under the tummy, between the testicles and inside the back legs, so that only the outer areas need to be groomed. Thinning out the longer remaining coat with thinning scissors should further reduce grooming time, and a fortnightly to three-weekly bath and groom should suffice. Nevertheless, have a go at giving your dog a show bath – the admiring glances will be your just reward.

If the coat has already gone past the point of no return and it would cause your Afghan too much discomfort to groom it out, cut through the knots vertically with thinning scissors and gently tease them out, or consider having your dog trimmed all over twice a year, in spring and autumn, at a grooming salon.

Many show dogs are trimmed down after finishing illustrious show careers, free from the restrictions of being unable to be exercised in woods and long grass for fear of slicing off precious leg coat and getting twigs and brambles entwined in their hair. Without this encumbrance they can gnaw happily at large marrow bones held between their front paws and enjoy life to the full. Furthermore, when a dog becomes older it does not want to stand for long periods whilst its grooming ritual is completed, and there is the added risk of it catching a chill.

Problems associated with coat

For reasons known only to themselves, some Afghans persist in chewing their coats. Sometimes it's just the odd nibble here and there, with others making it their life's work to chew themselves away. Anti-chew products can be bought with names such as *bitter apple* and *sour grapes* but, however bitter or sour they may be, the chewer will still continue with the destruction. A concentrated French perfume with a really heavy scent, regularly applied, tends to do the trick and ultimately works out cheaper than experimenting with all the different products on the market.

Coat chewing on a show dog can be a nightmare and can only be resolved if the cause can be identified. Puppies between the ages of four and nine months usually start to chew on a joint or an area where growth plates are beginning to fuse together and it could be that they are experiencing those awful aching, growing pains that some children experience. They can't rub their little legs so automatically suck and chew the area to administer comfort, and the fact that the area happens to be covered in coat is inconsequential to them. Likewise, if the chewing is to a bony area, the dog may well have knocked itself playing, and will naturally lick where it feels sore. Unfortunately, the comfort factor associated with coat chewing becomes habit forming long after the pain is gone and it is very difficult to break. It is important never to over-exercise a puppy during this critical growing period.

Toe chewing could possibly indicate a nail-bed infection or the presence of rabbit mites, picked up on a walk, and the regular application of a good pest control spray that kills fleas, lice and mites may just do the trick. If your dog merely has a one-off chew, it has probably picked up a flea and its first reaction will be to bite the little perisher. However, more serious biting and scratching resulting from an infestation by fleas or lice can do untold damage to a show coat if left untreated. If the coat has been sliced straight across and looks a mess, all is not lost. Careful blending with thinning scissors in the opposite direction to the line of the slice may help in its disguise until grown out.

Dogs will chew the odours on body and leg coat when they become sexually

The old-fashioned coat pattern.

active and some bitches in season will chew dried blood from their trousers if this is left unattended. If you want to keep coat, be vigilant and help by rinsing these areas down regularly.

Some dogs carry typical old-fashioned coat patterns with deep, smooth, natural saddles, receding top-knots, and bare pasterns and hocks that may give the illusion of small feet. This is often accompanied by a sparse coat of a fine, cotton-wool texture and is one of the most difficult to grow and maintain for the show ring. Extreme care must be taken when exercising not to let twigs entangle and break delicate leg and body coat. The wearing of a protective coat during exercise will assist in keeping length.

Many bitches lose coat after a season and any woolly hair that has grown through the saddle will fall out, sometimes spreading further down the sides of the body than the owner would wish. As long as the loose hair is not allowed to mat into the longer coat and is brushed away with care, this is not too serious. The psychological effects associated with a false pregnancy, however, are a problem, and bitches will lose belly coat in preparation for the birth of their imaginary puppies, exposing teats and even producing milk. By carefully keeping length on the side coat to conceal a bare tummy and not allowing the felts caused by licking to accumulate, I have known many bitches appear quickly back in the ring looking just as wonderful as ever.

chapter nine

Afghan Hound activities

Showing

Of all the Afghan activities, showing is the most popular and, whether you attend shows where Afghans are scheduled in Great Britain or anywhere in the world, you can be assured of meeting up with friendly, like-minded enthusiasts who are willing to share their experiences. There is no need to feel apprehensive about going to a show on your own, because by the end of the day I can guarantee that both you and your dog will have made many new friends.

If you so wish, you can attend a show every weekend but, to gain some insight into the breed and knowledge of the dog show world in general, it is a good idea first to order copies of the weekly dog newspapers from your newsagent. *Our Dogs* and *Dog World* are essential reading for everyone connected with breeding and showing, and the 'Afghan Breed Notes' therein will keep you up-to-date on forthcoming events and shows, as well as reporting show results and printing interesting features.

All Afghan Hounds registered with The Kennel Club are allowed to enter shows, provided that they are at least six months old on the day of the show.

Types of show in Great Britain
Exemption shows: These are frequently held in aid of charities and are a great day out for all the family. They are usually held in local parks in the summer months and have classes scheduled for show dogs as well as non-pedigree dogs. Entries are taken on the day of the show and, as well as being good fun, exhibitors find them good opportunities for socialising their puppies without placing them under any pressure. The last exemption show that I attended was judged by a well known character from a leading 'soap', who knew nothing whatsoever about dogs, but nevertheless had us all in stitches. At the end of the day a great deal of money was raised for a worthy cause and everyone, dogs included, had an enjoyable day.

Open shows – all breed: All dogs registered at The Kennel Club are eligible to enter an open show and, depending on the size of the show, several classes may be allocated to Afghan Hounds. These shows are advertised in advance in the weekly dog press and the judge will usually be an Afghan or general hound specialist. If you are new to the show scene, it is usually recommended that you start with this type of show to understand the mechanics and gain confidence. Many venues around the country hold this type of show, organised by different canine societies. Occurring most weekends, they are less expensive to enter than championship shows and you should not have to travel too far to find one.

Open shows – breed club: These are undoubtedly the best places for the newcomer to start. All 12 British Afghan Hound Societies (see **Useful Addresses**) hold at least one open show a year, where you can meet up with other enthusiasts and ask as many questions as you like. Held around the country, these shows have specialist judges, large rings, numerous rosettes and special prizes on offer, and the happy atmosphere of people just enjoying their hobby. Afghan memorabilia, from snoods to sweatshirts, can be purchased from the organising Club's stall and, if the bug bites, you will soon find yourself participating in all the Club's other activities, such as training days and dinner dances.

Showing – on the bench. Photo: David Paton

Championship shows: To become a British champion, a dog must be awarded three Kennel Club Challenge Certificates (CCs) under three different judges, and these are only on offer at championship shows. At present there are 36 shows where CCs are on offer, of which 11 are organised by the breed clubs. Championship shows are benched, which means that each dog has a bench allotted to it, bearing the same number as its ring number, which is listed in the catalogue. The rules state that the dog must be on its bench, secured with a collar and chain, when not being exercised or shown. Championship shows attract the largest number of entries, despite the fact that entry fees are high, prize money is seldom given and you may have to travel 300 miles to get there. However, only by winning a prize at a championship show can a dog qualify for Crufts or gain a Kennel Club Stud Book Number.

Ring training
If you have followed the suggestions in my chapter on training, your dog will be walking well on the lead, responsive to your commands and well socialised. Making your debut in the ring can be nerve-wracking, but by knowing what to expect you are halfway there. Attending a few ringcraft classes, where emphasis is placed upon handling and showmanship rather than obedience, will help develop your confidence immensely, and your dog will

benefit from being gone over (examined) by many different people acting as judges. As well as standing, your dog will need to learn to trot at its best speed in an absolute straight line, displaying correct head and tail carriage. Many training clubs and canine societies organise ringcraft classes and these are often advertised in local newspapers and pet shops.

When you attend your first show, try not to reveal the fact to the judge but to give the impression that you have been doing it for years.

Equipment for the show

You will need to put together a 'show bag' containing the following:

- Show lead/fine check chain. There are many types from which to choose and these are on sale at most shows.
- Leather collar and benching chain. The end of the benching chain has a spring-loaded clip which can be undone quickly in an emergency. However, many exhibitors prefer the extra security of keeping their dogs in a cage that fits inside the bench, or alternatively a metal cage front can be attached to the bench.
- Blanket or small duvet.
- Drinking bowl and water. Although water is available at the show, it is wise to take your own to prevent tummy upsets.
- Dog coat and towel. If it is wet or there is dew on the grass, walking into the show from the

(Top) Training the show 'Stand'.
(Below) Getting the dog to the show clean and dry.

car park can result in very damp feet and trousers.
- Clip or large elastic arm band to hold your ring number.
- Brushes and water spray.
- Dry cleaning powder, in case of accidents. These products can cause static, so it would be wise to change your brush before going on to groom the rest of the coat.

If you are attending an outdoor show, keep a waterproof coat and wellingtons in the boot of the car for yourself. Even in the marquees, the ground gets wet after heavy rain.

Capes and boots.

Various further items of show equipment can be bought, such as grooming tables, cages and trolleys for wheeling your equipment into the show from the car. These items are not essential if you just have one dog, but can be added gradually if you decide to continue with showing.

The day of the show

Always arrive an hour before judging is due to start. Remember that there are hundreds of people of the same mind, all trying to get through one gate into the car park, and this can sometimes involve a long walk to the benching area. Buy a catalogue and give your dog time to relieve itself before going on to its bench; otherwise it will go into the ring feeling uncomfortable and will not move at its best. If you are unfortunate enough to be benched next to an unruly dog who is going to upset your own dog, request permission from the Show Manager to be moved; there is no reason for your dog to be upset in this manner. Likewise, if your own dog has a reputation of being unruly, it is unfair to other exhibitors if you leave him unattended.

It is a good idea to familiarise your dog with the ring before grooming it. If it is not self-assured, this will boost its confidence. The extent of the final preparation will largely depend on how much work you have done beforehand and how clean its arrival into the showground. Afghans never arrive anywhere in an immaculate condition. Groom your dog through, starting at the feet and working upwards, using clips as discussed in chapter 8 and paying attention to the inside of the legs, which are sometimes overlooked. A spray of water will settle the coat and help to straighten kinks, but this should not be brushed in vigorously, or it will cause static. Many finishing sprays on sale at shows to enhance shine and final appearance would contravene Kennel Club regulations if used, although, unless you are a top winning exhibitor, your dog is very unlikely to be chosen for random coat testing. I can only suggest that, if your dog has been prepared thoroughly and naturally on the day preceding the show as described in chapter 8, such products will prove unnecessary.

Handling: how to get the best out of your dog

Handling your dog in the ring is an art. First impressions count and, if the judge sees your dog float into the ring looking a million dollars, he or she will be keenly awaiting the opportunity to go over it to see if it is really as good as it looks. A good exhibitor can make a mediocre dog look good, and a poor exhibitor can make a good dog look mediocre, so it is in your interest to make the most of your exhibit, the aim being to present a balanced picture, both stacked and on the move. To do this you will have to bear in mind the points that the judge will be looking for – in other words, those required by the Breed Standard.

If the ring is outdoors, the ground may be sloping or uneven, in which case your dog will look much better standing with the front feet at a point slightly higher than the back feet. This is not to say it must display the topline of a German Shepherd but, if the front feet are in a hollow, the topline will slope upwards towards a raised rump, resulting in a totally unbalanced appearance. If the ring happens to be even, another point for consideration is the way that the wind is blowing. Afghans do not look good with the wind coming at them from behind, so face your dog into the wind if at all possible.

Always remember that, even when the judge is appraising another dog, he may just turn around and catch sight of your dog looking sloppy with topline slouched, front legs at 'ten to two' and rump in the air, while you are having a chat with a fellow exhibitor. When awaiting your turn, talk to your dog and not to your neighbour, and don't just pull your dog into a new position – ask it to move into it. Keep your dog on its toes and in a happy frame of mind until it is your turn to be examined.

Only by practising will you be able to stand your dog in front of the judge without it looking like a major effort. Walk your dog into the show stance and make a few quick adjustments that are undetectable to the judge. As the judge approaches, do not crowd the dog but lightly support its head and mentally say, 'Yes, the best one is here!'. Confidence is contagious. If requested by the judge to show its bite, lift the upper and lower lips away to give a good view of top and bottom teeth alignment.

Leads should be used only as a means of maintaining communication between you and your dog and as unobtrusively as possible. A well trained dog does not need a thick lead to restrain it and, if you have a good understanding with your dog, a light touch on the lead should convey your message. A fine lead and/or check chain held high up the neck, under the chin, will not string the dog up, but rather maintain contact at all times, allowing instant communication. A loose lead flapping around the dog's shoulders cannot tell it of an imminent change in direction and does not convey professionalism.

Never jerk the dog with the lead as you are going around the ring. This just puts it off balance and wastes strides as it gets back into balance. In a small ring you have only a short distance to demonstrate your dog's soundness to the judge and it is imperative that you make the best possible use of this opportunity to be seen. Additional showmanship can be displayed if you train your dog to stand free, looking up at you when you return to the judge. You can train your dog at home by offering its favourite food and teasing it a little

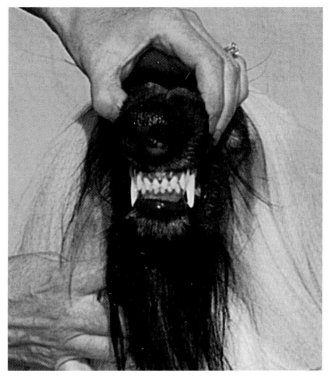
Showing the bite.

before giving it the treat. Your dog will soon come to expect the treat after a show-ring-type run-around and will automatically look up at you when the triangle is finished. An Afghan should never be trained to run around chasing a biscuit in an attempt to keep its head held high. Its head and neck carriage would be incorrect and it would not be looking where it was going – in other words, at the surrounding area – as a sighthound should. Neither will your hound convey the impression of a 'King of Dogs', owning the ground on which it walks, if it is pleading for a taste of biscuit held a short distance from its nose.

A well trained, but not over trained, confident dog with pride of race, sailing around the ring with head and tail held high, is a joy to behold. It is what we are all aiming for, and some dogs and exhibitors working together as a perfect team achieve this. Once seen, this image of teamwork will never be forgotten and should always remain your goal.

How to disguise faults

There is a saying that *the perfect dog is yet to be born*, but there is also another that says *beauty is in the eye of the beholder*. With this in mind it is worth discussing how the less-than-perfect points of a dog can be disguised in the ring. That is not to say that our judges are fools but, when judging a large class of dogs, they have an awful lot to store in their minds! The manner in which you present your dog for the final appraisal can make a lasting impression. Whilst the following suggestions will never be a substitute for correct conformation, they may just help the owner of the less than perfect dog score a few extra points. See also The show coat in chapter 8.

The main thing to bear in mind is keep corrections subtle and not to fuss with faults. By doing so you will only draw more attention to them.

To hide a rising topline in which the rump is higher than shoulders, pull the back legs out further behind than is normal. If the dog is lacking in rear angulation, widen the back legs a couple of inches beyond the width of the hips, 'fluff up' the hocks and brush the leg coat forward from the stifle joint. Dogs can also be taught to crouch ever so slightly to give more angulation behind, if you hold the dog's tail at the base and gently pull away and down. The dog will naturally lean against this slight tension, pull forward over its front and bend its back legs a little. This is also a good method to adopt if your dog tends to pull backwards on the stack. While not uncomfortable, this does need to be practised at home. You will soon find that, after a short time, you do not need to pull at all; as soon as you put your hand around the tail the dog will lean forward. Pushing on the dog's backside has the opposite effect. The dog will then resist this pressure and pull even farther backwards.

To conceal a narrow front, place the front legs so that they give a good hand's width between them, making sure the elbows are not protruding or the feet pointing at 'ten to two'. Hide a short neck by pulling outwards rather than upwards.

Choice of lead colour can also help disguise faults. A long back can appear shorter on the stack if broken up by using a brightly coloured lead, draped from the back of the shoulder to the point of shoulder to give the impression of long, sloping shoulder blades and shorter back. A short-backed dog should never be shown with a bright, contrasting lead placed in this manner, so conceal this either under the coat or use a lead which is the same colour as the dog. Stacking and use of leads varies from country to country.

If your dog has a superb outline, by all means show this off to its best advantage by wearing a contrasting colour yourself but, should the shoulders and topline be not so good, for example on a black dog, conceal the fact by wearing black yourself and stand directly behind your dog whenever possible. A dippy topline can be concealed either by encouraging the dog to lean forward (as before) so as to transfer more weight on to the front legs, or by positioning the offside hind leg forward underneath the body to give more support to the back.

Some dogs will hold a front foot in the air and refuse to put it down. A gentle push in the area of the ribs will force the line of balance over to the side in question, making the dog either replace the foot or fall over!

Brushing the top-knot forward to conceal a poor head and eye is rather obvious but, if you encourage the top-knot and ear fringes to grow long and luxuriant, they may just detract from a coarse head and untypical expression. Conversely, excess hair growth under the throat can detract from a good length of foreface and could be discreetly removed.

Movement

Having ensured that your dog has remained alert and happy throughout the waiting period, hopefully when requested to move it will do so eagerly with animation and style. Start off easily and adjust your speed to one that is comfortable to both you and your dog, aiming to achieve the balance between gayness and control. The judge does not want to see how fast your dog can move, but rather that it can move correctly. Too happy, and the dog will throw its legs around, wag its tail and appear to move out of alignment; too controlled, and it will appear dull. However, more control is necessary when moving towards and away from the judge, so that balance and soundness (correct foot placemen) can be assessed.

Extra exuberance can be displayed when moving in a circle to enhance the stride and style. If the head is held too high, the front legs will not reach full extension and the dog will paddle (throw its front feet out sideways).

When asked to return to your place, remember that you are still showing and the judge may still be watching. Stand the dog for the final appraisal, keeping your eye on the judge so that you do not miss your chance if you are pulled out into the final line-up. If you are fortunate enough for this to happen, never let your standards slip – it just may help you move up into a higher placing. Whilst you will be delighted to receive a prize card, it is more important that you stand your dog to perfection while the judge writes or dictates a report about it.

All first prize winners compete against each other within their sex, the winner then going on to compete against the opposite sex winner for Best of Breed (Best Afghan). The more glowing a report you can achieve at this point, the better your chances in the challenge, so be alert and on your toes at all times.

Always accept the judge's decision courteously and don't create a scene if the outcome of the judging has not been in your favour. If you lose, try to work out why – maybe the judge liked a different type and none of your dog's relatives won on the day. Unless you are aware that your dog did not perform at its best on the day or, indeed, was beaten by a better dog, you have the choice not to exhibit under that particular judge again.

Junior handling

Owning Afghan Hounds is a family affair and it is therefore a good idea for the junior family members to be encouraged to become involved in the training, grooming and showing of the dogs. Currently in Great Britain there are three junior handling organisations, all of which promote good sportsmanship, courtesy, loyalty and self-discipline amongst the youngsters, along with providing a very enjoyable social scene. The level of participation and the standards reached are largely up to the individual but, for most youngsters, it is not necessarily the winning, but the taking part that is the fun. Many canine societies and breed clubs feature junior handling classes at their shows and all juniors entering are usually rewarded, win or lose, by a small prize of some description.

The Kennel Club Junior Organisation (KCJO) (see **Useful Addresses**) was founded by The Kennel Club in 1985 to encourage young people aged 8–18 to develop skills and knowledge in all activities connected with dogs. Run on membership lines, it offers a wide range of events to suit every kind of interest and ability, and reaches its climax each year at Crufts. The KCJO organises events in Show Handling, Obedience, Agility and Triathalon competitions, plus educational events. Membership is split into regions, where annual competitions are organised to find each region's Best Show Handler within the age groups 8–11 years, 12–15 years and 16–18 years. The judging is based purely on handling and the winners of these regional competitions then go forward to compete at Crufts for the national title of KCJO Show Handler of the Year. The overall winner then usually goes on to represent Great Britain in the International Competition, which takes place on the final day of Crufts.

Another organisation that supports junior handling is the Junior Handling Association (JHA) (see **Useful Addresses**), which invites young people aged 6–17 to become members. Diplomas are awarded by participating canine societies and winners of the first three placings are invited to compete in a series of semi-final classes, held annually at Richmond Championship Show. The twelve finalists then compete for the title JHA Junior Handler of the Year, which is an annual event held at the Metropole Hotel in Birmingham.

The third organisation is the more recently formed United Kingdom Dog Handler's Association (see **Useful Addresses**), which is similar to the other two in that it arranges educational events, plus an annual international competition for both individuals and teams. Seminars in the training of junior handling judges are also held to ensure that the task no longer falls on the organising Society Chairman's wife!

The handler does not have to own the dog he or she is handling in any of these competitions, but it must be entered for competition at the show they are attending. Many handlers actually ask other owners if they might handle their dogs, as this is a good way to gain experience of handling different breeds. In top competition they will occasionally be asked to show another handler's dog.

Before taking part in any junior handling competition the handler and dog must be able to carry out a number of basic exercises, such as being able to move in a straight line or a triangle. This may sound somewhat obvious, but a judge will be watching that the alignment of these elementary movements can be performed in a competent manner. At a later stage, patterns such as the 'L', 'T' and circle can also be learnt.

Junior handlers often put the adults to shame when competing against them in a breed class at a championship show; the reason being that they are so well trained in the mechanics of moving their dog that they can demonstrate quite clearly the front, rear and profile movement, with the judge hardly having to move a step.

An important point observed by all junior handler organisations is dress, and in general a handler will want to look smart and professional without looking over the top. For both boys and girls, a clear-cut two piece suit is preferable, particularly in a plain material that will last the day without looking crumpled and untidy. When choosing the colour, the skillful handler will consider what colours would best complement the colour of their dog. If the dog is gold, then colours such as bright green and cobalt blue will enhance the dog and ensure that the pair look as one in the overall picture. In the case of parti-coloured dogs, it is appropriate to choose one predominant colour from the dog's coat and wear a colour which will complement that particular colour. Footwear is also very important, in that shoes should be quiet and have non-slip soles.

Lastly, to compete successfully, the handlers will need to demonstrate total compatibility with their dogs and have a definite will to win. It is also important that they enjoy themselves. All handlers and their dogs experience bad days and occasionally the competition does not go as well as was hoped, but determined handlers will rectify the points that have let them down and look towards the next competition.

Miss Hannah Bouttell and Miss Claire Millward are

Hannah Boutell and Claire Millward, first and second prize winners at the 1995 JHA semi-finals. Photo: John M Hope

Afghan owner/exhibitors who have experienced a great deal of success in junior handling competitions at all levels.

Racing in Great Britain

Given the chance, most Afghans love to chase. However, with fewer safe open spaces now available for them to exercise freely, the opportunities to do this for some are few and far between. Racing provides an excellent means of keeping them fit, promotes good muscle tone and really opens up their lungs. It is an activity to be enjoyed by show dogs and pet dogs alike and is not dangerous if the rules are adhered to. Racing will not make your hound aggressive or make it want to kill the cat; what it will do is make it fitter, happier and inject a new sparkle into its life. Whether it chases the other hounds or the hare is not apparent until you have given this sport a try.

Do take heart if your hound just wants to play around at first. By watching the other hounds and competing in a couple of trial runs, it will quickly realise what is expected and grow to love the sound of the approaching mechanical hare. Failing all else, it will at least provide you with a fun day out in the fresh air and widen your circle of Afghan friends.

The central controlling body for all Afghan racing in Great Britain is the Afghan Hound Association (AHA), and its representatives are on hand at all the meetings to give help and advice to all newcomers.

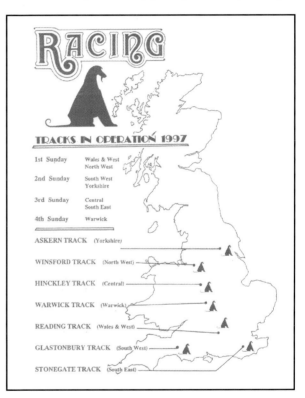

Map showing location of AHA tracks in operation, 1997.

Afghan Hound racing can be traced back to 1910, when it was reported that the imported dog Baz was raced alongside his Greyhound kennel mates by his owner, Mr Dunn. The next known recording was in 1929, when Mrs Phyllis Robson wrote that Mr W L Renwick's Watford Lou-Lou showed great aptitude for the sport and had easily won at Clapton Stadium when raced alongside other Afghans. Described as a cream-fawn dog sired by Khan of Ghazni, Lou-Lou was also a show dog, winning first prizes at Crufts and Birmingham Dog Show.

Mrs Molly Sharpe raced some of her Chaman Afghans in Scotland before the war, and

Afghan racing. Photo: David Paton

her Ch Garrymhor Faiz-Bu-Hassid, who gained his title in 1937, was reputedly one of the best and fastest racers of his day. From around this time there were groups of enthusiasts who would meet on private estates and flapping tracks all around the country to race their hounds for the sheer enjoyment of watching them run. Afghan racing had begun long before it was organised on a regular basis.

AHA Racing was started in Great Britain, originally with the intention of involving members whose hounds were not quite up to show standard. The late 1960s had seen an alarming explosion of often indiscriminate breeding and there were all too many owners to whom showing could be only a continual disappointment. Also worrying was the fact that many town dogs would never benefit from the experience of running free. It was around this time that Herta and Tony Buxey, originally from Hampshire, returned to Great Britain from Australia full of enthusiasm of their experience of the sport over there. They described their experience of racing to the then members of the AHA Committee, who decided it would be a great idea for this country too.

With safety as a major factor, the committee began the search for a suitable track. Whilst there were many greyhound kennels to be found with their own private flapper tracks, the majority of them were not available on a Sunday, that being the day when they either time-trialled their own greyhounds or gave their staff an afternoon off. Because this was to be a family-involved club event and also at the time there were no shows held on a Sunday, this was obviously the preferred day on which to hold the meetings.

After several months of searching, a small training track belonging to private greyhound kennels at Blindley Heath in Surrey was discovered. This was a somewhat makeshift affair with absolutely no facilities. The fact that the fencing was not very good and there were sheep grazing alongside was a cause for concern, but the owner Mr Vernon Ford was keen to have Afghans at the track and offered to give up a Sunday afternoon once a month to run the hare for £15 in cash. Afghan racing had found its first home in Great Britain.

Initially, Afghans were raced without muzzles but, as the sport progressed, the

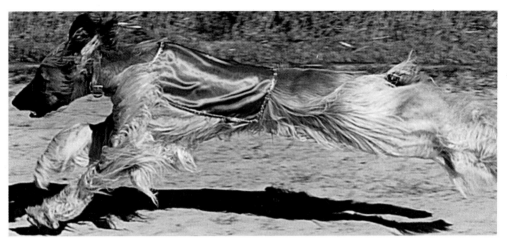

An Afghan in full chase is a magnificent sight. Photo: David Paton

committee took advice from the greyhound fraternity and introduced a few simple rules to ensure the safety and well-being of the dogs. Racing at Blindley Heath lasted for six years and an enjoyable time was had by its gallant band of originators: Herta and Tony Buxey, Ann and Ron Adams, Philip Holden, Geoff Northwood and David Paton (AHA Secretary at the time and near neighbour to the track). They were later joined by John Callow and Helen and Don Sheppard, who between them were to keep AHA Racing flourishing in the South East for most of the succeeding 20 years. Also lending a hand were many willing helpers who took along everything from gas bottles and stoves to sandwiches, coffee and soft drinks.

Initially there was a fair amount of opposition from some of the show fraternity, who were concerned about matters ranging from the likelihood of dogs breaking their legs to how the dogs would be captured at the end of the race. Fortunately, these objections and prejudices were soon dispelled when enthusiasts such as Jo Holden, Margaret Niblock and others allowed their champion dogs to participate.

Because of the obvious enjoyment of both owners and dogs, racing was soon in great demand and today it is possible for the enthusiast to go racing on most Sundays (see map). AHA Racing is held at several tracks around the country, between March and October and these can range from very modern stadiums to original flapping tracks. An array of trophies and awards is on offer, many to be won outright.

In 1975 the Show Race Competition, devised by Chairman Ron Adams, was introduced by the AHA to encourage the racing of more show dogs. Originally it was hoped that one day a dual show/racing champion would be crowned, but the idea was squashed at birth by The Kennel Club, who said the title of champion was exclusively for show dogs. However, over the years several have got near to it in spirit, if not in title, and it was a great cause of celebration when Pat and Pete Dollman's Ch Izmars Dizzy Dolly gained her title in 1982 and achieved the Fastest Bitch award at the Inter-Track meeting in the same year.

This competition is still held at today's tracks, with the Ron Adams Memorial Trophy on offer to the dog accumulating the most points between 1 January and 30 September in any one year. Each dog can be entered at one nominated track only and trophy points are gained by winning a place in a breed class at an Open or Championship show, which are then multiplied with the points accumulated on the race track.

By 1976 there were enough tracks around the country to hold an Intertrack event to find the top team of the year. Intertrack is now an annual event, represented by the cream of the racing dogs, and an important date on the racing calendar.

The fastest Afghan ever in Great Britain is Fox, owned by Gordon and Liz Ellis. He holds the track record at every track where he ran, and won his last Intertrack aged seven. Liz told me that it was always difficult to get a photograph of Fox with other dogs following, as he was always so far in front! Now aged twelve, he no longer races, but loves to chase around the fields near his home – and is still as fast as a bullet.

At a race meeting all novice dogs are *slipped* (held until the last moment and then let off the lead), not *trapped* (lined up in cages whose fronts are lifted automatically at the last moment). They line up at the start with their collars held by their owner and are 'pushed off' from behind when the hare comes around. They start in Green and, when qualified, progress to Yellow, which is one second faster. They continue to work through the grades, moving up to the next one when a qualifying time is achieved. Rosettes are presented for first time qualifiers and certificates presented when qualifying for a grade.

Track distances vary, so qualifying times are calculated accordingly.

AHA Grading

Short distance (approx 265m)	Medium distance (approx 465m)	Long distance (approx 700m)
Green)	Bronze)	Black) Trapped
Yellow) Slipped	Silver) Trapped	
	Gold)	
Blue)	Platinum)	
Red)		
Pink) Trapped		
Purple)		

Lure coursing in Great Britain

The cry goes out: 'Are the dogs ready?' The handlers nod.

'Are the judges ready?' They are.

The huntmaster gives a signal, and two white plastic bags start to whizz over the grass behind the dogs. As the lure approaches, the dogs try to break loose from their handlers, eager for the chase. As the lure passes there is a cry of 'Tally Ho!', and the dogs are released and free to charge after the lure.

This is the exciting sport of lure coursing and, if you have ever looked at the dogs in the show ring and wondered whether the beautifully-groomed exhibits could ever catch their own breakfast, this is the sport to answer your questions.

The aim of the sport is to simulate as closely as possible the blood sport of coursing, but without the blood. Chasing an animal or object that is running away is a natural instinct to most hounds and, when this is coupled with being released in a 15-acre field, most Afghans think that they are in Heaven! Even while a course is being run, the waiting competitors bay with excitement and impatience for their turn, proving that under all the coat the old hunting instinct still exists.

The sport of coursing has long been established in Great Britain, although generally Lurchers or Greyhounds were used. It owes its roots to the value placed on a good hunting dog which in turn provided yet another means of comparing the ability of one dog with another.

Modern lure coursing has gained a strong foothold in the United States and Scandinavia, where many well supported meetings are held during the year. In the United States, the title Field Champion is recognised by the American Kennel Club, although this prestigious status is not one currently recognised in lure coursing by The Kennel Club, which prefers the somewhat understated title Lure Courser of Merit.

The British Sighthound Field Association is modelled on the American Sighthound Field Association and was founded in 1989 by a small band of enthusiasts to cater for all breeds of sighthounds, with the intention of covering as large an area of great Britain as possible. Events are run monthly between March and October and, whilst many venues are in the south of England, at least two events each year reach the Midlands. Expansion to other areas was initially envisaged, but these have had to be curtailed due to lack of support from both competitors and helpers.

Whilst Afghans competed from the very first meetings, Afghan enthusiasts in general were a little slow to take up the sport, and it was not until 1993 that sufficient Afghans participated to qualify for points toward the title of Lure Courser of Merit. An early supporter was Anna Paton with Ch Amudarya Thanks a Million who, along with Janet Lear and Ch Krishan's Kribensis at Learael, proved that show champions were perfectly capable of giving chase. More recently, Ch Karaburan Be Be King has been a regular competitor. Age is not a problem to a fit hound; indeed, Anna's Amudarya Shushma's Image achieved a Best of Breed as a veteran.

During 1994, other breeds started to achieve the title of Lure Courser of Merit but Afghans had to wait until 1996, when a two-year battle between Trudy Doll's Am F/Ch Windcrest's Major Lee and Keith and Diana Searle's Salamkhan Ice Dancer was resolved in the latter's favour. Unfortunately, Major Lee had to return to America before he could gain his title.

How, then, does lure coursing work? The lure consists of two white plastic pedal bin liners tied onto a strong line. The line is led around a series of pulleys. These are set out to lead the hound around a field in an erratically circular direction, finishing at the same point as the start, with the line in a continuous loop. The line is powered by an electric motor and the speed of the lure is controlled by the Lure Operator.

Other key people on the field are the Secretary, who takes the entries and computes the scores, the Collecting Ring Steward, who handles the public address system and controls access to the course, and the Huntmaster, who is responsible for the running of the course and the safety of dogs and handlers during a course.

Hounds are normally run in pairs, one with a white jacket and one in red. Although it is possible to run hounds solo, they are not then eligible for Best of Breed or Best in Field.

Lure coursing is great fun, and good exercise, too!

Solo runs in competition are restricted to novices (the first three runs) and veterans. All sighthounds are allowed to compete and many owners take along more than one breed, although a dog will only be allowed to course with another dog of the same breed. Dogs competing must be registered with The Kennel Club.

At each event two judges are positioned at vantage points to give a whole view of the course and points are awarded to each dog on five different aspects of its performance:

- *Agility* counts for a maximum of 25 points and relates to nimbleness in negotiating terrain and making tight turns without losing momentum. It would obviously be unfair to compare different breeds in this respect – for example, a Wolfhound and a Whippet – which is why Afghans are only compared with Afghans.
- *Enthusiasm* is worth up to 15 points. Like most judging, this can be a rather subjective assessment, but strong indications are the dog's attitude at the start and its desire to 'kill' the lure. By the end of the session the lure bags are often torn to shreds.
- *Follow* attracts a possible 15 points and is a measure of how closely the dog sticks to the lure during the course. The lure may be a varying distance ahead of the dog, and dogs are expected to head for the lure, or even anticipate its movement, rather than follow the line taken by the lure. A dog who loses sight of the lure but quickly locates it again will not be penalised seriously.
- *Endurance* refers to the dog's stamina and mental concentration. This tends to show in negative ways, where the dog slows down or gives up. There are 20 points on offer for endurance.
- *Speed* is a difficult parameter to measure, but is worth 25 points. If a stopwatch is used to time the run from the start to the finish, a dog who cuts corners appears to be faster than one that covers the whole distance. For this reason the judges are supplied with the approximate time for reference purposes, but the speed score is arrived at subjectively. Once again, the speed is judged against other dogs of the same breed.

Penalties are applied if hounds are released by the handlers before the 'Tally Ho!' order is given and a hound may be dismissed from the course if it interferes with its partner during the course. A dog that fights another will be disqualified.

A total of 100 points is on offer for each run. The end of the first session normally coincides with lunch time, during which the direction in which the lure runs is reversed. Each hound then has a second run. After the two sessions are completed, the best score for each hound is used to declare the results.

Each breed is divided into four classes based on age: yearling, 2–4 years old, open (any age) and veteran (7 and over). A Best in Class is declared for each class in each breed. Each breed also has a Best of Breed if four or more dogs of that are breed competing. Under the latter circumstances, points are awarded that count toward the Lure Courser of Merit title. These points depend on the dog's position within the overall breed results and the number of dogs competing, as shown in the table below:

PLACE IN BREED

	1	2	3	4	5	6	7
4 hounds in breed	16	12	8				
5 hounds in breed	20	15	10				
6 hounds in breed	24	18	12	6			
7 hounds in breed	28	21	14	7			
8 hounds in breed	32	24	16	8	6		
9 hounds in breed	36	27	18	9	7		
10 or more hounds in breed	40	30	20	10	8	6	4

In other words, if 5 Afghans are competing and your dog is placed second in its breed, 15 points will be awarded towards its title.

To qualify for the title of Lure Courser, a hound must have aggregated over 200 points and have achieved three Best of Breeds while running with another hound.

It should be pointed out that certain qualities are required for a hound to be a successful lure courser. The natural instinct to chase must be strong, but this must be enhanced by the instinct to hunt. A good lure courser will take bites out of the lure, sometimes while running at high speed, in an effort to kill it. A hound which chases another hound will never do well at lure coursing. Your hound needs to be fit and well muscled to give protection to bones and joints when sharp turns are called for. Ideally, the dog should be fast, but straight line speed is not always an indicator of a good lure courser. Above all, a good lure courser is bold and determined, showing aggression towards the lure but not towards other dogs or people.

Any worries about catching your dog upon finishing the course can be dispelled, as most hounds allow themselves to be caught quite easily after the exhilaration of a 500-metre chase. Added to which, the perimeters of the fields are always well fenced.

If you feel you would enjoy a healthy Sunday outdoors whilst your Afghan enjoys the exercise for which it was bred, why not give lure coursing a try? If in any doubt, ask your dog how it would feel about being let off the lead in a 15-acre field and allowed to chase elusive prey – I can guess the answer! For your part, you will be able to enjoy a picnic lunch in good company while watching the best sight in the world – fully-coated Afghans running free.

Other activities

Other activities involving Afghan Hounds are Agility and Obedience and, although these are very popular in the United States of America, they have never really enjoyed great popularity with British enthusiasts.

Afghan Hound World Congresses

If there is anything Afghan owners enjoy more than showing their dogs, it is talking about their dogs, watching videos of Afghans and listening to other Afghan owners talking about their dogs, so what could be better than a World Congress devoted to the Afghan Hound.

The very First Afghan Hound World Congress, organised by the Yorkshire Afghan Hound Society, was held in July 1993 and attended by over 200 enthusiasts from all over the world. It was scheduled to follow the Hound Day at Windsor Championship Show, the international speakers and overseas visitors had the opportunity to see the British Afghan in the show ring and compare and assess the breed world-wide.

Among the speakers were Helen Furber (Australia), who spoke of the origins of the breed, with many slides of early canines, some of which in her opinion had formed the nucleus of the Afghan. Mike Canalizo (United States) spoke about *The Afghan Hound – King of Dogs*, using computer-generated pictures to show the difference that certain conformational faults can make to the breed. Lotte Jorgensen (Denmark), with her *Who is Right and Who is Wrong?*, directly involved the audience, and her allotted time was lively, entertaining and challenging.

Edwina Thomas (Australia), after a thumbnail sketch of the breed in her country, gave a personal view of what the Afghan Hound meant to her. Fukie Yoshimoto (Japan) explained, through an interpreter, her country's involvement with the breed and Lynn Schanzle (USA) attempted to unravel the intricacies of the American points system.

Norwegian vet and breeder Espen Engh had put together a delightful array of slides of Afghans he considered to have had major influences in the breed in Scandinavia and indeed, in the case of Int Ch El Khyrias Hazztafer, world-wide influence. Representing South Africa was Milan Anteglievic, a great supporter of the classic British lines.

Pirkko Konttinen (Sweden) talked in detail about the pedigrees of influential dogs and touched upon the importance of maintaining the breed as a disease-free specimen, both hereditary and otherwise.

A question and answer session followed in which many diverse subjects were discussed. A thoroughly enjoyable and informative event, the Congress drew to a close with Dave Frei claiming the next one for the United States of America, by the picturesque San Diego Bay, in November 1995. Again, it was a most instructive and entertaining gathering, with a wide variety of speakers from all over the world.

The Third Afghan Hound World Congress took place in June 1997 at Elsinore, Denmark, and was held over a day and a half to coincide with The Afghan Hound Club of Denmark's Silver Jubilee Show and the European Winners Show in Copenhagen. Again, a good time was had by all who attended. It ended with a presentation video on the Fourth World Congress, to be held in Sidney, Australia in the Year 2000, and a summary from the Belgian Organising Committee of their ideas for a Fifth World Congress in 2002.

Similar events, held every couple of years, will continue to give Afghan enthusiasts the opportunity to indulge in their favourite pastime and meet up with old friends in many interesting places in the world.

Ch Tazkindi Pharaohs Gold competing in an Agility competition.

chapter ten
Breeding

There was great demand for puppies between the late 1960s and mid-1970s, when the Afghan Hound was at the height of its popularity and considered a 'fashion accessory'. Fortunately, those days are behind us, and the advancement of the breed is now left largely to true devotees, who love the Breed dearly and have its welfare and future at heart, always looking to improve the quality of their stock with each generation. While there is still a handful of people who constantly have puppies in the nest, breeding litter after litter of invariably mediocre quality, they are, thankfully, in the minority and gain little respect from most of the Afghan fraternity. However, this is not meant to deter you from the pleasure of having a litter, as a great deal of satisfaction can be gained from the whole experience, if carefully thought out beforehand and carried out conscientiously.

Many important factors must be taken into consideration before making the decision to breed, the main one being that an Afghan is quite a large dog, capable of producing a large litter, so serious thought must be given to the future welfare of your bitch's offspring. You must be able to provide her with adequate, warm accommodation where she can whelp undisturbed by other dogs, and additionally there must be space outside where up to 12 puppies from the ages of five to at least nine weeks can play and do what puppies do (and believe me they 'do' an awful lot!) without causing undue destruction. If you go out to work you will need to arrange time to be at home when your bitch is due to whelp and also for the first week after the puppies are born to ensure that Mum is coping well. Subsequently, their needs will dictate you nipping home at lunchtime to provide their midday meal and clean up, or alternatively arranging back-up and paying someone to come in.

This introduces the financial aspect. Having a litter is not cheap. *Give them the best and you will get the best* is perfectly true of a bitch and her puppies. The enterprise cannot be undertaken without sufficient funds behind you, particularly in the case of a medical emergency, such as a caesarean section, as veterinary fees can be alarming. If all goes well and you have homes for your puppies, you should be able to break even, but you must be prepared to keep and feed all of your puppies until responsible homes can be found.

It is an old wife's tale that a bitch needs to have at least one litter of puppies for the sake of her health, and it does not follow that she is worth breeding from because she has a wonderful pedigree. If she is a well loved pet, do ask yourself honestly if you really want her to have puppies.

If you decide to go ahead you will need to select a stud dog and, if you have attended dog shows, you may well have noticed a couple of dogs you admire and feel are suitable, especially if they already have winning progeny in the ring displaying dominant characteristics that you feel will complement your bitch. Be critical in the appraisal of your bitch: know her faults and virtues and select a dog who excels in and can enhance the areas in which she is lacking. It does not follow that the mating of extremes will produce dogs with good conformation: if, for example, she is heavy in head and the dog you choose has an extremely fine head, the chances are that the resulting puppies will display both traits, without a typical head amongst them. Always choose a dog that is a good example of the breed. He doesn't necessarily need to be a champion but must have a good head, correct conformation, be of sound temperament and in excellent health and preferably come from a line of established winners and producers.

Seek advice from the breeder of your bitch and the owner of the stud dog, as they will have a good idea about the compatibility of the two pedigrees and kennel types. It will probably be remarked upon that the pedigrees *tie in well together*, are a *complete outcross* or are *far too close, my dear*, and these comments should be taken on board and given due consideration. At the end of the day it helps if these two key players are in agreement with your choice, as their knowledge and support can be an enormous help throughout. They may even be able to assist by redirecting puppy enquiries for their stock.

Planning a breeding programme

Three terms generally associated with breeding dogs are *line breeding, outcrossing* and *inbreeding*.

Line breeding

This has been the most widely accepted method of breeding Afghan Hounds and describes the mating of dogs that are closely related and descendants of one outstanding ancestor. The aim is to keep the relationship within the family of the particular ancestor by *doubling-up* progeny on both sides of the pedigree to perpetuate his or her qualities.

The best overall results occur only when the related dog and bitch are themselves good examples of the breed and have a family resemblance to their famous ancestor. Many breeders have established their own kennel type by gradually fixing the outstanding qualities associated with a greatly-admired forebear and maintaining them by continuing to breed mainly relations for further generations.

As the whole point of the exercise is to reproduce the outstanding characteristics of the famous antecedent, it is pointless to use dogs of mediocre quality. Their faults will be passed down along with their good points, eventually degenerating genetic potential. Should a weakness materialise after several generations of line breeding (for example, temperament deterioration, breeding difficulties, lack of substance, or extremes of size) the knowledgeable breeder will seek to redress the problem by outcrossing for one generation, thereby introducing new genes from different lines that are known to excel in the desired features. Once the faults are eliminated, breeding back within family lines can be continued.

Outcrossing

It would be very difficult to produce good stock consistently, generation after generation, from seemingly unrelated parents. You may achieve good results in the first and maybe the second generation, particularly if the parents themselves were outstanding, but it is unlikely that they would continue to breed true to type unless mated back to their close relations. Additionally, a minefield of faults would be introduced and certainly loss of breed type, resulting in the production of dogs of mediocre quality.

In-breeding

This is the term used for breeding very closely related dogs – brother to sister or parent to child – and is not to be recommended for the novice. It may be a quick way to secure type and, while the resulting puppies would carry the outstanding characteristics of the parents, they would also possess duplicate genes in respect of prominent faults and health problems. Before you attempt to in-breed, a complete knowledge of all ancestors is vital, as nothing new will be introduced. On the contrary, dormant faults will be reproduced, and breeders who carry out such matings must keep a close watch on the resulting progeny for signs of physical defects and weaknesses.

The stud dog

Owning a stud dog is a great responsibility and you will be doing the breed a great service if you have your dog tested for hereditary faults which, although not currently problematic, are likely to affect Afghan Hounds in future years. By having your dog's hips X-rayed under the British Veterinary Association/Kennel Club (BVA/KC) Scheme for the Control of Hereditary Diseases and his eyes tested for Progressive Retinal Atrophy (PRA), Hereditary Cataract (HC) and glaucoma (which may lead to blindness) you can at least enter into stud work with a clear conscience, knowing that your dog shows no clinical evidence of being affected and passing on serious defects to future generations.

If he is well bred and starting to make his mark in the ring, you are certain to receive enquiries for stud work, and it will help if his first encounter is with a bitch who knows the score and will take the experience in her stride. Maiden bitches can be very snappy, uncooperative and difficult, and a bad first experience can put a young dog off indefinitely. Once his confidence has been knocked it will take a great deal of patience on your part to help him regain it. Some dogs find handling during mating quite off-putting and should be trained from an early age to accept this as a matter of course.

On his first encounter it is your responsibility not to allow him to become frightened or hurt. In turn, he will feel quite secure to let you lend a helping hand in future, once this mutual trust has been established.

It is important to remember that, first and foremost, your stud dog is an integral member of your family and his stud work should remain a very low key affair. Stud dogs can live together quite amicably and, like all puppies, should be taught very early on that misbehaviour will definitely not be tolerated. After a mating, his genitals should be washed down with a mild disinfectant solution and checked to ensure that no hair has been drawn into the sheath. He should then resume life with his normal companions, whether they be in-house or kennelled, as soon as possible. They will of course be very interested in the scent of the bitch on him but, knowing your own dogs, you will know whether their inquisitive attentions will result in a fight.

An experienced dog will know when a bitch is due to come into season and will make a great fuss covering the ground where she has urinated, chattering his teeth, wimperingly excitedly and generally becoming sexually aroused. If your dogs and bitches live together, now is the time to separate them, especially if you are planning a mating between your own dog and bitch, as familiarity can sometimes lead to lack of performance when the time to mate arrives. Never reprimand your dog for his natural interest, as he will associate your displeasure with his mating instinct, and so become reluctant to perform. A loss of appetite due to frustration is commonplace at this time.

Stud fee and arrangements

A stud fee is generally payable for the services of a proven dog at the time of mating and is for the service, not the result. If no puppies are produced as a result of the visit, the stud fee is not returnable in whole or in part, but most stud dog owners will agree to a free service on the next season. This is regarded as customary rather than obligatory. Should alternative arrangements be made, for example a puppy taken in lieu of stud fee, a written agreement stating the exact terms should be signed by both parties, thus eliminating subsequent misunderstandings.

Coat

A word about coat: sometimes a show dog will have a long, thick belly coat which, when he mounts the bitch, can get in the way and impede penetration. If the long coat is tied up or he wears a light body jacket, the deed can be performed without hindrance or injury.

Sperm testing

If a dog has mated several bitches and they have not produced puppies, it is worth consulting your vet for a semen investigation to detect the extent of its motility. This may possibly involve a referral to a specialist in this particular field and, if the sperm count is low, the dog may derive benefit from hormonal treatment. Sperm production is ongoing, but can be affected by illness, trauma or following administration of certain drugs, such as steroids. Once interrupted, sperm production can take 63 days before fertility is re-established.

The brood bitch

As I have said before, the main purpose of breeding is to improve upon what you already have, and I cannot stress strongly enough the importance of only breeding from a sound, healthy bitch who portrays the typical characteristics of the breed.

Vaccinations and worming

If you are planning a mating, make sure that her vaccinations are up-to-date, as this will ensure her puppies are protected until their own immune systems are fully operational. It is not advisable to give live vaccine to an in-whelp bitch, as this may be detrimental to the puppies. She should also be free of worms, as puppies receive a much better start when born free of these parasites.

Season

Bitches are likely to have their first season between the ages of eight and sixteen months and these will continue at regular six- to twelve-monthly intervals throughout her lifetime. I use the word 'regular' with tongue in cheek, as there is nothing more contrary than an Afghan bitch and her seasons, particularly if you plan to mate her. It is inadvisable to breed her until she is over two years old, as Afghans before this age are notoriously immature themselves. If you have several bitches living together and one bitch comes into season, the others will generally follow suit, being stimulated by her behaviour and hormonal odours. They will tease, flirt and mount each other, simulating the act of mating, and can become quite frustrated if the subject of their attentions does not reciprocate.

The first noticeable signs of an oncoming season are that she will urinate more often than normal and lick herself repeatedly. Her vulva will become slightly swollen, with an almost colourless to pink discharge, and gradually increase in size, becoming blood-stained. She will not welcome the attention of male dogs at this pre-oestrus stage of her cycle, and is best kept under your constant supervision to prevent accidental mating.

The vulva will continue to bleed, swell and harden during this pre-oestrus stage, which can last up to 15 days from the start of the season, although you will need to check her regularly from around the ninth day. If you are unsure how far your bitch is into the pre-oestrus stage, or if she is experiencing a colourless season, your vet will be able to give some indication of the correct day to mate by taking a blood test.

It is when the discharge begins to pale in colour and the vulva shows signs of softening at the top (becoming wizened and prune-like) that the oestrus stage is beginning, and mating normally takes place within the next 48 hours if puppies are to be conceived. She will also switch her tail to the side when her vulva is touched, indicating her desire and cooperation to allow mating to occur.

It is all too easy to panic and make a premature visit to the stud dog for fear of missing the vital ovulation days. I have found that Afghan bitches conceive later rather than earlier, and I would always advocate two matings 24–48 hours apart. If your bitch was not quite ready on the first mating but reluctantly allowed the dog to mate her, the sheer act of mating will usually stimulate the onset of ovulation, resulting in a productive second mating.

In the case of a bitch who has had a successful first mating, there is probably no need for a return visit, as many will not let the dog near a second time, having 'closed down'. This is usually a good indication that she has conceived. Similarly, it is a good sign if the experienced dog shows total disinterest after the first sniff.

It is important to telephone the owner of the stud dog as soon as your bitch comes into season to pencil in possible dates for mating.

The mating

Bitches are normally taken to the home of the stud dog when ready for mating, and an experienced dog will know exactly why she is visiting. About an hour before a bitch is expected for mating, I tell my own dogs that we have a 'lady coming', and they know exactly what I mean and will wait by the gate and watch for her.

On arrival, allow the bitch to relieve herself before she is introduced to the dog. It is not advisable to let the mating pair run freely together, as the dog may force unwelcome attentions and the bitch, who may need more time to become acquainted, could become aggressive. The area where the pair are to mate should be enclosed, with a non-slip floor, as the dog will need to feel sure-footed when mounting the bitch. Alternatively, a small piece of rubber-backed carpet can be laid for this purpose. Should the dog and bitch be of differing heights, with the dog probing too high or low of the vulva, the floor level will need to be adjusted accordingly.

Fasten a leather collar on the bitch and let her owner take hold of this, standing in front to avoid interfering with the dog. The stud dog owner should kneel at the side of the bitch putting a hand underneath her abdomen to support her. This will also give an indication as to how close the dog is to the vulva as he probes. If necessary, her tail can be held to one side with the other hand. Should the bitch show any indication of growling when the dog makes advances, it would be wise to bind a wide crêpe bandage around her muzzle, which is then fastened behind her neck so that she cannot bite. While some people take a different view, I have found that a gentle internal examination with clean hands and a smear of Vaseline prior to mating is often helpful to determine just how easily she can be mated. To avoid cross infection, it is important that the same jar of Vaseline never be re-used on another bitch. Some bitches are extremely tight inside, some have a steep angle of ascent, and some are very roomy. The stud dog owner can bear these factors in mind when assisting the dog. Also, at this stage, a vaginal stricture (which could just be a tight sinew of tissue across the vaginal opening or, more seriously, a total restriction) will be detected. This would make penetration impossible and requires veterinary advice.

The dog, stimulated by her hormonal scent, will lick her vulva, chatter his teeth and tug at her coat in his excitement. He will climb on her back, gripping in front of her hips with his front legs, and probe with his penis until penetration takes place. At the base of the penis are large bulbous glands, which become engorged with blood and swell immediately after penetration, causing some bitches to emit a shriek or cry. As the muscles of her vagina contract around these glands, a *tie* will result, and the pair will be locked together until these glands have reduced in size, enabling the bitch to release the dog. The pair should be gently restrained during the tie and, if the bitch has had her muzzle bound, this can now be removed.

The thrusting movements of the dog cause the sperm to be ejaculated early on in the mating process, after which he will drop his front legs to one side of her and turn around to face the opposite direction by lifting one hind leg over her back. The dog may require assistance in lifting his leg into position but, if he shows no desire to turn around, leave him where he is most comfortable for the remainder of the union. This can last anything from just a few minutes to up to an hour (usually 15–20 minutes) and, during this time, the seminal fluid carrying the sperm travels towards the uterus where the ova are to be fertilised. The size of the litter is dependent upon how many eggs are released from the ovaries and fertilised.

Sometimes, if a bitch has shown aggression towards a sensitive or inexperienced dog, he will mount her, but will hesitate in climbing too far over her back for fear of being snapped at again. He will penetrate, possibly ejaculate, but quickly withdraw before the bulbous glands can swell inside her and allow a tie. This is known as a *slip mating* and, although there is a possibility that puppies may have been conceived, it cannot be considered particularly successful. It would be not only unethical to take the bitch to a second-choice stud dog after such a mating, but also unacceptable, as she may already have conceived. If the dog has ejaculated, give him an hour's rest before trying again, and be ready to hold the two firmly together, following penetration, to prevent withdrawal before the glands have swollen inside her.

Views differ, but I prefer to pop my bitches back in the car following mating, without giving them the opportunity to urinate. Having said that, this did happen on one occasion immediately after mating, and the owner of the stud dog, upon seeing the dismay on my face at the puddle on the floor, remarked dryly, 'Well, you can't put it back!' Thankfully, my bitch produced puppies, but I am still reluctant to take the chance.

Once mated and back home, the bitch will still be sexually desirable to other males and should be housed securely until her period of oestrus is completely finished. She may continue to bleed for another week or so, but this is no cause for concern. She is also quite capable of seeking out another mate and giving birth to puppies from both sires in the same litter, in which case the sire of an individual puppy could only be identified by DNA testing, which is very expensive.

Mismating

If you discover your bitch mating with a wandering opportunist who has infiltrated your security system and they are already tied, there is little you can do, as ejaculation will probably already have occurred. Don't try and separate them as injuries can result, but wait until the end of the tie. An injection can be given by the vet to bring her back into full season, but do contact your vet immediately as the administration period is dependent upon the type of drug used at your surgery. For example, Oestradiol Benzoate by Intervet can be given after 24 hours and up to four days following mating but, because this drug can only be given once in the oestral cycle, it is important not to let the incident recur. Many breeders are of the opinion that excessive hormonal interference can lead to uteral problems (pyometra) later in life, since an hormonally open uterus can be receptive towards bacteria entering from the vagina.

If, after a successful mating to a proven stud dog, the bitch has failed to conceive, take her to the vet to be checked over. It is quite possible that she has a streptococcal infection, which can be successfully treated with a course of antibiotics.

Artificial Insemination (AI)

Artificial insemination can be particularly beneficial to breeders wishing to introduce new bloodlines from overseas into their stock or store valued semen from a top winning dog for use at a later date. AI has been carried out successfully overseas for many years but in the past has not been generally encouraged in Great Britain, which is probably why there are presently only a handful of vets specialising in this country. Information on the subject can be obtained from The Kennel Club and, as it stands at present, you would need a valid reason and written permission from them before carrying out AI on your bitch.

A few breeders in Great Britain have semen already stored from their own valued genetic stock, in the hope that Kennel Club permission will be granted for its use in the future. They are finding alternative ways around all the red tape by exporting sperm for use overseas and importing the resulting puppies back through quarantine or the Balai Directive (see Chapter 2). At present, permission will only be granted for semen to be used from a live dog who is unable to mate naturally because of physical injury, not from one that is deceased. A new development overseas (and one worth taking on board) is the requirement that a rabies and leptospirosis test be carried out on the dog by a Government Pathology Laboratory prior to collection, which would mean that his semen could still be exported and used, in the event of his death, to those countries that specify these tests as requisite for the importation of frozen semen.

Importing semen into Great Britain is a considerably cheaper alternative to quarantine but, nevertheless, the Ministry of Agriculture, Fisheries and Food (MAFF) and Customs and Excise still lay down very stringent requirements and an import licence is required. Frozen semen is transported in liquid nitrogen, which is considered to be a hazardous cargo, so the containers must comply with Airline Regulations. The use of an agent to clear the cargo through customs is advisable.

Semen is easier to import into Great Britain from Europe, Australia and other recognised rabies-free countries, because one of the requirements is for there to have been no evidence of rabies in the exporting country in the twelve months prior to it's collection. In the case of non-rabies-free countries, the semen must be stored in its country of origin for at least six months prior to export.

Before the semen is collected, the donor dog will have specific blood tests to ensure he is free from disease and issued with a health certificate. He must not have been vaccinated against rabies in the previous six months. The semen is usually frozen in straws and has to be stored in a specific way following collection and prior to export. Most of these requirements are dealt with by the exporting country and, as long as the paperwork is correct, they should not pose a problem to the importer.

Obtaining Kennel Club permission is all-important when embarking on AI, and this will only be granted for a specific bitch with semen from a named dog. This means that you can't change your mind and use a different bitch at the last minute without first obtaining their permission and sufficient time should be allowed for this to be granted before the bitch is due to come into season. Additionally, it is recommended that AI be carried out on a proven bitch.

When the bitch comes into season, blood tests are taken every other day (this may vary from vet to vet but many will give a 48-hour forecast) to determine progesterone levels so that an accurate assessment can be made about the best time to inseminate. This can be performed in a number of ways.

Vaginal insemination: This involves inserting a catheter approximately 30cm long and syringing the semen through. During a normal mating the purpose of the tie is to encourage the semen to go one way (into the uterus), and this is simulated, following the removal of the catheter, by the insertion of a finger around which the bitch can contract. Her hindquarters are also raised. Because the semen has further to travel using this method, it must be of good quality (medium to high activity), with the use of fresh rather than frozen recommended.

Uterine insemination: This goes further than vaginal but is not practised to a great extent in this country because of the difficulty in passing the catheter through the cervix, causing possible damage to the wall of the uterus.

Surgical insemination: This involves the bitch undergoing a general anaesthetic for a few minutes whilst a small mid-line incision is made (similar preparation to that for spaying). The uterus is taken out and the semen injected centrally into both horns, before being 'milked' manually into the fallopian tubes and ovaries. This method is generally considered to be the most reliable. Because the semen is implanted directly, puppies are usually born earlier than the average 63 days, so a close watch should be kept on the bitch for signs of whelping from around the 57th day.

For obvious reasons, the semen is checked under a microscope for activity prior to insemination.

The first British Afghan bitch to be given permission by The Kennel Club for AI was Jarnay Miss Trotwood from Quaisuma, in 1992. She was inseminated twice to Day, Sinclair and Hickie's Aust Ch Aboukir High Priority, but there were no resulting puppies. There have since been several other attempts with Afghans, but again with no resultant live puppies. However, Drishaun Desdemona made British breed history in April 1998 when she gave birth (naturally) to five puppies after being inseminated with frozen semen from Am Ch Gazon Say What You Mean. The insemination was carried out surgically and vaginally on consecutive days by vet Miss Gillian Averis BVMS, MRCVS.

Exporting semen

In the past, several top-winning British dogs have had semen collected for exportation, and more information on the subject can be obtained from The Kennel Club. The semen is collected (with the co-operation of a 'teaser' bitch in season) on the premises of a specialist veterinary surgeon, and is then frozen into straws before being exported.

The most recent Afghan to have had semen successfully collected is Chris and Julie Amoo's Ch Viscount Grant, and this was subsequently exported to Norway, where 14 puppies were produced as a result.

chapter eleven
Whelping and Rearing

Care in pregnancy

Although the gestation period is 63 days from the date of a natural mating, puppies can arrive a few days either way. I have known pups to be born four days early with no detrimental effects and, if the bitch has been well nourished during pregnancy, giving birth a few days early will pose no problem. However, I would be concerned if she went three days overdue with no signs of the impending birth and would take her to the veterinary surgeon to be checked over. The effects of the internal examination performed by the vet to establish the likely imminence of whelping, combined with the car ride, would in all likelihood trigger the birth of the first puppy and stimulate her into bearing down when she arrived home.

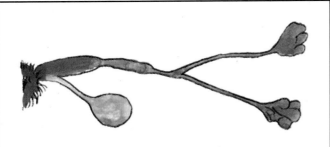

Fig 11.1: Reproductive tract of the bitch before mating.

Fig 11.2: Foetuses implanted along the horns of the uterus.

You will not see any visible signs that your bitch is in whelp for about five weeks, when you will probably notice a slight widening of the rib cage. The vulva will have remained slightly enlarged, not having returned to its pre-season size, and the teats will become pink and more pronounced. I prefer to let nature take its course up until this time, and it is usually upon greeting the dogs first thing in a morning that I will look down on her and notice that her shape has thickened overnight. Up until this time she will live a normal life with the other dogs, have regular exercise and be fed her normal diet.

Between two to three weeks into the pregnancy the fertilised eggs move into the two horns of the uterus and become implanted into the uterine wall to be nourished through the mother's bloodstream. It is around this time that my own bitches will often refuse their breakfast and generally lose their appetite for a few days, experiencing morning sickness and vomiting small amounts of bile.

False pregnancy
Unfortunately, bitches can experience the foregoing symptoms whether they were mated or not and will mimic all the signs of pregnancy to the letter. I know only too well the optimism and disappointment that a false pregnancy in a mated bitch can cause and call to mind one occasion when I was totally convinced my bitch had a puppy tucked up high behind the ribs, which had been overlooked by the vet in his diagnosis. Blood and urine tests are not possible as the hormonal changes that occur are just the same as those resulting from a normal pregnancy, the only real diagnosis being an X-ray. Bitches who experience false pregnancies after each season generally continue to do so, even more so after successfully rearing a litter, and in the long term spaying is the only real solution. In the short term, your vet will be able to give hormone treatment and maybe tranquillisers if she is very distressed. Raspberry leaf tablets can be a preventative aid, if given from the first sign of coming into season and continued for a 12-week period.

Pregnancy scanning
If you are particularly anxious to learn whether your bitch is pregnant, scanning by ultra-sound is inexpensive, reliable and can be performed between 28 and 35 days after mating. When it is carried out between these days the pups can easily be counted but, as they increase in size, they overlap, making the exact number difficult to assess. If your bitch was mated more than once, the specialist can indicate on which mating she conceived, 28-day images being tiny and 35-day images much more developed. The scan is carried out with the bitch in a standing position. Gel is pasted on to her belly and the rotating probe passed along the centre between the teats, displaying images on to a screen. The equipment cannot scan through fresh air, hence the use of gel to connect the sound waves to the tummy. There is presently no register of animal scanning specialists, but they advertise in the weekly dog press and many conduct home visits. Not all vets have the equipment and those who do are inclined to clip off the belly coat unless instructed otherwise. If a bitch has experienced a problematic birth previously, scanning at eight weeks when there is no longer space for the pups to turn around can help by detecting awkward positioning such as breach, lying sideways or obstruction.

Palpation
Your vet may be able to feel the foetuses by gentle palpation at four weeks after mating. After this time, the outlines become more difficult to distinguish from other abdominal

organs because of increased fluid in the surrounding amniotic sacs.

Supplements

Foetal growth increases rapidly from around six weeks after mating and the bitch will require supplements to her diet by way of calcium and protein obtained from extra meat and milk. She will also benefit from a nutritional supplement, such as SA-37, Stress or Canovel, either in tablet or powdered form, which will aid foetal bone development, build up her strength for their approaching birth and help prevent eclampsia. I am a firm believer in giving raspberry leaf tablets at this time, which I find helpful in combating delivery problems. She will still require exercise to

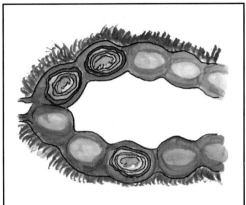

Fig 11.3: Foetuses growing within the uterine wall (about 28 days after mating).

maintain her muscle tone but should be restrained from boisterous play with other dogs. Allow her to eat as much as she wants within reason and split her daily food into three meals towards the end, to alleviate indigestion and abdominal discomfort.

Care of the coat

Believe me, you will eliminate 50% of the stress associated with the first few weeks from the birth of the litter if you trim your bitch's coat to be no longer than four inches all over, including her ears. You cannot watch her 24 hours a day and it is so easy for puppies, until their eyes have fully opened, to crawl through the long coat and hang themselves as she stands up to turn around. Pups at this age nuzzle and knead the bitch quite vigorously in their search for milk and it is almost impossible to keep coat constantly tangle free.

If it is important that your bitch retains as much coat as possible because you wish to get her back into the ring, prepare yourself for a considerable amount of hard work and total vigilance. Lightweight maternity coats, similar to those worn in wet weather but made of cotton, can be worn to protect her coat. A couple will be required, as they become soiled very quickly and will require daily laundering. Firstly, wrap up the longer sections of hair

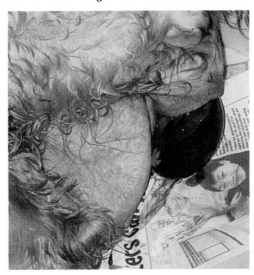

The embryo puppy appears, enclosed in its fluid-filled sac. This is a breach presentation – note the back paw.

into parcels (see chapter 8), using Jay-cloths instead of polythene, and secure with light rubber bands. Trim the coat short under the belly and around the nipples because, no matter how careful you are, the bitch will naturally discard coat in this area after a few weeks of nursing. The cotton coat must be removed and the parcels taken out and groomed through daily and it may help strengthen the hair if a little baby oil is brushed through before the parcels are re-wrapped. The main drawback to wearing a coat is that very young puppies can crawl inside and may get trapped. Therefore, constant supervision is required for the first week or so until they become stronger. Weekly bathing in a mild shampoo will keep her fresh and should be performed as quickly as possible so to avoid risking a chill or keeping her from her pups for too long.

Equipment for the whelping

My own tried and tested whelping box is 120cm x 120cm (4ft x 4ft), with the sides 60cm (2ft) high and the front split into three removable sections. If space is limited, the minimum

size is 110cm x 90cm (3ft 6in x 3ft). Made of melamine-covered chipboard, it was inexpensive and is easily cleaned and wiped down.

Whilst Afghans are not particularly clumsy mothers, precautionary guard rails to prevent the bitch from lying flat against the sides of the box and possibly suffocating a newborn pup can be fitted about 15cm (6in) from the floor and removed when the pups are stronger and have opened their eyes. The floor of the box

Another puppy emerges, this one hind leg and tail presentation. The puppy is safe from drowning while the sac is intact.

should be covered with several layers of newspaper, which can be changed easily when soiled, and undoubtedly the best bedding for puppies is the green-backed, white veterinary type such as Vet-bed, which is non-allergic, washable and moisture absorbing, keeping puppies warm and dry. The bitch should be encouraged to sleep in the box in the latter stages of pregnancy.

Whelping quarters should be light, clean, well ventilated and free of draughts. It is vital that newly born puppies are kept warm and a steady temperature of 24°C (75°F) maintained throughout the first few days of their life. Warmth is more important than food and, if they are allowed to become too cold, they will reach a point from which recovery is very difficult, no matter how quickly you endeavour to reheat them. Various types of heaters can be used, either fixed to the wall or suspended 1.25m (4ft) over the box, and the chosen heater should be thermostatically controlled. A dull-emitter infra-red heat lamp with aluminum reflector suspended over the box is ideal.

Additional equipment to hand should be a thermometer, sharp, blunt-ended scissors, sterilised thread, kitchen scales, rough towels, kitchen roll and pen and paper to record details of the puppies such as weight and sex. Also, a small feeding bottle with a narrow teat and a good brand of puppy milk. Whelping can be somewhat messy, so plenty of newspapers and large black sacks for waste will be needed. Newborn puppies will need to be kept warm while the bitch is attending to her latest-born, and a small box with Vet-bed over a heated pet-pad or wrapped hot water bottle is ideal, but must be positioned out of ear-shot to save her from distress. Until recently, brandy was the recommended remedy for limp pups fighting for life, but there is now a concentrated blend of micronutrients called *Nutri-drops* that is absorbed rapidly into the bloodstream and reputed to be a life saver. They can also be used to good effect on an exhausted bitch suspected of having uterine inertia, which mainly occurs when blood sugar levels become very low. Available from the vet, they are well worth having to hand should problems arise.

Whelping

From the eighth week onwards you will be able to feel the puppies rolling and moving in her abdomen when she is laying on her side. She will be quite uncomfortable and sit quietly with a matronly gaze on her face, sometimes wincing if given a fair old kick by one of her pups. The vulva will be very large and droplets of milk may be seen at the teats. A good sign that she is due to start whelping within the next 24 hours is a fall in temperature to about 37.5°F (99.5°F): normal temperature is 38.6 (101.5°F). In her discomfort she will rip up the newspaper in the box and attempt to make a nest. The vulva will begin to soften

and become distended, and there will be a clear discharge to lubricate the birth passage. While some bitches will accept food right up to giving birth, this is best avoided just in case the bitch eventually needs an anaesthetic for a caesarean. It is courteous to inform your vet that whelping has started, just in case you require advice or assistance at some unearthly hour.

A brief, simple explanation about what is happening internally, prior to birth, may be helpful to

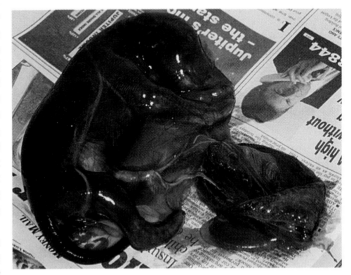

The puppy is born in a water sac, attached to the afterbirth by its umbilical cord.

the reader at this point. The cervix, situated at the top of the vagina, must expand and open before birth can occur. It is the first puppy, not the bitch, that triggers the actual start of whelping by pushing against the cervix and encouraging it to open.

Each embryo puppy is enclosed in its own double-walled, fluid filled bag. It also has its own placenta, which is embedded in the wall of the uterus, providing nourishment from the bitch's bloodstream. The umbilical cord connects this placenta to the puppy and is the vehicle through which the oxygen and nourishment have been transmitted from the bitch to the puppy, and any waste products have been carried away. Anyone who has had a litter will be familiar with the dark green, fluid discharge that stains the bitch's coat, your fingernails and anything with which it comes into contact. As each placenta separates from the wall in the uterus, this fluid is released and is normally seen after one or two puppies have been born. However, should this dark green staining be seen before any pups at all are born, it is an indication that something is going wrong and veterinary advice should be sought immediately.

Once the strong abdominal contractions begin, the foetus has started its journey and you can expect the birth of a puppy within the hour. Keep a discreet watch on her, lifting her tail occasionally to check for the appearance of the dark, outer water-sac, balloon-like in appearance, which has safely surrounded the puppy in the uterus. Once this has burst, allowing its fluid contents to gush out and lubricate the passage, a pink nose or paw can usually be spotted within the second, inner sac. If the sac is intact, allow the bitch to produce the puppy at her own pace. However, if she continues to strain without a result, a gentle internal examination will detect the advancement of the puppy in the birth passage. If the puppy is very high up and just within reach of the tip of your finger, showing no signs of advancement with each contraction, it is probably unable to pass through the cervix and down the pelvic passage, so veterinary assistance must be sought without delay.

Some bitches are extremely laid back during whelping. They offer a few contractions, push with their feet against the box, raise the base of the tail with each strain and produce a puppy with seemingly no effort at all. Others, especially maiden bitches, frantically scratch and rip up their bed, pant, shiver and attempt to give birth standing up, impatient to tear the sac from the half-born puppy in their panic. Such bitches should be restrained gently and encouraged to lie down until further contractions either produce the puppy naturally, or at least push it down far enough for you to take hold of and draw downwards with each strain.

Upon birth, the bitch will tear open the water sac and lick the puppy vigorously, stimulating it to start breathing and breaking the cord joining it to the placenta. If she chooses to ignore it, which is very unlikely, you will need to break open the sac in the region of the mouth, releasing the fluid to prevent drowning when it starts to breathe. Attached to each puppy by the umbilical cord is the placenta (afterbirth), which has the appearance of a piece of liver and, if the cord is not broken by the bitch, you will need to sever it. This is best done by pinching the cord tightly, pressing the blood towards the pup to seal off blood vessels and severing it at least 2.5cm (1in) from the puppy with your fingers. Sterilised scissors can be used and the cord tied with thread if bleeding persists. Take care not to pull the puppy by the cord, as this could result in an umbilical hernia, necessitating surgery when the puppy is older.

The bitch will gobble up the afterbirth eagerly and, while this will do her no harm, it will result in extremely loose motions over the next few days. An afterbirth will quite often be passed just before the birth of the next puppy, but do ensure that every afterbirth is accounted for, as they can rot inside her and cause infection.

Puppies are normally born head first, but breech presentations (rump first) are quite common and should not pose a problem if the puppy is of average size with the feet tucked under the body and within the water sac. Difficulties arise when the sac becomes broken in the birth channel and there is not enough lubrication to ease the dry puppy downwards. If the back legs are outside the bitch's body you are halfway there and should be able to bring about a successful delivery by wrapping a small towel around as much of the body as possible and gently pulling downwards, working with the bitch's contractions. If the bitch has been straining for a while with no results and an internal examination detects a lone, dry tail which keeps withdrawing just out of reach of your finger, veterinary assistance will be required quickly. Lodged high in the pelvic passage without its sac, this puppy is in danger of asphyxia and is preventing the birth of other pups. Some puppies are remarkably resilient and I have known such pups to be born alive before the vet arrives, but you cannot risk the delay.

If you have a puppy that appears dead, clean the mouthway and rub its back and sides briskly with a clean towel. Then hold it gently upside down with both hands, supporting the head and spine to avoid breaking its neck, and swing it vigorously in downward motions to clear any mucous in the respiratory system before rubbing again. Keep working on it – some puppies can take up to 20 minutes before giving their first squeal. If the puppy turns blue, blowing very gently into its mouth may encourage breathing. Failing all else, immerse alternately into bowls of cold and warm water, followed by more vigorous towel rubbing.

Afghans pace themselves between births, giving the occasional contraction to move the pups along the horns. If the bitch is relaxed and shows no sign of distress, allow her to proceed at her own rate, offering regular drinks of water, milk and glucose. As each puppy

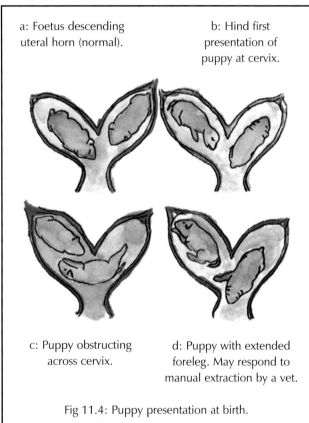

a: Foetus descending uteral horn (normal).

b: Hind first presentation of puppy at cervix.

c: Puppy obstructing across cervix.

d: Puppy with extended foreleg. May respond to manual extraction by a vet.

Fig 11.4: Puppy presentation at birth.

is born it should be placed on a teat and encouraged to suckle, which in turn stimulates the bitch into producing another puppy. For the first 48 hours the bitch's milk contains colostrum, which is rich in nutrients and is absorbed directly into the puppy's bloodstream. Also included in this first milk are essential antibodies that protect against infection. Settle the bitch and puppies under the lamp, ensuring that they are warm enough, and hook the smaller ones on to the milk bar. Puppies will cry if they are cold or hungry, but there is always the possibility that a persistent crier has an internal problem and will not thrive. The bitch often senses this and will push it to the edge of the box with her nose. You can offer it a bottle and lots of tender loving care, but in all probability it will not gain weight and should not be allowed to suffer. Also, should a puppy be blowing milk down its nose whilst suckling, check inside the mouth for a split in the roof, which is a deformity known as a cleft palate. Whilst this can be repaired, it is difficult to keep the puppy alive until it is old enough to have surgery and therefore more humane to have it painlessly put to sleep.

Possible problems during and after whelping

Caesarean section

Several conditions that could prevent puppies being born naturally may arise during whelping. Inertia, meaning inactivity, occurs when the bitch shows all the signs of starting to whelp but makes no attempt, or is unable, to push. This can happen at any time during whelping and can render a puppy already in the birth channel quite helpless. The vet must be called in quickly and the decision made either to give Oxytocin injections to contract the muscles behind the next puppy to be born or to perform a Ceasarean section operation at the surgery, to deliver the rest of the litter safely.

You may be called upon to assist the vet, particularly if the hour is late and the practice has no resident nurse, in which case it will be helpful if you are familiar with the procedure. For a caesarean, the bitch is anaesthetised and a central abdominal incision made. The uteral horns are lifted out, usually one side at a time, and a small incision just large enough to squeeze the puppies through is made. The vet will ensure that each horn is clean before stitching up, pushing back, stitching together the abdominal muscles and finally the outer skin. Everything happens very quickly, the vet's main concern being for the welfare of the bitch and, if you are handed puppies in their sacs, break them open and work on them as discussed earlier. The bitch will recover quickly from the anaesthetic to make the return journey home with her puppies, which should be kept warm in a small box.

Metritis

It is advisable to arrange for your vet to visit the following day to check the bitch and her puppies, as problems can arise immediately after giving birth. Retained afterbirths can lead to infection in the uterus (metritis), which can result in a very poorly bitch. Signs to look out for are a high temperature, listlessness and a lack of interest both in food and her puppies. As a precaution, an injection of Oxytocin may be given to shrink down the womb and expel any debris. A brownish discharge for the next few weeks is quite normal, although contact your vet if it becomes foul smelling with the presence of pus.

Mastitis

Mastitis is inflammation of the milk glands and generally occurs when the puppies are about three weeks old and beginning to teethe. Affected teats will become hot, hard, swollen and very painful and the bitch will require immediate antibiotic treatment or she may reject her litter. Puppies claws should have the tips trimmed with small nail clippers and be kept short while they are with you.

Eclampsia

Eclampsia or milk fever is a metabolic illness resulting from a severe drain on the bitch's calcium store, induced through feeding her puppies. An affected bitch will lose interest in her litter, initially appearing distressed and nervy before becoming unsteady on her legs and eventually collapsing, with symptoms similar to fitting. This condition is life threatening and immediate veterinary attention is required. Injections of calcium will soon put her back on her feet, but you will have to assist in feeding her family until calcium reserves are re-built, only allowing the pups an occasional suckle to relieve the build-up of milk.

Break the water sac from around the mouth area first, before cutting the cord.

Supplementary feeding

Should the mother's milk supply fail, or dwindle due to the number of puppies she has to rear, you will have to bottle feed them until they can lap. Specialist milk substitutes (for example, Canovel or Welpi) are formulated to simulate the bitch's milk and contain a better nutritional balance than ordinary cow's milk. Read the manufacturer's instructions carefully, and time will be saved in mixing the product if you have a hand blender. You will also need a couple of feeding bottles with long, thin teats, sterilising equipment and infinite patience.

If the pups have already been drinking from their mother, introducing a rubber teat into their mouth may be intolerable to some. By laying them on Mum's tummy and, just when they think they are taking her teat, whipping the rubber one quickly into their mouth, you may just be able to fool them. With a towel in your lap, cradle the puppy in your hand when giving a bottle and you will feel its tummy expand as it takes the milk. If it starts to resemble a fat-bellied toad you are giving too much. Take care also that the hole in the teat is not too large for the pup, causing it to choke or receive fluid into the lungs.

Once accustomed to drinking from a bottle, pups thrive very quickly, some being downright greedy. Tube feeding can be attempted on very weak puppies who are unable to suckle, but only following veterinary advice.

If the bitch is well in herself but just lacks milk, the pups can be passed back to her for washing and toileting. Otherwise, gently rubbing the abdomen with damp cotton wool after every feed encourages them to relieve themselves.

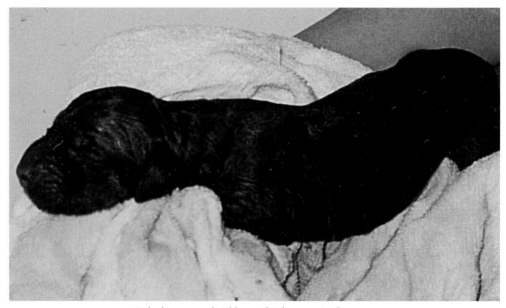

Rub the puppy briskly until it lets out its first cry.

Weaning

Puppies should be encouraged to lap as soon as possible and can be offered milk from a shallow dish while supported on your lap, so that they can get the hang of it. Once they have better control over their heads and necks, with their eyes fully open (about two weeks old), you will undoubtedly have more success. Between the ages of two to three weeks they can be introduced to a specially formulated puppy weaning food (for example Pedigree Chum Advance Formula Weaning Food) that contains all the essential nutrients to help the digestive system adapt from milk to solids. Do not be upset if the bitch offers her own regurgitated food to the puppies at this stage as this is how she would have fed them in the wild.

How the puppies are to be weaned is entirely a question of the indiviual breeder's preference. However, before the introduction of complete foods, weaning took the form of gradually adding a cereal food such as Farex to the puppies' milk. Finely scraped raw meat,

12 hours after birth – all present

minced cooked chicken, soaked puppy biscuit and a calcium/vitamin supplement were introduced at around four weeks old. A point to watch here is that too much porridge at breakfast could result in loose motions for the greedy, which would need to be rectified by giving a more binding meal at lunchtime to firm them up. While the home-prepared food looked appetising, the imbalance of vitamins, minerals, fats and carbohydrates could result in a multitude of growth problems, many of which were undetected until later in development.

The complete proprietary puppy foods now available are excellent, particularly as they remove all the guess work from providing a balanced, nutritional diet, so essential to a growing youngster. Because they are also easily digested, they result in the puppy producing well formed motions, eliminating the risk of diarrhoea and subsequent loss of condition.

The family at 10 days old.

From four weeks of age the puppies will be investigating everything and should be allowed to lead an interesting life, with plenty of free play and fresh air (weather permitting), before falling asleep, only to wake and do it all again. They will now have full hearing capacity and this vital learning period in their lives should be spent in the company of people as often as possible. If the bitch whelped in a quiet corner where she and her young family would be undisturbed, now is the time to relocate the whelping box, pups and all, into a central location where they can be the focus of the whole household and its visitors. If they are to grow into confident, friendly adults the importance of early socialisation cannot be stressed strongly enough.

They will still be sleeping at night in the whelping box, but Mum will probably take the option of sleeping away from them and just looking in occasionally, as their teeth will be coming through and they can be quite rough with her.

Puppies begin to lose the maternal antibodies passed through the bitch's colostrum from about six weeks, so it is advisable to take care that visitors do not bring in germs from the street on their shoes until the pups have received their first vaccinations.

Worming

See also Chapter 12. Puppies should be wormed for roundworm (*Toxocara canis*) and your vet will recommend a suitable product and tell you how often it has to be given. Dogs wormed regularly throughout their lives will thrive better and the slight risk of children ingesting eggs shed in the faeces is eliminated.

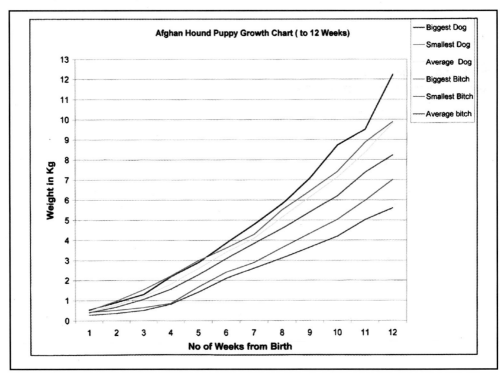

Development

From six to eight weeks the puppies will be growing rapidly and will still be receiving four meals a day at breakfast, lunch, dinner and supper time. Most complete puppy foods contain milk so it is not necessary to give milk, but it is important that water should be freely available. They will have received their first vaccinations and be playing in the fresh air, with access to warm sleeping quarters, although during the night newspapers can be laid away from the box in case they need to relieve themselves. Rawhide chews and cooked marrow bones provide comfort to the teething puppies as well as giving lots of pleasure. Companies such as Nylabone produce a range of products that help dogs' teeth to stay clean and plaque-free as the dogs play with them. Puppies can be quite destructive at this age if allowed to become bored.

Regular weighing helps you to be sure that the puppies are thriving.

Growth – birth to 12 weeks
The graph opposite is a growth chart of an average Afghan litter from birth to 12 weeks.

Going to their new homes

It is wise to insure the puppies to safeguard the transitional period from leaving you to going into their new homes, and many specialist insurance companies will forward you a book of cover notes, one to be issued with each sale (for instance, Pet Plan Ltd or Dog Breeders Insurance Company Ltd). You should have registered the litter with The Kennel Club, but it may well be that the puppies' individual registrations have not arrived before they leave you, in which case they can be forwarded to the new owners for transfer at a later date. Be sure to provide new owners with a sample diet sheet, giving them a couple of days' supply from your own stores if necessary, to minimise the risk of any digestive upset. New owners should also be advised that the puppies, having received their first vaccination, should not be taken out on walks until two weeks following the second vaccination, and then only for short walks, as it is not wise to over-exercise the young. They

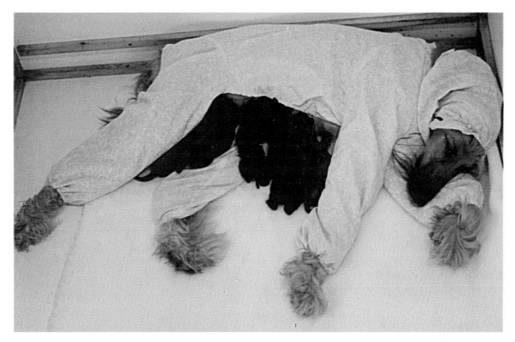

An Afghan bitch in her maternity coat.

should also be given a copy of the puppy's pedigree along with the name and address of the secretary of their nearest breed club. It is only natural that, having lovingly reared them, you will want to keep in touch with their new owners and will follow up the sale with telephone calls about their progress and be on hand to give any necessary advice.

At twelve weeks of age the number of meals can be reduced to three, then at six months to two and at twelve months to just one meal per day, although quantities should be increased accordingly. Fresh water should be freely available.

Aftercare of the bitch

It is natural for the bitch to miss her puppies for a short time. Nursing the litter will have taken quite a lot out of her, but she will quickly return to her old self if fed on a nutritious diet and allowed to rest. If you feel that she enjoyed the experience, had no untoward problems and was a good mother, you may wish to have a further litter from her in 12–18 months' time, but it is important to see how the first litter develops before embarking on a second. If the whole thing was a disaster and you ended up with an unhappy bitch, large vet's bills and many sleepless nights, the experience of mating her again is just not worth repeating. She will continue to come into season regularly throughout her life and, to avoid the complications associated with these hormonal changes, it is much more sensible to have her spayed (the removal of the ovaries and uterus). However, should you wish to resume her show career, first check the Canine Controlling Body's regulations in your country, as some do not permit spayed bitches to be shown.

Pyometra

Pyometra is a condition which occurs between one and two months following a season and is caused by bacteria entering the hormonally-receptive uterus from the vagina. A bitch suffering from pyometra will lose her appetite, drink excessive amounts of water and have a high temperature. This may be accompanied by a bloody/pussy discharge or alternatively a build-up of fluid in the uterus, giving a barrelled appearance to the body. This condition, if not treated as a matter of urgency, can be life threatening and, if you suspect it at all, you must contact your vet without delay. Antibiotic treatment may be successful if the condition is diagnosed in the very early stages, although there is still the risk that the infection will render the bitch infertile. Because a pyometra is likely to recur after the following season, the most appropriate course of action is to have her spayed.

Ch Bondor It's A Kinda Majic with her well reared eight-week-old pups.

chapter twelve
Health Care

Afghan Hounds are robust, energetic dogs that do not succumb easily to illness and disease. If correctly fed, given regular exercise and kept in clean living conditions they will remain physically fit and mentally alert. However, like humans, even the healthiest can become unwell and veterinary advice in respect of an early diagnosis and subsequent treatment will need to be sought.

The guiding principle in health care is knowing your own dog so well that you can see changes almost before they start, and the important thing for any layman is to be able to recognise certain symptoms quickly. As a matter of routine, have a good look at your dog first thing in the morning as it greets you. It should be 'bright eyed and bushy-tailed' and, if it is not, you should look for a reason. Its nose should be cold and slightly moist and it should show no signs of listlessness. Gums should be salmon pink in colour. Check its motions for any signs of looseness or diarrhoea and its coat for wet patches where it may have been licking, indicating a hidden sore area. Keep an eye on its water; is it drinking more than normal? It should also be eager for food and its bed should be clean with no signs of mucous or blood.

Health insurance

Owning an Afghan Hound is a great source of pride and pleasure, but it can also cause great anxiety and expense if illness or injury should arise. Veterinary fees have escalated in recent years and, in view of the fact that two out of every three pets require veterinary care each year, considerable reassurance can be gained from taking out health insurance.

Various policies are currently marketed and details will be found on display at your veterinary surgery or through advertisements in the canine press. All offer substantial cover against veterinary costs and third party liability, and only by careful study of the small print will you be able to decide upon the one most suited to your needs. Most policies dictate that you pay the first £30 of any one claim, but remember that routine treatments such as vaccinations and worming are exempt.

Many owners have a high regard for the benefits offered by alternative or complementary medicine and there are now policies providing cover for homeopathy, acupuncture, physiotherapy and herbal treatments.

Choosing a veterinary surgeon

If you intend to breed and show your dogs, a good veterinary surgeon who is genuinely interested in your successful achievements is someone to be clung to through thick and thin. Many dog owners know their vet better than their doctor, the relationship being just as personal and at times more emotional. But unfortunately, there are still vets to be found who have little regard to the career of a successful show dog, and persuading them that the retention of your Afghan's coat is of utmost importance can sometimes be an uphill struggle. A congenial vet will understand this requirement and endeavour to accommodate where at all possible, but there will obviously be occasions when coat loss is inevitable. This is an important consideration and the subject would be better discussed with your prospective vet sooner rather than later.

Probably the best way of choosing a vet is by recommendation and, more often than not, a 'small animal' practice will be better equipped for your purposes than one that concentrates mainly on farm animals. If you are interested in homeopathy as a means of veterinary treatment, you should enquire whether the practice concerned uses 'alternative' as well as conventional veterinary medicine.

Your dog should be willing to allow the vet to examine it and, if it is show-trained, this should not present a problem. However, if you are in any doubt about your dog's temperament, take along a muzzle or request that the vet uses one. If you are starting out with a young puppy, try to ensure that its first visit is stress-free; otherwise the whole experience will remain with it for a long time and future visits will be regarded with apprehension.

If a major illness is at any time suspected, do not be afraid to ask questions about the treatment and prognosis. Also, ascertain how much the treatment is likely to cost, as veterinary treatment can sometimes run into several hundreds of pounds. If your dog is not insured and the estimated costs amount to more than you can pay, enquire whether deferred payments will be permissible.

At the end of the day, if your vet is unwilling to answer your questions or you feel in any way intimidated, the relationship is clearly not working and you should find another vet.

Home nursing

A sick Afghan or one recovering from anaesthetic must be kept warm and comfortable and away from all disturbances, although it will want to remain in close proximity to its owner. If suffering from an infectious disease it should not be allowed to come into contact with your other dogs and you should also exercise precaution against the disease spreading to them. Its bed should be dry and comfortable, the green-backed, white veterinary bedding being ideal because it is warm, moisture-absorbing and washable. Drinking water must be accessible and, if the dog cannot drink on its own or reach the bowl, water must be offered frequently. If the patient is unable to move, it should be turned onto its other side regularly.

Diet will vary according to the illness, but a tempting light diet of fish or chicken, liquidised if necessary, will usually be acceptable and it is important to note whether the dog has its bowels open or passes urine. If the dog is receiving veterinary attention, instructions should be followed to the letter. In other words, if pills are to be given three times a day, they should be given every eight hours – religiously. After an operation your dog may need to wear an 'Elizabethan collar' around its head to prevent it from licking parts of its body or scratching its ears and face. Whilst this is not very comfortable, sometimes drastic measures have to be taken for the good of your dog and you will find that it will adapt to the cumbersome object quite quickly.

Giving pills

To open the dog's mouth, hold either side of the upper jaw with your left hand on top of the jaw, the thumb at the right side and the index finger at the left. Press gently behind the canine teeth to open the mouth. With your other hand, depress the tongue and slip the pill to the back of the throat. Close the dog's mouth and encourage it to swallow by stroking the throat or tickling just below the nose, until the tongue emerges just a little, indicating that it has swallowed. Afghans conceal pills very well and will quietly spit them out when they think you are not looking, so always double-check that they are not still in the dog's mouth.

Taking the temperature

The best way to take a dog's temperature is rectally, and a blunt-ended thermometer should be kept specifically for your dog. The best thermometers are digital ones which, although more expensive, are far safer and easier to read. Raise the dog's tail and insert the thermometer about 5cm, holding it in place for about a minute according to the instructions supplied with your thermometer. Normal body temperature is 38.3–38.7°C (100.9–101.7°F).

Immunisation against specific diseases

Up to 50 years ago, viral diseases for which there were no known cures killed thousands of dogs annually. Fortunately, immunisation now effectively controls the major canine diseases such as distemper (hardpad), leptospirosis, infectious canine hepatitis and parvovirus.

Normally, puppies are vaccinated from the age of eight weeks old and vaccines should not be administered if the dog is at all off colour. Whether it is wise to give everything in one multiple inoculation is currently a cause for concern, as many breeders feel there may be a connection between giving such a large cocktail of micro-organisms in one initial dose and auto-immune disease (caused by a failure of the bodily defence mechanisms when antibodies become active against some of the dog's own cells). The spacing of initial administration should therefore be first discussed with your vet. Personally, I rely on my vet's advice and have my puppies vaccinated and would have them boosted throughout their lives, but that does not mean to say that I will not keep a close watch on current developments and arguments against this procedure.

Alternative programmes of protection are available, and the address of a homeopathic pharmacy is given in **Useful Addresses**. However, should you wish to board your dog at any time, an up-to-date regular vaccination certificate will be required by most kennels, many of which do not recognise homeopathic alternatives. The inoculation is repeated at 12 weeks and sometimes again at 16 weeks if it is felt that the puppy is likely to pick up infection as a result of close proximity to other animals.

All puppies receive initial immunity from their mother (transmitted via the colostrum in her early milk), which tends to wane around the age of six weeks. The danger is that, if the puppy still has its mother's immunity, vaccination will not give full protection. Should you be in any doubt, blood tests can be carried out by the vet to determine the antibody levels present at the time.

Distemper

Distemper is a viral disease that can affect dogs of all ages, although youngsters between the ages of three and twelve months are the most susceptible. It is characterised usually by a rise in temperature, listlessness and loss of appetite, and in the later stages by a cough and catarrhal discharge from the eyes and nostrils. Sometimes, the first sign of the disease (apart from the fact that the dog has seemed unwell) is a fit or a change in temperament with a tendency to viciousness

An early diagnosis by the vet is vital and, after recovery, the dog is left vulnerable to other viral infections. Vaccination is the only effective method of control.

Canine Viral Hepatitis

Dogs of all ages may be affected, even puppies a few days old, but the disease occurs most frequently in young dogs of three to nine months old. As its name suggests, the disease affects the liver and is likely to produce the symptoms of jaundice, a noticeable sign being the yellowing of the mucous membranes inside the mouth. The illness is sometimes also known as 'blue-eye', because of the characteristic opacity that develops over the eyes in about 25% of cases approximately a week or two after the beginning of the illness, but this usually disappears gradually.

The blood-clotting mechanism is also affected to the extent that haemorrhaging may develop within the body. Dogs that have recovered may continue to harbour the virus and act as 'carriers', spreading the disease to other dogs via their urine. Vaccination, however, provides good protection against this illness and a strain of vaccine has been developed that gives all the advantages of a live vaccine but without the 'blue-eye' risk.

Leptospirosis

Dogs who are likely to come into contact with rats at any stage are particularly at risk from this bacterial illness and the effects depend upon the bacterium involved. *Leptospira canicola* is 'dog-to-dog' transmission (for example, by sniffing lamp-posts in urban areas) and strikes primarily at the kidneys, causing damage likely to be permanent. *Leptospira icterohaemorrhagiae* is 'rat-to-dog' and can affect the liver in humans, in which case it is known as Weil's disease. Infection of the disease spreads easily and is difficult to control because most of those dogs that recover excrete the organisms in the urine for long periods afterwards (sometimes up to 18 months).

If you are caring for a dog suspected of suffering from leptospirosis, it is important to wear gloves to prevent the bacteria entering through a break in the skin. A severe infection in humans can result in the kidneys, liver or heart being damaged: hence the importance of vaccination against this dreadful disease.

Parvovirus

This infection appeared as a new disease in 1978–9 and, not having encountered the virus previously, dogs proved highly susceptible. Serious outbreaks occurred throughout the world and many dogs died as a result. The illness takes the form of severe gastro-enteritis and there may be blood in the motions, accompanied by a foul smell. Treatment must include measures to overcome the severe dehydration caused by vomiting and diarrhoea, with a light diet during convalescence. In young puppies, typically around five weeks old, the virus can attack the heart muscles, causing myocarditis and resulting in sudden death, although the disease can still prove fatal at any age.

In the early days of parvovirus outbreaks, the only vaccine available was one given to cats to protect against feline enteritis, but today dog-specific vaccines are available. The virus is extremely resistant, survives well in the environment and can be walked into kennels on your shoes, so extra care should be observed when you are in contact with un-vaccinated puppies. Disinfectants specifically formulated to combat the disease (for instance, Parvo-Virucide, obtainable from The Animal Health Co) act as a safeguard.

Rabies

Rabies is derived from the Latin word for *madness* and is undoubtedly the most serious viral disease associated with dogs. The relaxation of border controls across Europe means that the likelihood of the disease reaching Great Britain (currently free from the virus) is now somewhat increased. In mainland Europe, dogs have long been protected against rabies by vaccination, but at present this is not permitted in Great Britain except for dogs being exported and those arriving in quarantine.

The rabies virus is transmitted in saliva and it is not necessary to be bitten to be infected. If you have an open cut on your hand and come into contact with a contaminated dog, you could be at risk. Should you have the misfortune to be exposed to a rabid animal in this way, or be bitten, wash out the wound with alcohol as an emergency procedure and seek medical help immediately.

The length of time for clinical signs of rabies to develop in the dog depends largely upon where the virus was introduced into its body. If it was bitten close to the foot, the virus will need to track up through the peripheral nervous system into the central nervous system and the effects will then become obvious. A bite close to the neck is more likely to result in rapid emergence of symptoms, possibly within three weeks rather than two months later.

Kennel cough

Although less serious than the diseases already mentioned, kennel cough is a troublesome complaint, most likely to be acquired where dogs are in close proximity to each other such as at shows or in boarding kennels. While no single organism is responsible for kennel cough, a vaccine has been developed that gives good protection against the most common causes of the illness. Unlike other vaccines, the kennel cough product is given intra-nasally, simply being squirted up the dog's nostrils. Two doses are usually recommended, spaced about a month apart, to be followed by an annual booster.

Usually only the upper air passages are involved, the chief symptom being a dry, rasping cough that is aggravated by exercise or excitement. In most cases, the cough abates after about five days, although it may persist for longer, and the bacteria can still be found in the respiratory tract for up to three months after the initial infection. Complications can include a nasal discharge or even broncho-pneumonia, but these symptoms are more likely to occur in the old or very young.

Because of the less serious nature of kennel cough, some owners take their dogs to shows while they are still infectious. This is irresponsible and unfair.

Testing for hereditary problems

Certain hereditary diseases reared their ugly heads and affected Afghans during the 1960s and 1970s, and it was largely thanks to the efforts of certain conscientious breeders that the problems were nipped in the bud before they escalated to serious proportions. To my knowledge, the current situation in Great Britain is that the breed is free from hereditary disease, but that does not mean we can afford to become complacent. Breeders cannot be forced to have their stock tested, but by so doing they will be acting responsibly to ensure that eye and hip problems never re-emerge.

Hereditary eye disorders
Progressive Retinal Atrophy (PRA), **Hereditary Cataract** and **Glaucoma** are all serious hereditary eye conditions that could affect Afghan Hounds. Testing dogs under the British Veterinary Association/Kennel Club/International Sheep Dog Society (BVA/KC/ISDS) Eye Scheme is a means of identifying the presence or absence of inherited eye disease. Details can be obtained from your veterinary surgeon or The Kennel Club.

Hip dysplasia
Hip dysplasia (HD) describes a badly fitting hip joint, occurring when the head of the femur (thigh bone) is not correctly shaped and does not make a perfect union with the acetabulum (hip socket). The BVA/KC operate a similar scheme for hip scoring, Again, you can obtain details from your vet or from The Kennel Club.

Other problems
These aside, there are less serious but just as debilitating conditions, namely **entropion** (in-turning of the eyelids, resulting in the eyelashes irritating the corneal surface) and **epilepsy** (see fits and seizures), which are creeping into the breed. While not always hereditary, they do need to be carefully monitored and must not be allowed to escalate. It is hoped that conscientious breeders will keep a watchful eye on the situation.

Routine maintenance

Anal gland impaction
Each dog has two of these glands, one each side of the anus and slightly below it. The glands produce a particularly smelly fluid whose purpose is possibly to act as a lubricant to aid defecation, and they are also the dog's means of depositing its own individual scent on its faeces. Each gland has a duct opening just inside the anus, and sometimes the ducts become blocked, so the secretions cannot escape and the glands swell. The dog usually attempts to relieve the discomfort by dragging its rear end across the ground – contrary to popular thought, this does not indicate worm infestation.

While not a particularly pleasant task, it is not difficult to empty these glands, and many breeders attend to the matter themselves. Raise the dog's tail, grasp behind the sacs or glands and squeeze outwards. You should have a wad of cotton wool in your hand in front of the anus, as the fluid will shoot out when you squeeze. Otherwise, your vet will empty them for you and show you what to do if it recurs. If you do not feed your dog on a complete food, adding more fibre to the dog's diet in the form of bran may help.

Dental care

Tartar is caused by salts in the saliva and, if deposits are allowed to build up, they will lead to inflammation of the gums, eventually resulting in loss of teeth. The length of time tartar takes to build up varies from dog to dog and two litter-mates housed together and fed the same diet can develop the problem at different rates, and some not at all.

Whilst tartar is not problematic in youngsters, it will help if puppies are accustomed to having their teeth brushed at an early age so that they do not resent the procedure when they are older. Prevention is better than cure, and there are several ways of keeping tartar at a minimum. Special toothbrushes and toothpaste are available for dogs, although ordinary toothpaste will suffice as long as it is not the minty, foam-in-the-mouth variety. I have not yet owned a dog who particularly enjoys this procedure, so I tend to

Gnawing on a marrow bone helps to keep teeth and gums healthy. Photo: David Paton

regularly give marrow bones which have been bought raw and roasted in the oven. The dogs seem to prefer these to the smoked ones which can be readily purchased, not tiring so quickly of them. Some companies, such as Nylabone, sell a range of products designed to clean and exercise dogs' teeth as they play with them. Chewed legs and ears on a show dog can be prevented by first kitting them out in wet weather coats and snoods, or even a pair of old socks. Do take care to keep dogs separate when giving bones, as this is one of the few times that they can become possessive. Alternatively, as part of your bath-time routine, rub the teeth with the corner of a towel dipped in bicarbonate of soda.

If existing tartar is particularly bad it can be removed with a descaling tool, obtainable at dog shows, or, failing that, a visit to your vet, who will clean the dog's teeth under a light anaesthetic.

Ear problems

Shaking the head, holding it to one side or scratching the ears are all symptoms of irritation in the ear and they should be examined for signs of inflammation or a nasty brown discharge. Never poke down the ear canal with a cotton bud as you could easily damage the ear drum. Instead, arrange an early appointment with your vet, who can inspect the interior carefully with an auroscope, ascertain whether the infection is fungal or bacterial, and provide you with the appropriate treatment. Massaging behind the ears after giving the medication will help in its effective distribution. If irritation and inflammation persist, ask your vet to take an ear swab to investigate the problem in more detail.

Otodectic mites are the most frequent cause of infection of the external ear canal and can be recognised by a distinctive, smelly, brown discharge. Curing them effectively is often difficult as the eggs and larvae are extremely resistant and survive the treatments that kill the adults. Oterna ear drops, containing a mite-killer plus an analgesic to reduce the irritation caused by the mites, are often prescribed by the vet and will clear them in most cases. An alternative remedy is Thornit Canker Powder, used by many breeders with spectacular results (see **Useful Addresses**). If the condition is left untreated in the early stages, complications of the inner ear may result, necessitating an operation.

When conditions involve **bacterial** or **fungal infections**, the appropriate drugs (anti-bacterial or anti-fungal) will be prescribed.

Sometimes, persistent shaking of the head due to untreated ear infections, can cause a large, fluid-filled swelling on the flap of the ear, known as a **haematoma**. This condition requires an operation to remove the fluid, the flap being stitched up in such a way as to prevent the collection of more fluid. However, try not to let the problem reach this stage, as the operation occasionally results in deformation of the ear flap.

Eye care

Because an Afghan's eyes are set to the side of the head, they are well protected and not particularly vulnerable to injury, so will generally require little in the way of routine maintenance. Healthy dogs may require the occasional removal of 'sleep' from the lower corner of the eyes, but they do not demand the daily irrigation required by those breeds that have large, front-facing eyes.

In the case of an acute eye infection, seek veterinary advice as soon as possible.

- *To insert eye drops* gently pull up the upper lid, exposing the cornea, and squeeze the drop on to it without touching the eye.
- *To insert eye ointment*, pull down the lower lid and squeeze the ointment along the bottom of the eye. Do not touch the eye.

Nail care

All nails must be trimmed regularly, but dogs with good feet who are given plenty of road work rarely require attention. I have never found it necessary to have dew claws removed but, because they do not come into contact with the ground, they require trimming from time to time. If neglected, these nails can grow right around, penetrating the soft pad behind. If this has happened, the nail should be cut short and an antiseptic powder applied to the sore area.

To cut nails, use the guillotine type of nail clipper and cut to within about 1/8in of the quick, which shows pink in an uncoloured nail. With black nails, the quick is impossible to see, so clipping should err on the side of too little rather than too much. Your Afghan will soon let you know if you overstep the mark! However, if you do cut a little too much, dip the nail into potassium potash crystals and the bleeding will soon stop.

Afghans occasionally get an infection in the nail bed, which can be extremely difficult to cure. Bathing the affected foot twice daily in warm salt water may help but, if the condition does not improve, veterinary advice should be sought.

External parasites

Fleas

Fleas in any long-coated breed are a nightmare and, fortunately, there are now many excellent preparations that eliminate them quickly and effectively. Fleas can be picked up from a show or just out and about and are easily detected as the dog will repeatedly scratch himself. If you suspect or see fleas, spray the dog with a preparation such as Nuvan Top, obtainable from the vet.

A flea spends only a small percentage of its life time on a pet and does not lay its eggs on the dog, but in nooks and crannies around the dog's bedding in the house, or outside on the grass. The eggs then develop into maggots, and then into fleas, which jump on to the nearest living animal. The warm environment of today's centrally-heated homes means that fleas can prove a problem throughout the year, not just in summer. Therefore, it is equally important when ridding the dog of fleas to spray around bedding areas with products such as Nuvan Staykil or Flea Ban (available from the vet) to destroy any eggs and break the life cycle.

Flea shampoos are most effective, as are drops applied to the back of the dog's neck, preventing it from being badly bitten in the first place. There is also a flea treatment that can be given once a month in tablet form, rendering infertile any fleas your dog may pick up. Treatment at an early stage is important, not only to prevent the destruction an Afghan will cause to its coat by constant scratching, but also to minimise the risk of tapeworm infestation, caused by swallowing a certain type of flea.

Flea allergy occurs when the dog becomes extremely sensitised to flea saliva, in which case a single flea bite can cause severe irritation, resulting in eczema.

Lice

Lice are very small and pinkish-white in colour. They do not jump, but burrow their heads into the dog and are spread only by direct contact with an infected dog. Typically, the dog will scratch more than normal. The eggs, or nits, are laid on the sides of the hairs and look like small particles of scurf but, unlike scurf, they will not brush off. Two distinct families of louse are found on the dog: the sucking louse and the biting louse. It takes about a month for their life cycle to complete and infected dogs should be treated with suitable insecticides such as Nuvan Top or repellent powders and shampoos at regular, four-weekly intervals.

Ticks

Ticks can be a problem in farming and moorland areas, where they lie concealed in long grass and become attached to the dog as it brushes past. They are bluish-black in colour and resemble a small bean in appearance. The tick anchors its mouth parts into the dog's skin and then walks around in a clockwise movement as if trying to 'screw itself in'. It then gorges on the dog's blood, swelling noticeably in size as a result. At this stage ticks are sometimes mistaken for skin cysts, but careful examination will reveal the presence of legs and biting mouth parts near to the dog's skin.

An effective way of dislodging ticks is to smear the tick's body with Vaseline, which will block the breathing pore and cause them to drop off, but this can be somewhat messy in the coat of an Afghan. Probably a better way is to spray the tick with Nuvan Top or a similar flea and tick repellent. However, if the tick is on the dog's face or near its eye, do not attempt to spray. Greater accuracy is offered by soaking a cotton wool bud with the spray and wetting the tick thoroughly, whereupon it will die within seconds and is then best left to fall off on its own. If pulled, it will break off, leaving its mouthparts still buried in the dog's skin, which will set up irritation and localised infection. Once the tick has been removed, cleanse the area of the bite with diluted antiseptic solution.

Cheyletiella

Cheyletiella mange mites are commonly called *walking dandruff* and should be suspected if your dog has what appears to be scurf or dandruff on the nape of the neck and down the back and is scratching frequently. Whilst it is barely visible to the naked eye, if you stand your dog on a dark, flat surface like a black plastic bin liner and comb out some of the 'scurf', note whether it moves.

Cheyletiella is not usually detected until a human member of the family becomes allergic to it and develops a rash. In some cases, the advice given is to get rid of the dog to which they are allergic, but this is totally unnecessary. Your vet will advise the appropriate shampoo to kill off the mites and, to prevent re-infestation, bedding, furnishings and crevices should be attended to with a suitable repellent.

Harvest mites

Harvest mites are microscopic in size, orange-red in colour and can just be seen with the naked eye. The mite burrows under the skin and engorges with blood, appearing as a red spot in the centre of an inflamed area. In two or three days the spot becomes a blister and ultimately a scab, which falls off. They are particularly found in cornfields, grasslands and the chalky soil of woodlands, most often attacking the face of the dog where it has been sniffing. Irritation will also occur between the cleft of the toes.

As before, obtain the necessary shampoo to kill the mites from your vet. Residual sprays and baths will kill larvae and prevent re-infestation. Dipping the feet in a diluted citronella or eucalyptus solution may help.

Demodectic mange

The main symptom is hair loss on the head, particularly around the eyes and feet, but it is less likely to be itchy. Skin scrapings under a microscope will show mites. Conditions are much more serious when the lesions are pustular, as secondary bacterial infection can occur. Treatment is made difficult by the fact that the mites are sometimes living at a depth difficult to reach; however, Ivermectin is effective.

Ringworm

A contagious skin disease caused by the growth of certain fungi, which appears in the form of circular patches from which the hair has fallen. Whilst not especially common in dogs (long-haired cats are more likely to be affected), it is serious in that it can be transmitted to people, typically causing red circular patches on the forearms. Always contact the vet at once if you suspect ringworm. He or she will examine your dog under a Wood's lamp, which causes the affected areas to fluoresce or glow in some cases. The disease is treatable with specific antibiotic drugs and precautions such as hand-washing in Dettol should be taken after contact with known affected animals.

Internal parasites

Roundworms

Virtually all puppies are born infected with the roundworm *Toxocara canis*, including those born to bitches regularly wormed pre-mating. Immature larvae lie dormant in the tissues of the bitch and become active during the second half of the pregnancy, when they migrate into the lungs of the developing pups. By the time the pup has reached three weeks of age, toxocara larvae will have developed into adults – each capable of producing thousands of eggs per day. By using an effective wormer, such as Panacur, which removes both larval and adult stages of the worm, the level of environmental contamination is minimised and the toxocara lifecycle is broken.

Roundworms resemble thin white pieces of spaghetti and symptoms of a poor appetite, dull appearance and a hard, pot belly may be found in an un-wormed puppy. In extreme cases the puppy will cough up or vomit worms.

To reduce infection of puppies, bitches may be given Panacur from day 40 of pregnancy to two days post-whelping at the recommended dose rate, and this will decrease pre-natal transmission of *Toxocara canis* by approximately 89%. It will also minimise the transfer of worms from the bitch to the puppies via the milk, and re-infection of the bitch when cleaning her litter. The puppies should be treated from around three weeks of age, and again at five, eight and twelve weeks depending on your vet's advice. Further treatment at six months is usually recommended, with regular de-worming carried out at six monthly intervals throughout the dog's life.

Care should be taken not to allow small children to play where dogs and cats defecate, as not all pets are de-wormed regularly. In very rare cases it has been known for children to ingest *Toxocara canis* eggs, which have subsequently hatched and migrated to the eyes, causing blindness.

Tapeworms

Tapeworms are most often found in adult dogs that are fed on raw tripe or have fleas. Tapeworms are flat and ribbon-like in appearance and a mature worm sheds segments. These are passed out of the dog's body in the faeces. They can sometimes be seen sticking to the underpart of the tail, resembling small grains of dried rice.

The most common tapeworm in the dog is *Dypilidum caninum*. When the mature segments of this tapeworm are passed by the dog they contain many thousands of microscopically tiny eggs, which are then eaten by fleas. Should a dog swallow an infected flea while grooming itself or eating grass, the worm then becomes established in the dog's gut. Fleas provide a constant source of reinfection, so effective flea control is very important.

The actual amount of food consumed by tapeworms is so small as to be of no consequence, and it is only when the worms are present in large quantities that they may interfere with normal digestion. In most cases it will be sufficient to treat dogs for tapeworms every six months, although those fed on raw tripe should be routinely dosed every two months. Drontal Plus (obtainable from the vet) is an effective treatment for tapeworms and will also kill roundworms, hookworms and whipworms.

Other conditions and emergencies

Many conditions have already been dealt with in their respective chapters and I will mention only the ailments and diseases that I have known to affect Afghan Hounds. A good

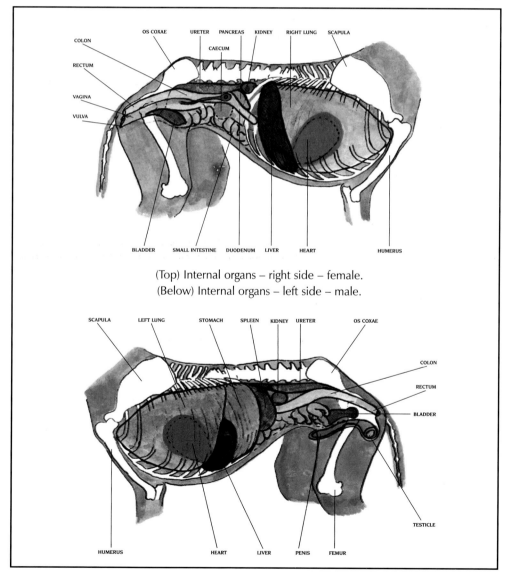

(Top) Internal organs – right side – female.
(Below) Internal organs – left side – male.

veterinary book will certainly be of more help, and a comprehensive one to have to hand is *Veterinary Notes for Dog Owners*, edited by Trevor Turner BVet Med MRCVS.

Abscesses

Occurring almost anywhere, abscesses are extremely painful. The first signs are inflammation, redness, warmth, and swelling, followed by a rise in temperature when the abscess is well developed. When the abscess bursts or it is emptied by lancing, the pain disappears, the swelling subsides and the temperature falls. If all the pus has been withdrawn the cavity heals rapidly, although it is best left uncovered.

Afghan Hounds can occasionally develop anal abscesses, which are usually the result of an impacted anal gland becoming infected. They tend to recur in some dogs, in which case surgical treatment may be the only solution. Your dog will draw your attention to the abscess by constantly licking the affected area. Hot fomentations may afford relief and draw the abscess to a head, although early antibiotic treatment may just help the abscess to subside before reaching that point. Early consultation with your vet will ensure a speedy recovery.

If it occurs in the mouth, an abscess will cause your dog to go off its food and feel generally miserable. Check around the gums for an infected tooth root and treat it with antibiotics.

Arthritis

Arthritis is a very painful condition caused by inflammation of the joints. It can be brought on by injury or infection and, in the case of older dogs, by a gradual wearing of ligaments or cartilage. The most common symptom is stiffness, particularly noticeable after a period of rest. The condition is often made worse by cold, damp weather. If your dog injures itself as a youngster, be it to the shoulder or any other limb, the importance of resting the dog and restricting its exercise until it has completely recovered cannot be stressed too strongly.

Apart from conventional treatment, other long-term ways of easing arthritis can involve acupuncture and homeopathic remedies, and these should be discussed with your vet. Additionally, to prevent undue stress being placed on ligaments, tendons and joints, an arthritic dog should not be allowed to become overweight.

Artificial respiration

In the event of an emergency, knowing how to give artificial respiration could save your dog's life, particularly in cases of drowning (when the dog has been rescued from water), electrocution, or asphyxia from smoke or fumes.

Lay the dog on its side with the head at a lower level than the rest of the body, if possible. Extend the head and neck to allow a straight passage of air into the lungs, open the mouth and pull the tongue well out. Place one hand flat over the upper side of the abdomen and the other on the rib cage, lean heavily on the hands and, in a second or two, release the pressure, observing a slight pause before each rhythmic movement.

If this fails, mouth-to-nose resuscitation can be attempted and, as long as the heart continues to beat, no matter how feebly, attempts at resuscitation should be pursued.

It should be mentioned here that, although the physical signs of death are well known, there are occasions when it is difficult to state whether an animal is dead or not. In deep coma, an animal may have all the superficial appearances of being dead, and yet recovery is possible if effective measures are taken.

When an animal dies, the essential sign of the cessation of life is said to be the stopping of the heart. This, however, is not strictly correct, for it is possible by massage to resuscitate an already stopped heart and to recover an apparently dead animal. It is generally considered that death has taken place when the heart and respiration have ceased and when the eyelids do not flicker if a finger be applied to the eyeballs.

Auto-immune disease

This disease is due to a defect or failure of the bodily defence mechanisms in which antibodies become active against some of the host's own cells. Auto-antibodies can be produced at any time, by any individual, but in most cases they are eliminated by suppresser cells.

Specific auto-immune diseases include:

* *Canine auto-immune haemolytic anaemia*, where the antibodies attack and destroy the red blood cells.
* *Immune mediated thrombocytopenia*, where the antibodies attack the platelets (blood-clotting process).
* *Lupus Erythematosus*, of which there are two types: the *discoid* form, characterised by symmetrical lesions of the face, nose and ears, hair loss and redness of the skin, and the *systemic* form, causing damage to kidneys, lungs, joints, the central nervous system and other tissues.

Also commonly associated with auto-immunity are Diabetes Mellitus, Addison's Disease, thyroiditis and rheumatoid arthritis. Whilst many auto-immune diseases are associated with a preceding infection, other contributing factors can be genetic predisposition, hormonal influences (especially of sex hormones), infections (usually viral) and stress.

Bloat

Owners should be aware of this life threatening condition, which has been known to affect Afghan Hounds. Signs to look out for are acute distress, salivating from the mouth and the stomach blowing up like a balloon. The stomach twists upon itself and air and gases build up which, unless relieved immediately by the vet, will result in death.

Never allow vigorous exercise immediately before or after a meal. If your dog has suffered with bloat previously, give it two small meals instead of one large one, or feed it once last thing at night, as the condition may recur.

Bursitis

These fluid-filled swellings are common in many of the larger breeds and are usually found on vulnerable areas such as the elbows and points of buttocks. Boisterous youngsters are particularly prone and a bursa can swell to the size of an orange in some cases. Whilst being uncomfortable to the dog, they are not known to be painful and, if left alone, have a tendency to disappear. However, this can take several months, and your vet may decide to withdraw the fluid by syringe, followed by an anti-inflammatory injection into the sac. Unfortunately, until such time as they decide to repair themselves, they do have a habit of recurring. Also, when they eventually disappear, the skin on the elbow can remain flabby, although coat growth ultimately conceals any unsightliness.

Cancer

The occurrence of cancer in Afghan Hounds is quite high and, as with humans, can develop at any age. The term refers to both malignant tumours and to leukaemia (commonly referred to as *cancer of the blood*) and it is a sad fact of life that this awful disease will possibly cause you to lose your beloved Afghan.

On the positive side, the treatment for cancer improves each year, particularly if discovered in the early stages, and more help is available to improve the quality of life of your hound. It is therefore important to check your dog regularly for any unusual lumps or bumps, particularly in the lymph nodes in the neck under the jaw, at the shoulder and at the back of the stifle and thigh. If discovered, they should be brought to the attention of your vet promptly.

Cataracts

Normally found in dogs over eight years of age, cataracts are an opacity or clouding of the lens, which prevents clear vision. Because the change is very gradual, the dog has time to adapt to the new situation of approaching blindness as it develops.

Conjunctivitis

The eye appears red as a result of infection and inflammation, and this is often accompanied by an excessive discharge of tears and a tendency to keep the eyelids closed. Bathe with warmed eye lotion and, if the condition does not respond, your vet will be able to provide a suitable remedy. If only one eye is affected the cause may be because of irritation by a foreign body. Windy conditions and draughts further exacerbate the condition.

Constipation

If the dog is straining without passing a stool, it is probably constipated. The condition often occurs in older dogs, as a result of loss of elasticity in the bowel, or in dogs fed on a lot of bones. It can also be caused by dry, bulky foods without enough water or inadequate exercise. A dessertspoonful of medicinal liquid paraffin, a bowl of warm milk or the addition of raw liver to the diet should have a laxative effect but, if the condition persists, you should seek advice from the vet.

Cuts and abrasions (minor)

These are successfully treated by cleaning with a weak salt solution (about half a teaspoon of ordinary household salt in approximately 570 ml (a pint) of warm water), twice daily. If infection has started up, your vet will probably recommend a course of antibiotics.

Cystitis

Inflammation of the bladder is generally caused by infection, urinary calculi (stones) or a growth. In acute cystitis, small quantities of urine are passed very frequently, or the dog may strain without actually urinating. Blood may also be seen in the urine. The condition is quite painful and requires veterinary attention so that an appropriate antibiotic, and in some cases a pain reliever, can be given. To aid diagnosis, a fresh sample of urine should be taken along for the vet to test, as these symptoms also correspond to those of urinary calculi (stones) or a growth.

Cysts

This term is applied to swellings containing fluid or soft material other than pus and to hollow tumours (usually non-malignant). Sebaceous cysts are mainly caused by a blocked sebaceous gland, caused by normal secretions being unable to reach the skin surface because of a blockage of the duct. Some can be drained, while others need to be removed if they become infected. They are more commonly found on older dogs, usually occurring on the neck and body.

As a general rule, cysts are distinguishable from tumours in that they are moveable, are not raw on the surface and do not bleed.

Diabetes

This condition exists when the pancreas fails to produce sufficient insulin, resulting in a rise in sugar levels in the blood. A diabetic dog develops an excessive thirst, urinates more frequently and has a ravenous appetite. Veterinary attention should be sought at the onset of these symptoms, as the dog will lose weight progressively and become sluggish. Take along a urine specimen to be tested by the vet for an abnormal amount of sugar content.

Once the condition is diagnosed, the only effective method of control is by attention to diet and daily injections of insulin. Diabetes is more common in females than males, particularly in unspayed, middle-aged or elderly bitches, and, because treatment is impeded by hormonal activity such as seasons, diabetic bitches will need to be spayed.

Diarrhoea

Diarrhoea is not a disease in itself but merely a symptom, which may indicate nothing more than the result of a sudden change of diet. Continuous diarrhoea, however, is serious: not only are the digestive processes and the absorption of nutrients impaired, but the loss of fluid gives rise to dehydration. If diarrhoea persists for 48 hours or more, veterinary advice should be sought, as this symptom can be associated with many serious diseases, including parvovirus. The dog's temperature is a useful guide to the severity of the condition and, if high, is an indication that there is some other condition complicating the diarrhoea.

If you suspect a mild tummy upset rather than infection or poisoning, food intake should be withheld for 24 hours and, when feeding is resumed, it should be limited to an easily-digested, light diet fed several times a day. Milk should be avoided. A short starvation will do no harm and will give the intestinal lining time to repair.

Much more serious is a condition called **colitis**, an inflammation of the large bowel (colon). This is indicated by completely fluid or semi-solid faeces accompanied by mucous and/or fresh blood. Acute colitis can be treated successfully by your vet with specific antibiotics, although the condition in its chronic form can recur over a period of several years. The exact cause is difficult to determine, but a diet low in fat and high in fibre seems to help dogs prone to this condition.

Eye ulcers

Ulcers can be caused by irritation from a foreign body or infection resulting from conjunctivitis, but are more commonly found in Afghans after illness. The dog will be in some pain, rub its eye and generally feel miserable. You may be able to see the ulcer or the eye may have an opacity over the cornea, stemming from the inflammation below the surface.

The vet will identify the ulcer by means of a dye test and, if the ulcer is shallow, it will respond well to treatment. A healed ulcer can leave scar tissue, seen as a white mark on the eye.

Fits/seizures

Fits can manifest themselves at any stage of a dog's life and can occur for a variety of reasons. However, the onset of epilepsy, a common cause of fitting amongst all breeds, generally occurs from the age of two years onwards. The owner may not immediately be aware of the cause of the fit so, when the fit/seizure has subsided and the dog recovered, veterinary advice should be sought to obtain diagnosis and treatment if appropriate. Epilepsy can be controlled effectively by the use of drugs, enabling the dog to live a full, long and active life.

For the owner who has never previously experienced a fit in either humans or dogs, the first experience can be as traumatic for the person as for the animal. Fits can vary in degree, duration and frequency. At the lower end of the scale, the dog may only experience nocturnal fitting – in other words, at night when it is asleep. In such circumstances the owner may never witness the episode, but a wet or soiled bed may provide the evidence.

At the other end of the scale, the effects are more visible. For a matter of seconds or even minutes (which, to the stunned owner, will seem like hours) the dog will go into muscular spasm and collapse. In the case of an epileptic dog, this is brought about by a discharge of energy from the brain. The body and limbs will appear rigid and may thrash about, making involuntary paddling movements similar to those observed when the dog is asleep and dreaming about a chase. The dog will salivate excessively and probably lose control of his bowel and bladder.

Until the dog comes out of the fit there is little the owner can do except ensure that it is not in contact with furniture or hard objects that could cause injury. If you own other dogs, it is advisable to separate them until the dog has fully recovered, for fear of an attack.

The length of recovery time is influenced by the severity and duration of the fit and the age of the dog. The senses will remain dull and it may take some time before full co-ordination returns. It is not always wise to make immediate physical contact with the dog as, in this state of disorientation, it may perceive this contact as threatening and respond accordingly. Allow the dog space and offer calming verbal assurance and encouragement.

Ensure that water is available following the episode, as considerable amounts of body fluid may have been lost.

Gingivitis
This is the name given to inflammation of the gums and is usually accompanied by a build-up of tartar on the teeth and poor dental hygiene. The infection responds well to antibiotics and can be prevented from recurring by keeping the teeth clean and feeding a diet containing hard or chewable food. See **Routine Maintenance - Dental Care**.

Grass seeds
Although not an illness, grass seeds can be quite dangerous when they enter the body and, once under the skin, are extremely difficult to locate. A grass seed will lodge itself in soft tissue such as between the pads of the feet, under the arms, in the ears or even up the nose, where they invariably result in the formation of an abscess.

Hair balls
Afghans occasionally vomit a sausage-shaped wad of hair, and I must admit that, when I first encountered this problem, I did not know which end it had come from! Hair balls are invariably associated with the coat chewer and, if the mass is not too large, will pass out of the stomach through the intestines. If your dog is particularly prone to this problem, a teaspoonful of olive oil in the food daily may help to lubricate its system.

Heart attacks
A common cause of heart failure is the degeneration and narrowing of the mitral valve, situated between the upper and lower chambers in the left side of the heart. It is a condition more likely to affect middle-aged or older dogs. The dog will suddenly collapse and may appear to be dead, although it usually recovers in about five minutes. There may be involuntary emptying of the bowel and bladder and the eyes may rotate upwards.

    The dog should be kept warm and quiet whilst recovering from the attack and you should contact your vet as a matter of urgency.

Heart disease
A good vet will check your puppy's heart as a matter of course before giving initial vaccinations, enabling faulty heart action to be detected early. As with humans, heart troubles are much more common in old age, and it is very difficult to tell the nature of the heart condition as symptoms are not always apparent. Tiring easily when walking short distances and a dry cough are usually symptoms found in the elderly.

    Some young dogs with heart murmurs continue to lead perfectly normal lives without medication, while others may require treatment, which is likely to be for life.

Heat stroke
Many dogs die each year as a result of heat stroke and it is hoped that, by now, all owners are aware of the danger of leaving dogs in cars in warm weather. It should be borne in mind that the temperature inside a car parked in the sun, with two windows opened to the extent of 5cm each, will rapidly soar to over 32°C (90°F), even if the shade temperature outside

the car is only 18°C (65°F). The symptoms are great distress, rapid panting and drooling, with the dog quickly becoming weaker, until unable to move.

The dog should be removed to a cool place immediately and cold water applied to the skin, particularly to the head and neck areas, to reduce the body temperature. Place a wet towel all over the dog's body or douse with a fine hose, but do not use ice-cold water as this can be equally damaging. Let the dog rest in the cool and ensure that the temperature does not start to rise again, repeating the dousing until the dog's breathing slows down. Allow the dog to drink as much as it wants and, if possible, add a pinch of salt to the water. If you can do so, get the dog to a vet as soon as possible for drug administration to raise his blood pressure.

In severe but non-fatal cases, the dog's recovery will probably be slow and the dog may appear dull for several weeks afterwards.

Kidney disease

This can be *acute*, from sudden infection, or *chronic*, due to gradual breakdown as a result of past disease when the kidneys have been over-taxed. It is particularly common in older dogs and symptoms include excessive drinking, passing large quantities of dilute urine, loss of weight and general dullness. If your suspicions are aroused by any of these symptoms, you should consult your vet and take along a urine sample for checking.

Laryngeal paralysis

Affecting mainly long-throated animals, this is a condition sometimes seen in Afghans, particularly those over nine years of age. It is often confused with heart or lung failure. Symptoms include noisy, laboured breathing, a moist, retching cough, muted bark and early fatigue when taking exercise. The condition is caused by a degeneration of the unusually long nerves that motivate the muscular contractions of the voice box (larynx), resulting in an obstruction of the airway.

Treatment is by an operation to tie the voice box back into a semi-open position, out of the path of the entering stream of air. Although both sides of the larynx will be affected, an operation to pin back only one side has the desired effect. Despite the advanced age of many of the dogs involved, the results are generally excellent, giving the sufferer a new lease of life. In the past, affected dogs were referred to a specialist to conduct the operation, but many local practices now have vets trained in the procedure.

Liver disease

The liver is described as the chemical factory of the body, and its cells carry out a large variety of metabolic functions. Signs of liver disease include weight loss, jaundice, vomiting, diarrhoea, depression and excessive thirst. A blood test will establish whether there is a deterioration of liver function.

Pancreatic insufficiency

If the dog has a ravenous appetite, but remains thin, with a poor coat and unusual faeces, pancreatic insufficiency could be the cause. Veterinary advice should be sought.

Poisoning

As a general rule, poisoning should be suspected if a dog becomes ill suddenly. It must be emphasised that the symptoms of some illnesses are the same as some poisons, and vice versa. For example, not only vomiting and diarrhoea but also abdominal pain, rapid breathing, convulsions and salivation, any of which will require a professional diagnosis as a matter of urgency.

Many cases of poisoning result from the careless use of Metaldehyde (slug killer) and Warfarin (rat poison), along with various weedkillers and chemicals used in the spraying of fruit trees. Some medicines intended for human use, for example paracetamol, can result in poisoning and should be not be administered to dogs. Always keep pills and tablets out of reach.

It is a safe rule to regard all garden trimmings as unsafe for animals, with the exception of vegetables, such as cabbages and turnips. Clippings from shrubs, especially from yews, rhododendrons, lupins, laurels and laburnums, are at their most toxic when they begin to wither and should never be discarded in a heap at the bottom of the garden.

When a poison is believed to have been taken by mouth, an emetic that can be safely used in an emergency is a strong solution of ordinary household salt. In a few minutes the dog will regurgitate its stomach contents and, once this has been accomplished, you should contact your vet.

Prostate gland problems

An enlarged prostate gland may be due to acute infection. The dog will be in pain and walk with an arched back, appearing stiff-legged. Depending upon where pressure from the enlarged gland is placed, the dog will either have difficulty passing urine or be troubled with incontinence. Treatment by drugs can be effective; otherwise the removal of the testicles will render the gland inactive and it will decrease in size.

Puppy head gland disease

Puppies can start with this disease as early as two to three weeks old and breeders should be vigilant for early signs of tiny pustular spots developing around the eyelids, lips and nose. Specific antibiotics should be administered as quickly as possible to prevent the disease spreading all over the face. If the condition is left untreated, the neck glands become swollen, and this is usually accompanied by a rise in temperature. Severe cases can lead to entropion (turning in of the eyelids), blockage of the tear ducts and a leathered appearance to the muzzle, caused by damaged hair follicles.

Road traffic accidents

Always be aware that an injured or frightened dog may bite and approach with it caution – even your own trusted Afghan could react out of character if panic-stricken and in pain. In an emergency, a makeshift muzzle can be fashioned from strips of cloth or a bandage, wrapped around the dogs nose, and crossed under the jaws, with the two ends tied at the back of the neck.

In the event of severe bleeding, apply a pressure bandage and seek professional help quickly. If broken bones or internal injuries are suspected and it is necessary that the dog be moved, lay it carefully on its side, slide a blanket underneath and transport it hammock-style to avoid further injury.

By law, all collisions involving a dog must be reported to the police. If the accident happens in an unfamiliar area at night, the local police should be able to direct you to their duty vet.

'Sticky Puppy'

A relatively recent condition, this is a term relating to the appearance and texture of the coat at birth. Whereas a normal puppy is born with a coat resembling that of a sea-lion, drying off to a beautiful shine, the coat of a 'sticky puppy' appears dull and dry at birth, with a tacky feel to its texture. Food and debris stick to the coat and the puppy never looks clean. The eyes take four to five days longer to open than normal, often accompanied by a dryness due to the absence of tear ducts. This being the case, it may be much kinder to put the puppy to sleep at birth, as there can be nothing more painful than it having to suffer sore, dry eyes for the rest of its life.

Whether this problem is hereditary (as was first thought) or auto-immune related (a later theory) is still a subject undergoing serious discussion. My personal view is that 'sticky puppies' should never, under any circumstances, be bred from, as they offer no contribution towards the betterment of the breed.

Stings (wasp and bee)

Stings are most noticeable when sited around the nose and lips, although more serious if in the mouth or throat. The face can swell to unrecognisable proportions within minutes and, if the dog experiences an allergic reaction or its condition deteriorates within the hour, veterinary advice and possibly antihistamine drugs will be required.

Bee stings should be removed either with your fingers or with tweezers, and the area swabbed with a solution of bicarbonate of soda and water. Wasp stings should be bathed liberally with vinegar.

Thyroid (underactive)

Caused by an insufficiency of thyroxin (which slows down the rate of metabolism), the thyroid gland can become underactive at any stage of your dog's life. Symptoms include lethargy, poor coat and a possible loss of appetite despite an increase in body weight. Diagnosis is by blood test and the condition can be controlled effectively.

Vomiting

Dogs eat grass from time to time as a self-administered medicine, usually to induce the vomiting up of something that is lying uncomfortably and not totally digested. The grass usually eaten is couch or twitch grass and, while young couch will be eaten for pleasure, it is the older, coarser leaves that are eaten as an emetic. Caution should be exercised when using weedkiller on grass in the garden, Paraquat being particularly dangerous.

Warts (pappillomas)

Single small warts are commonly found on the eyelids, lips, ears and paws as well as upon the general surface of the body. They usually grow very slowly and may be present for years without causing any pain or inconvenience. If they become unsightly or uncomfortable (usually only when growing on eyelids), arrange with your vet to have them removed.

Care of the older dog

Afghan Hounds have a lifespan of 12–15 years, although they usually begin to slow down around the age of 10, when greater attention to diet, exercise and health matters will be necessary. I know of many elderly Afghans who lead full and active lives, and feel they can be likened to some elderly people in that, for their own well-being, they occasionally need a little encouragement to leave the comfort of the home and take exercise.

Looking back over the years, you will remember how quickly the puppy stage passed as your dog progressed into a gawky junior, and recall how much you enjoyed its clowning companionship and free spirit. Then, between the ages of two and four, came the lively adolescent who had discovered sex and wanted to become leader of the pack. At four years old your hound was fully developed, both mentally and physically, having earned and established its position in the household – and then suddenly it was seven years old, approaching middle age and eligible to compete in the veteran classes at shows. Where did the time go?

Ch Ifmaraf Go-Man-Go winning Best Veteran at eleven-and-a-half.

Caring for an elderly Afghan is something very special and, if you have been particularly close, you will be aware of all the small changes taking place as your friend slowly winds down. Its physical appearance gradually alters. Muzzle hairs begin to turn grey and the eyes take on an opaque haze due to changes in the lens. Hearing tends to be less clear although, to be fair, the true Afghan is now genuinely experiencing something that has been 'functional' for most of its life – rattling the biscuit tin will establish the true extent of the problem!

Your hound's normal loud bark now becomes a half-hearted, somewhat gruff affair, and the blood-curdling howl that drove you mad when it was young is merely now a whisper. Bad breath can also become a problem, which can be avoided if tartar is not allowed to build up on the surface of the teeth.

Exercise is essential to keep ageing joints supple and aid circulation, but your hound may not be up to walking as far as in the past. When circumstances allow, let it off the lead to investigate sounds and sights at its own pace. With age, Afghans become more reliable, so you will hopefully find it easier to catch. At all costs, don't leave your dog to sleep all day as this will soon make it lose all interest in life; even accompanying you on a short walk or drive to the shops will add variety to the day.

As dogs become older, their energy requirements decline, and some dogs put on too much weight. A balanced diet should be maintained, but bear in mind that fewer calories will be required and adjust the diet accordingly. My own dogs love food, especially the oldies, who really look forward to their meals. Rather than reduce the amount of food given, I prefer to feed them a balanced light diet twice daily, which not only gives them something to look forward to but also aids digestion.

On the other hand, some Afghans lose weight as they get older and become so thin and bony as to appear a cause for concern. Having ascertained that they are not experiencing failing health, you will find them as fit as the next, eating well and having an excellent quality of life. However, be aware that, with less fat, this type of dog feels the cold more quickly than its well-covered counterpart and will benefit from wearing an old jumper or body jacket when being exercised in cold weather.

Continue to keep the coat tidy, although you may now wish to trim the length with scissors to around 5–10cm (2–4in). Regular brushing is still important, as this will stimulate circulation and alert you to any lumps and bumps that may appear on the skin. If you give your dog a bath, keep it warm until it is completely dry.

As the dog gets older, rising from its bed will take longer, and some dogs begin to lose the use of their hind legs, going *down on their hocks* as the muscles waste away. This is particularly distressing to the dog who has been fit all its life and still has an active mind; getting around proves very frustrating. Arthritis is another extremely painful condition more commonly seen in older animals and it may help weakening joints and muscles to cope better if the dog is not overweight.

The bladder may not be as strong as it used to be and the odd accident in the house is bound to happen, calling for tolerance on your part. All organs eventually deteriorate as a result of wear and tear, and diseases of the kidneys, liver or heart can all sadly lead to premature death. Pyometra (pus in the uterus) and mammary tumours are frequently seen in veteran bitches, whether they have been bred from or not, and can be successfully treated by the vet if discovered early. Indeed, all unexplained lumps should be viewed with suspicion and brought to the attention of the vet.

Whether you should introduce a youngster into your home as a companion for your elderly dog is a matter only you can decide. Your main consideration has to be the senior citizen's care and welfare and only you know your dog well enough to understand whether it would feel pushed out of your affections and resent the newcomer. A further consideration must be the state of its health and general activeness. It would be very unfair for it to be pestered by a boisterous new puppy if it was frail and sleeping most of the day.

Ch Barnesmore Imperial Wizard aged twelve-and-a-half.

A different viewpoint, however, is that introducing a youngster to an older hound can have a rejuvenating effect, with the older one exerting a controlling influence over the younger and showing it the ropes, so to speak. Some owners hope that forming a relationship with their new puppy will give them comfort and help them cope better when the time comes to say good-bye to their oldie.

At the end of the day, it is well to remember that dogs are social animals who maintain a rigid pack structure. My personal opinion is that an older dog deserves a little peace and respect in its twilight years, without having the additional stress of defending its role as pack leader.

Saying good-bye

The bond between Afghan and owner strengthens as the years go by and the prospect of ever being parted is unthinkable. We all hope that our dogs will slip peacefully away in their sleep; in the comfort of their own homes, but unfortunately it rarely happens that way. In illness, Afghans are fighters who cling to life until the bitter end. All too often we find ourselves faced with the agonising decision of saving them from further pain and suffering. Throughout their lives we have made decisions based on their well-being and longevity – how on earth can we now make the decision to end it? Our vets will help by giving advice and support, but it is not up to them to make the decision for us.

Inevitably, there comes a time when your dog is experiencing such a poor quality of life that it is selfish to prolong its suffering any longer. If it is terminally ill, cannot stand on it own, is in pain, is rejecting food when it once had a healthy appetite, has trouble going to the toilet or is incontinent, then you must have the strength to do what you know is for the best. Making the decision to have your old friend painlessly put to sleep is the last service of kindness that you can perform.

My own vet will pay a house call on such an occasion but, if you do have to visit the practice, be sure to make an appointment at a time known to be quiet, say at the end of surgery. There is nothing to fear; the vet will give an injection into the forearm and, as it enters the bloodstream, the dog will rapidly lose consciousness and stop breathing almost immediately. It is a very peaceful end.

An important part of coming to terms with your loss is having the opportunity to say good-bye. This may be from holding and talking to your dog whilst the vet is putting it to sleep, or it may take the form of scattering its ashes in a favourite place, or maybe planting something in memory. I gain great comfort from having reminders of my oldies around the house, by way of paintings and photographs.

We all react differently to losing a dog, and the final task of laying your dog to rest should be carried out in a manner that is comforting and acceptable to you. If you have the space you may wish to bury your dog at home; alternatively, many pet cemeteries will arrange for cremation and return the ashes in a small wooden casket, which is my preferred method. My dog is then back home, and I am content knowing that it has returned home, where it belongs.

Making provision in your will

Because the life-span of an Afghan is much shorter than that of a human, we tend to overlook the possibility that our dog may be left alone in the event of our premature death. Unfortunately, tragedies can occur at any stage in our lives and, by giving some thought to their future welfare, we are acting responsibly. If you have relatives or close friends whom you would trust to honour your wishes, then by all means discuss the matter with them. Alternatively, you may wish to make a more formal provision to safeguard your pets' welfare, in your will. This being the case, you should instruct your solicitor that, in the event of your death, an immediate financial payment must be made available to provide for their upkeep. This will prevent the new carer having to wait for the final winding-up of your estate before any funds can be released. Wills can be altered at any time and keeping them up-to-date is a simple matter.

appendix a
Kennel Club Registrations

1945–1997

1945	1946	1947	1948	1949	1950	1951	1952	1953	1954	1955
143	274	278	262	273	278	323	217	220	205	280

1956	1957	1958	1959	1960	1961	1962	1963	1964	1965	1966
247	237	257	250	273	335	450	388	537	576	774

1967	1968	1969	1970	1971	1972	1973	1974	1975	1976	1977
1096	1486	2194	2853	3606	4379	4820	4890	3867	1836	1106

1978	1979	1980	1981	1982	1983	1984	1985	1986	1987	1988
1830	2098	1606	1187	933	763	911	643	665	645	504

1989	1990	1991	1992	1993	1994	1995	1996	1997
538	429	460	400	370	419	303	457	356

appendix b

Afghan Hound Champions

Name	Sex	DOB	Sire	Dam	Breeder	Owner
1927						
Buckmal	d	14.2.22	Ooty	Pushum	Maj G Bell-Murray	Miss J C Manson
Sirdar of Ghazni	d	?.6.23	unknown	unknown	An Afghan Shikari	Mrs M Amps
Ranee	b	?.3.19	Rajah	Begum	Maj G Bell-Murray	Miss J C Manson
1928						
Taj Mahip of Kaf	d	17.4.24	Khym	Daghai	Maj G Bell-Murray	Mrs J Barton
1929						
Shadi	b	27.7.24	Baluch	Oolu	Maj G Bell-Murray	Mrs A B Willans
Asri Havid of Ghazni	d	4.3.27	Ch Sirdar of Ghazni	Roshni of Ghazni	Mrs M Amps	Mrs P Robson
1930						
Alfreda	b	3.9.26	Shahzada	Afroz	H Duffy	Miss A Simmons
1931						
Sirfreda	b	26.1.28	Ch Sirdar of Ghazni	Ch Alfreda	Miss A Simmons	Mrs E M Squibb
Nush-ki of Ruritania	b	17.9.27	Ch Sirdar of Ghazni	Tarza	Mrs M B Cooper	Miss A Doxford
Ashna of Ghazni	d	18.8.29	Ch Sirdar of Ghazni	Shireen of Ghazni	Mrs M Amps	T G Chamberlain & T H Watt
Marika of Baberbagh	b	23.4.28	Ch Sirdar of Ghazni	Sada of Ghazni	Mrs G S Cannan	Mrs L Prude
1932						
Garrymhor Souriya	b	13.7.31	Ch Ashna of Ghazni	Ch Alfreda	Miss A Simmons	Mrs O Couper
Badshah of Ainsdart	d	28.5.30	Ch Sirdar of Ghazni	Ku-Mari of Kaf	Mrs Morris-Jones	Mrs M Wood
1933						
Maharani of Cheltside	b	29.8.32	Ch Raj	Ch Marika of Baberbagh	Mrs L Prude	Breeder
Yakub Khan of Geufron	d	2.3.30	Omar of Geufron	Zabana of Kaf	Mrs E E Drinkwater	Miss A Doxford
Mahaprajapati of Geufron	b	16.4.31	Omar of Geufron	Zabana of Kaf	Mrs E E Drinkwater	Breeder

Name	Sex	DOB	Sire	Dam	Breeder	Owner
1934						
Westmill Tamasar	d	28.1.32	Int Ch Badshah of Ainsdart	Ranee of Geufron	Mrs M Wood	Breeder
Raj	d	28.6.30	Kymn	Ch Sirfreda	Mrs E M Squibb	Mrs N Coombes
Westmill Ben Havid	d	26.1.31	Ch Asri Havid of Ghazni	Elsa of Ghazni	Mrs M Wood	Breeder
Agha Lala of Geufron	d	16.4.31	Omar of Geufron	Zabana of Kaf	Mrs E E Drinkwater	Breeder
1935						
Zandi of Enriallic	b	26.12.32	Rupee	Souriya of Enriallic	D I Cronin	Breeder
Chankidar	b	17.1.33	Ch Firdausi of Geufron	Safiya	Mrs E Carlton	Breeder
Westmill Karabagh	b	6.6.33	Kymn	Ranee of Geufron	Mrs M Wood	Mrs S Rhodes
1936						
Chota Sahib	d	17.1.33	Ch Firdausi of Geufron	Safiya	Mrs E Carlton	Mrs A Bhanubandh
Westmill Natanz	b	9.7.34	Mukhlis Saramad	Illima of Geufron	E P Holford	Mrs M Wood
Firdausi of Geufron	d	16.4.31	Omar of Geufron	Zabana of Kaf	Mrs E E Drinkwater	Breeder
1937						
Azura Goldstar	b	1.10.35	Int Ch Chota Sahib	Madirekshana of Geufron	Mr & Mrs Bhanubandh	Mrs F E Peake
Wanawallari of Geufron	b	28..6.34	Omar of Geufron	Sheba of Wyke	Mrs E E Drinkwater	Mrs H Gibson
Shah Shuja of Geufron	d	16.4.31	Omar of Geufron	Zabana of Kaf	Mrs E E Drinkwater	Dr B Porter
Kisagotami of Geufron	b	21.3.33	Lakki Marwat	Sita of Geufron	Mrs E E Drinkwater	Breeder
Garrymhor Faiz-Bu-Hassid	d	23.3.35	Ardmor Anthony	Ch Garrymhor Souriya	Mrs O M Couper	Mrs M Sharpe
1938						
Taj Akbar of Chaman	d	24.4.36	Kulli Khan of Kuranda	Safiya	Mrs M Sharpe	Breeder
Malati of Geufron	b	11.5.36	Omar of Geufron	Sheba of Wyke	Mrs E E Drinkwater	Mrs A Bhanubandh
Kinsuka of Geufron	b	25.9.34	Omar of Geufron	Ch Sirfreda	Mrs E E Drinkwater	Mrs S Rhodes
Westmill Bayezid Ansari	d	25.4.32	Int Ch Badshah of Ainsdart	Elsa of Ghazni	Mrs M Wood	Miss F G Ide
1939						
Westmill Kariza	b	14.10.33	Ch Westmill Ben Havid	Westmill Matta	Mrs M Wood	Breeder
Westmill Purdil Khan	d	6.2.35	Westmill Azadulla	Westmill Matta	Mrs M Wood	Breeder
Faxhill Bathsheba	b	16.9.37	Faxhill Dost Hammad	Faxhill Kalana	B F Hall	Mrs S Rhodes
1947						
Ravelly Patrols Ali Bey	d	3.6.43	Turkuman Dammar Pine Tree	Patrols Creme Chenille	Mrs R Y Harrison	R A Floyd
Ajawaan Chita Mia	b	16.12.45	Nosnikta's Nissim Tango	Silvercaul Sa-De-Miranda	Mrs King	Mrs S Rhodes
1948						
Vendas Tash Down	d	6.8.39	Tash Gariff of Pushtikuh	Fay Down	Mrs V J Smith	Mrs M O'Toole
Mitzou of Acklam	b	25.5.39	Ch Westmill Ben Havid	Ch Wanawalleri of Geufron	Mrs H Gibson	Breeder
Rajah Bey of Ravelly	d	3.10.45	Ch Ravelly Patrols Ali Bey	Buko of Bletchingley	Mrs E D Clarke	Mr R A Floyd

Name	Sex	DOB	Sire	Dam	Breeder	Owner
Taj of Chaman	d	27.3.39	Ch Taj Akbar of Chaman	Thofar	Mrs M Sharpe	Breeder
Netheroyd Turkuman Camelthomb	b	18.9.43	Turkuman Pomegranate	Golden Ranee	Mrs J V Polson	Mr & Mrs E Abson
1949						
Ajawaan Ranee Tamba	b	17.1.47	Azad of Chaman	Silvercaul Sa-De-Miranda	Mrs King	Mrs S Rhodes
Bletchingley Zara	b	28.4.47	Ch Bletchingley Tajomeer	Ravelly Badrea	Mrs F C Riley	Breeder
Bletchingley Tajomeer	d	21.6.45	Taj Ameer of Chaman	Shiba of Chaman	Mrs F C Riley	Breeder
1950						
Patrols Ali Khan	d	19.7.44	Turkuman Dammar Pine Tree	Patrols Creme Chenille	Mr Kent	Mrs R Y Harrison
Netheroyd Alibaba	d	10.11.47	Netheroyd Ansari	Netheroyd Camelthorn	Mr & Mrs E Abson	Breeders
Marika of Three Streams	b	29.7.48	Zhuba of Chaman	Watmor Amber	J H Parker	Breeder
1951						
Netheroyd Red Eagle	d	24.11.48	Ch Bletchingley Tajomeer	Ch Netheroyd Turkuman Camelthorn	Mr & Mrs E Abson	Breeders
Mohamed Ali of Acklam	d	19.5.46	Turkuman Dammar Pine Tree	Ch Mitzou of Acklam	Mrs H Gibson	Breeder
Moonbeam of Khorrassan	d	1.8.47	Kassim of Khorrassan	Water Lily of Khorrassan	Miss E Snelling	Breeder
Cleopatra of Khorrassan	b	9.5.50	Ch Moonbeam of Khorrassan	Sunrise of Khorrassan	Miss E Snelling	Breeder
Portrait of Khorrassan	b	9.6.47	Chota Nissim of Ringbank	Natara of Westover	Miss E Snelling	Breeder
Bletchingley Tribesman	d	13.9.48	Ch Bletchingley Tajomeer	Ravelly Badrea	Mrs F C Riley	Breeder
Taj Abu of Chaman	d	12.8.46	Taj Ameer of Chaman	Flavia of Chaman	Mrs M Sharpe	Breeder
Kyronisha el Kabul	b	25.8.47	Kuranda Turkuman Opium Poppy	Zara el Kabul	Dr B Porter	Breeder
1952						
Carloway Sharmain of Virendale	b	30.5.50	Jalalabad Barwala of Carloway	Shireen of Kenavon	Miss I Trevitt	Mrs S Devitt
Taj Avia of Chaman	b	21.6.45	Taj Ameer of Chaman	Flavia of Chaman	Mrs M Sharpe	Breeder
Tanza of Acklam	b	19.5.46	Turkuman Dammar Pine Tree	Ch Mitzou of Acklam	Mrs H Gibson	Breeder
1953						
Jabari Tango	d	5.3.50	Ch Netheroyd Alibaba	Ajawaan Ranee Sabina	K F Parrat	J F Parrat
Circe of Khorrassan	b	3.6.51	Ch Moonbeam of Khorrassan	Sunrise of Khorrassan	Miss E Snelling	Breeder
Bletchingley El Basrah of Ravelly	d	28.4.47	Ch Bletchingley Tajomeer	Ravelly Badrea	Mrs F C Riley	R A Floyd
Taj Amrit of Chaman	d	4.5.48	Int Ch Taj of Chaman	Ch Taj Avia of Chaman	Mrs M Sharpe	Breeder
1954						
Yussef of Carloway	d	28.6.52	Zog of Carloway	Dana Khan of Carloway	Mrs S Devitt	Breeder
Bletchingley Hillsman	d	27.6.51	Jalalabad Barwala of Carloway	Ch Bletchingley Zara	Mrs F C Riley	Breeder
Taj Aleh of Chaman	d	20.3.51	Ch Mohamed Ali of Acklam	Taj Alfreda of Chaman	Mrs M Sharpe	Breeder
Taj Arab of Chaman	b	20.3.51	Ch Mohamed Ali of Acklam	Taj Alfreda of Chaman	Mrs M Sharpe	Breeder

Name	Sex	DOB	Sire	Dam	Breeder	Owner
Bletchingley Bedra el Kabul	b	15.5.53	Ch Bletchingley Hillsman	Bletchingley Badrea	Mrs F C Riley	Dr B Porter
Kumari of Three Streams	b	4.3.50	Ben Havid of Three Streams	Zulieka of Khorrassan	J H Parker	Mrs W Leest
1955						
Bletchingley Tolo-Na-Kha	b	1.6.50	Ch Bletchingley Tribesman	Shurakhan of Barukhzy	Mrs F C Riley	Mrs B M Francks
Marjanah of Khorrassan	b	21.12.51	Ch Moonbeam of Khorrassan	Taj Aziz of Chaman	Miss E Snelling	Breeder
Taj Asum of Chaman	d	13.10.52	Ch Taj Aleh of Chaman	Ch Taj Avia of Chaman	Mrs M Sharpe	Breeder
1956						
Baluch Ranee Ashraf	b	14.2.54	Bletchingley Barzara of Carloway	Havmora's Wild Rose	Mrs McGregor-Cheers	Breeder
Bahia of Khorrassan	b	28.5.52	Sirdar of Khorrassan	Sunrise of Khorrassan	Miss E Snelling	Mrs E Mitchell
Achilles of Khorrassan	d	3.6.51	Ch Moonbeam of Khorrassan	Sunrise of Khorrassan	Miss E Snelling	Breeder
Tijah of Carloway	b	10.10.54	Ch Yussef of Carloway	Ch Carloway Sharmain of Virendale	Mrs S Devitt	Breeder
Horningsea Majid	d	31.5.54	Horningsea Turridu	Ch Marika of Three Streams	Mrs M M Dods	Breeder
1957						
Taj Akmed of Chaman	d	1.5.55	Ch Mohamed Ali of Acklam	Ch Taj Arab of Chaman	Mrs M Sharpe	Breeder
Bletchingley Talookdar	d	13.5.53	Ch Bletchingley Hillsman	Stonesby Asmara of Khorrassan	Mrs F C Riley	Breeder
Saleh Bey of Khorrassan	d	7.4.54	Montezuma of Khorrassan	Ajamais Amber of Menthe	Mrs Craik	Miss E Snelling
Fantasia of Carloway	b	14.2.54	Bletchingley Barzara of Carloway	Havmora's Wild Rose	Mrs McGregor-Cheers	Miss H Barnes
1958						
Enchantress of Tarjih	b	29.11.55	Ch Yussef of Carloway	Bletchingley Aurora	Miss P Leyder	Mrs W Gent
Khymn of Carloway	d	29.11.55	Ch Yussef of Carloway	Bletchingley Aurora	Miss P Leyder	Mrs S Devitt
Bletchingley Statesman	d	15.11.54	Ch Bletchingley Talookdar	Ch Bletchingley Zara	Mrs F C Riley	Breeder
Wild Iris of Khorrassan	b	7.2.55	Montezuma of Khorrassan	Zenella	Miss Lamphill	Miss E Snelling
Mir Kush Farida	b	10.9.54	Montezuma of Khorrassan	Safia of Three Streams	Mrs P Wills	Breeder
1959						
Nanda Devi of Khorrassan	b	13.11.54	Ch Moonbeam of Khorrassan	Ch Portrait of Khorrassan	Miss E Snelling	Breeder
Khanabad Azravi of Vishnu	d	27.3.56	Ch Horningsea Majid	Khanabad Azrar	Miss E M Niblock	Mr & Mrs C H Harrisson
Khanabad Aztrajid	b	27.3.56	Ch Horningsea Majid	Khanabad Azrar	Miss E M Niblock	Breeder
Krishna of Barbourne	d	18.11.52	Zabu of Barbourne	Kishkinda of Kabul	Mrs O'Sullivan	Mrs M F Masters
Pasha of Carloway	d	21.9.56	Ch Yussef of Carloway	Shiba of Carloway	Mrs S Devitt	Breeder
Muphytt of Khorrassan	b	29.11.55	Bletchingley Barzara of Carloway	Vashti of Carloway	Mrs S Devitt	Breeder
Yashmak of Khorrassan	b	3.12.57	Ch Saleh Bey of Khorrassan	Ch Cleopatra of Khorrassan	Miss E Snelling	Breeder

Name	Sex	DOB	Sire	Dam	Breeder	Owner
Rifka's Tarquin of Carloway	d	3.10.54	Ch Yussef of Carloway	Ch Carloway Sharmain of Virendale	Mrs S Devitt	Mrs C Race
1960						
Horningsea Sheer Khan	d	20.5.58	Ch Horningsea Majid	Tilluh of Carloway	Mrs M M Dods	Breeder
Taj Althea of Chaman	b	18.2.57	Ch Taj Amrit of Chaman	Taj Abida of Chaman	Mrs M Sharpe	Breeder
Jil of Carloway	b	4.5.58	Watsatari of Carloway	Undine of Carloway	Mrs S Devitt	Breeder
Mandodari of Carloway	b	30.3.57	Ch Yussef of Carloway	Pari Banu Bin Sreebas	Mrs S Devitt	Breeder
Netheroyd Elibaba	d	22.6.58	Ch Achilles of Khorrassan	Yasmin of Shibakhan	Mrs Stainton	Mrs I M Morton
Bletchingley Houndsman	d	12.5.57	Ch Bletchingley Hillsman	Bletchingley Shirin	Mrs F C Riley	Breeder
1961						
Tranwells Yana of Carloway	b	8.9.56	Ch Horningsea Majid	Tilluh of Carloway	Mrs M M Dods	Mrs G K Jackson
Horningsea Khanabad Suvaraj	d	16.9.57	Am Ch Horningsea Salim Dar	Khanabad Azrar	Miss E M Niblock	Mrs M M Dods
Bletchingley Saluna	b	2.1.58	Ch Bletchingley Talookdar	Bletchingley Yana	Mrs F C Riley	Breeder
Bletchingley Zelda	b	18.3.60	Ch Bletchingley Hillsman	Bletchingley Lana	Mrs F C Riley	Breeder
1962						
Shere Khan of Tarjih	d	29.8.57	Tajammul of Tarjih	Bletchingley Tara of Tarjih	Miss P Leyder	Miss M Willis
Conygar Janze of Carloway	d	15.5.56	Ch Yussef of Carloway	Conygar Gabel	Miss D Venn	Mrs D Bowdler-Townsend
Jinga of Carloway	b	4.5.58	Watsatari of Carloway	Undine of Carloway	Mrs S Devitt	Breeder
Badakshan Rani	b	3.8.58	Ch Khanabad Azravi of Vishnu	Rahane of Ladysmyle	Mrs A Adams	Breeder
Kubla Khan el Kabul	d	17.1.57	Khanabad Abdul Hamzavi	Ch Bletchingley Bedra el Kabul	Dr B Porter	Breeder
1963						
Waliwog of Carloway	d	21.3.61	Ch Horningsea Sheer Khan	Ilexis of Carloway	Mrs S Devitt	Breeder
Zaza of Khorrassan	b	10.3.60	Rajput of Khorrassan	Ruanda of Khorrassan	Miss E Snelling	D McCarthy
Jali of Vishnu	d	7.4.59	Ch Khanabad Azravi of Vishnu	Woodland Lassie	Mrs R E Hughes	Mrs M Harrisson
Barbille Houri of Carloway	b	15.10.58	Ch Conygar Janze of Carloway	Horningsea Samsie	Mrs S Devitt & Mrs M M Dods	Mrs D Hall
1964						
Empress of Carloway	b	11.4.60	Ch Pasha of Carloway	Alida of Khyber	Mrs D Bowdler-Townsend	Mrs W Gent
Mazari of Carloway	d	15.5.62	Ch Pasha of Carloway	Crown Crest Zardeeka	Mrs S Devitt	Breeder
Bondor Serenade	b	18.10.62	Ch Wazir of Desertaire	Yazeena of Carloway	A Brooks & E Swallow	Breeders
Kismati Khan of Tarril	d	4.7.62	Ch Wazir of Desertaire	Chandi B'Har of Tarril	Mrs J Pollock	Breeder
Kalbikhan Ravi	d	1.10.61	Ch Kalbikhan Ali Bey of Carloway	Woodland Lassie	Mrs R E Hughes	Breeder
Horningsea Mitanni	d	21.10.61	Ch Horningsea Sheer Khan	Horningsea Marue	Mrs M M Dods	Mrs B Clark

Name	Sex	DOB	Sire	Dam	Breeder	Owner
1965						
Pina of Carloway	b	8.2.62	Anzari of Takabbor	Narriman of Carloway	Mrs F Etheridge	B & Miss K Ross
Ueda of Carloway	b	1.7.61	Watsatari of Carloway	Horningsea Samsie	Mrs B Crosby	Mrs E A Andrews
Alphonse of Khyber	d	4.6.57	Ch Yussef of Carloway	Hanuman Takrityah	D V Walmsley	Breeder
Patchouli Khanabad Surasu	b	16.9.57	Am Ch Horningsea Salim Dar	Khanabad Azrar	Miss E M Niblock	Mrs J Purdue
Shemsuki Deva Raya	d	21.4.62	Ch Horningsea Sheer Khan	Riffari of Davlen	Mrs S Young	Mrs S Efford
Aryana Shalym	d	7.8.61	Ch Horningsea Khanabad Suvaraj	Sharima of Davlen	Mr & Mrs C A Robbins	Rev D Ford & Miss H Barnes
Tara of Pooghan	b	31.12.61	Ch Pasha of Carloway	Gina of Anzani	D McCarthy	Breeder
1966						
Bondor Lezah	b	20.8.61	Ch Pasha of Carloway	Bletchingley Zuleika	A Brooks & E Swallow	Breeders
Chandi Bibi of Kushra	b	27.8.59	Subadar Karim Khan	Sha Sha of Fu-Tu-Yu	Mrs H Morgan	Mrs H Morgan & A Hedges
Takabbor Tiaga	d	8.3.64	Horningsea Kublai Khan	Ilexis of Carloway	Mrs F Etheridge	Rev D Ford & Miss H Barnes
Conygar Kanika	b	25.4.59	Chitral Kirkuk	Conygar Judana	Miss D Venn	Mrs V Gilligan
Kalbikhan Ali Bey of Carloway	d	5.6.60	Ch Yussef of Carloway	Ch Muphytt of Carloway	Mrs S Devitt	Mrs R E Hughes
Horningsea Mustaph Ata	d	30.11.63	Horningsea Sagittarius	Horningsea Marue	Mrs M M Dods	Breeder
1967						
Rifka's Musqat D'Rar	b	28.4.65	Ch Horningsea Khanabad Suvaraj	Rifka's Rajena of Carloway	Mrs C Race	Breeder
Rifka's Tabaq D'Rar	d	28.4.65	Ch Horningsea Khanabad Suvaraj	Rifka's Rajena of Carloway	Mrs C Race	Breeder
Takabbor Golden Eagle	d	9.4.62	Chandra of Takabbor	Ilexis of Carloway	Mrs S Devitt	Mrs F Etheridge
Rifka's Moti of Carloway	b	15.5.62	Ch Pasha of Carloway	Crown Crest Zardeeka	Mrs S Devitt	Mrs C Race
Horningsea Kayacci	b	30.11.64	Horningsea Sagittarius	Khorissa of Carloway	Mrs M M Dods	Breeder
1968						
Horningsea Tiger's Eye	d	29.8.62	Ajman Branwen Kandahar	Horningsea Sardi	Mrs M M Dods	Breeder
Wazir of Desertaire	d	29.7.59	Am Ch Crown Crest Mr Universe	Am Ch Zar-Kari of Shamalan	Mr & Mrs J Buchanan	L Bridges
Kalbikhan Kara	b	10.7.65	Ch Kalbikhan Ali Bey of Carloway	Ch Pina of Carloway	Mrs R E Hughes	Mr & Mrs F J Severn
Safiya of Sacheverell	b	11.6.65	Ch Horningsea Sheer Khan	Zena of Sacheverell	Miss M J C Booth	Breeder
1969						
Ranjitsinhji of Jagai	d	17.4.65	Ch Waliwog of Carloway	Sahri of Amudarya	Mrs D M Gie	Mrs J Holden
Moonraker of Moonswift	d	23.11.63	Ch Horningsea Sheer Khan	Indira of Carloway	Mrs D Bowdler-Townsend	Breeder

Name	Sex	DOB	Sire	Dam	Breeder	Owner
Ophira of Davlen	b	12.8.65	Ch Aryana Shalym	Takabbor Shiraz	Rev D Ford & Miss H Barnes	Mrs G E Woolley
Myhorlyns Maharanee of Davlen	b	12.7.65	Ch Aryana Shalym	Myhorlyns Tullah of Davlen	Mrs Brennan	Mrs E S Montgomery
1970						
Bondor Kumari Khanum	b	10.5.66	Ch Moonraker of Moonswift	Ch Bondor Serenade	A Brooks & E Swallow	Mr & Mrs R G Elmore
Tzara of Pooghan	b	28.8.67	Ashley of Pooghan	Arafekh of Pooghan	D McCarthy	Breeder
Bondor Azim Khan	d	10.5.66	Ch Moonraker of Moonswift	Ch Bondor Serenade	A Brooks & E Swallow	Mrs D & Miss L Sams
Xzari of Carloway	b	5.5.65	Ch Waliwog of Carloway	Yazmin of Carloway	Mrs D Bowdler-Townsend	R M Allison
The Caliph	d	23.3.64	Miltonsay Alpine Merlin	Red Sheba	Mr & Miss Sutton	Mr & Mrs F J Severn
Khonistan El Cid	d	4.9.65	Sabu Barakzai of Fartonia	Khonistan Weirwater Azur	Miss D Heaton	W Walker, R Wilson & Mrs A Faith
Bondor Dera Ghazi Khan	d	10.5.66	Ch Moonraker of Moonswift	Ch Bondor Serenade	A Brooks & E Swallow	Mr & Mrs P Harris
Hajubah of Davlen	d	15.1.67	Ch Takabbor Tiaga	Khandi B'Har of Tarril	Rev D Ford & Miss H Barnes	Breeders
Rasta of Jagai	b	17.4.65	Ch Waliwog of Carloway	Sahri of Amudarya	Mrs D M Gie	Breeder
Miyasht Empress	b	17.12.66	Horningsea Aramis	Ch Ueda of Carloway	Mrs E A Andrews	Mrs A Doe
1971						
Sherrendale Brandy	d	24.10.67	Khanabad Wadi Mango	Horningsea Sindah	Mrs L J Milligan	Breeder & A J Hupka
Miyasht Chare Toqmar	b	11.11.64	Ch Horningsea Tiger's Eye	Miyasht Hebe of Carloway	Mrs E A Andrews	Mrs M Barlow & F S Lowbridge
Horningsea Tiger Doll	b	7.8.68	Ch Horningsea Tiger's Eye	Ch Horningsea Kayacci	Mrs M M Dods	Breeder
Khinjan Lorcah	d	7.4.67	Khinjan Banzai	Horningsea Lorabellah	Mrs A Hattrell	Breeder
Vishnu Sitara of Jagai	b	28.6.68	Ch Kismati Khan of Tarril	Ch Begum Kanda of Jagai	Mrs D M Gie	Mr & Mrs C H Harrisson
Bondor Sayonara of Fiazabad	b	2.1.69	Ch Horningsea Tiger's Eye	Bondor Cinnamon	A Brooks & E Swallow	J Edmonds
Begum Kanda of Jagai	b	3.2.66	Ch Pasha of Carloway	Kuzanda van de Emelenburg of Jagai	Mrs D M Gie	Breeder
1972						
Mustard Seed of Davlen	b	13.8.68	Tartu of Davlen	Khandi B'Har of Tarril	Rev D Ford & Miss H Barnes	M Docherty

Name	Sex	DOB	Sire	Dam	Breeder	Owner
Crown Crest Samarra	d	8.7.68	Hakim of Kethligarne	Gigi of Veschambre	Miss B Stone	Mrs I J Dyke
Dame Johanne of Anzani	b	3.3.67	Anzani Musketeer of Moonswift	Gigi of Anzani	Mrs B Appleton & E Walton	Mrs B Appleton & Mrs Ritchie
Khinjan Black Orchid	b	13.7.69	Ch Khinjan Lorcah	Rifka's Barbary Coast	Miss Jutsum	Mrs A Hattrell
Khanabad Peach Blossom	b	3.10.69	Khanabad Azure Azami	Khanabad Jaginda Jid	Miss E M Niblock	Mrs G D North
Koolaba Horningsea Eboni Earl	d	1.10.69	Horningsea Surivor	Ch Horningsea Kayacci	Mrs M M Dods	Mr & Mrs J T R Taylor
Khonistan Calypso	b	9.5.69	Khonistan Bondor Kohendil Khan	Zarakhan Shamoura	Mrs P Corbett	W Walker & R Wilson
Alyshan Hassan Shabbah	d	24.3.69	Ch Khinjan Lorcah	Alyshan Rosamund	Miss C Walkden	Breeder
Hanif Khan of Tarrif	d	30.8.65	Ch Kismati Khan of Tarril	Midj of Carloway	Mr & Mrs S J Pollock	Breeders
Shireena B'Har of Tarril	b	6.5.67	Ch Takabbor Tiaga	Shuja B'Har of Tarril	Mr & Mrs S J Pollock	Breeders
Netheroyd Regal John	d	24.5.68	Ormerod Bayezid of Fartonia	Netheroyd Ajman Shaduh	Mrs I M Morton	E Morton
1973						
Bondor Barbarella	b	2.1.69	Ch Horningsea Tiger's Eye	Bondor Cinnamon	A Brooks & E Swallow	Mrs S Rhodes
Top Peg of Daville	b	4.8.70	Tartu of Davlen	Tampa Bay of Davlen	M Docherty	Mr & Mrs A Macdonald
Saringa's Abra Cadabra	d	5.6.70	Ch Horningsea Tiger's Eye	Rifka's Kazinga	Miss J Dove	Breeder
Khanabad White Warrior	d	12.12.68	Khanabad Branwen Sheen Khalifa	Isfahan Micha of Torpaz	Miss E M Niblock	Breeder
Koolaba Tajma Zai	b	10.12.70	Ch Horningsea Tiger's Eye	Koolaba Mazai	Mrs B Taylor	Breeder
Khanabad Blue Pearl	b	17.2.67	Khanabad Branwen Sheen Khurram	Isfahan Micha of Torpaz	Miss E M Niblock	Miss M Baster & Breeder
Retaog's Sato	d	22.9.68	Horningsea Kabundi Bhai	Retaog Thillana	J H Goater	Mr & Mrs R C Biagioni
Jahana of Hazuki	b	22.4.69	Tajeer Khan of Tarril	Suki of Rabiouw Wahad	Mrs H Kinread	Breeder
Marquis of Anzani	d	3.3.67	Anzani Musketeer of Moonswift	Gigi of Anzani	Mrs B Appleton & E Walton	Mrs B Appleton
Bletchingley Marguerite	b	24.5.70	Bletchingley Patrolman	Bletchingley Krista	Mrs F C Riley	Mrs M Fairburn
1974						
Ghuura Khan of Tarril	d	22.9.68	Tajeer Khan of Tarril	Astura B'Har of Tarril	Mr & Mrs C Scope	Mr & Mrs S J Pollock
Masquerade of Moonswift	d	21.7.67	Ch Horningsea Khanabad Suvaraj	Mimosa of Moonswift	Mrs D Bowdler-Townsend	Mrs C V Winstone
Alyshan Michele	b	18.3.70	Ch Ranjitsinhji of Jagai	Alyshan Esmeralda	Miss C Walkden	Breeder
Sacheverell Zukwala	d	4.10.70	Ch Ghuura Khan of Tarril	Ch Safiya of Sacheverell	Miss M J C Booth	Breeder
Bamertag Zhivago	d	21.3.69	Khinjan Lancer	Goldcloud Azreefa	Mrs Raison	Mrs H W Hood

Name	Sex	DOB	Sire	Dam	Breeder	Owner
Khanabad Diablo of Whodeanie	d	21.6.69	Khanabad Branwen Sheen Khalifa	Khanabad Sayyid Tazi Salome	Miss E M Niblock	D J McCann
Horningsea Salome	b	29.3.69	Horningsea Silver Fox	Horningsea Bletchingley Shelagh	Mrs M M Dods	Mrs J Wright
Khinjan Sudi Shan	d	23.10.66	Horningsea Sagittarius	Shahmena of Shawville	Mrs P A Hattrell	Miss J Nicholls
Amudarya Khala	b	27.4.71	Bondor Moon Mist	Amudarya Mikhala of Moonswift	Mrs A Paton	Breeder
Amudarya The Pagan	d	10.9.69	Horningsea Aramis	Amudarya Mikhala of Moonswift	Mrs A Paton	Breeder
Chaman Taj Ayana	b	3.9.70	Maestro of Shirini	Taj Alanna of Chaman	Mrs M Sharpe	Breeder
Tarril's Azuur B'Har	b	24.4.71	Tajeer Khan of Tarril	Shastri B'Har of Tarril	Mr & Mrs S J Pollock	Mr & Mrs J Dryden-Bell
Saringa's Amira	b	5.6.70	Ch Horningsea Tiger's Eye	Rifka's Kazinga	Miss J Dove	Breeder
1975						
Vanathan Priam	d	21.3.70	Ch Khonistan El Cid	Putali of Whiteash	Mrs J Van Schaick	Dr G Hemmings
Khanlidar Zuzini	b	15.9.69	Mohamed Ali of Kushra	Shana Kuchi	Mrs B Morgan	W Walker & R Wilson
Alyshan Xtra Dandy	d	28.4.68	Reegan Washir	Princess of Zebedee	Mrs I Bastian	Mmes M & P Sexton
Xanaghan Tarquin	d	22.5.73	Xanaghan Sacha	Xanaghan Bah-Bah-Lu	Mrs N Thorpe & Miss M Turland	Breeders
Amudarya Phara	b	7.10.72	Ch Moonraker of Moonswift	Amudarya Phari	Mrs A Paton	Mrs C Buck
Shalmaneser's Ramesses	d	28.9.70	Ch Khonistan El Cid	Kaisi of Hazuki	Mrs J Kernaghan	Mr & Mrs W G Kernaghan
Mucmul-Gee of Jabigandal	d	7.7.67	Ashley of Pooghan	Tanya of Pooghan	Mrs J M Haag	Mr & Mrs K G Newitt
Khinjan Angelique of Sharazah	b	9.10.70	Ch Khinjan Lorcah	Khinjan Afrar	Mrs A Hattrell	Mr & Mrs D Arris
Taiwara Nazzari Chare	b	17.2.73	Ch Moonraker of Moonswift	Ch Miyasht Chare Toqmar	Mr & Mrs R Barlow	Breeders
Am Ch Huzzah Excelsis of Horningsea	d	1.7.68	Ch Horningsea Mustagh Ata	Red Rock Duhst	Mrs P Ide	Mrs M M Dods
Davlen Petite Etoile	b	26.5.71	Dahir of Davlen	Khandi B'Har of Tarril	Rev D Ford & Miss H Barnes	Mrs G Haywood
1976						
Khanabad Honeydew	b	6.9.70	Khanabad Azure Azami	Khanabad Jaginda Lu	Miss E M Niblock	Mrs G D North
Leaonora of Shamoon	b	22.9.71	Ch Bondor Azim Khan	Wantzala Black Velvet	Mmes Kimberley & Gurton	Mr & Mrs G Ellis
Zendushkas Dazravi	d	2.12.71	Ch Bondor Azim Khan	Zendushkas Dazla	Mrs N K Hitch	Mrs L Mawdsley
Kharisar Karibh Khan	d	16.5.73	Alyshan Omahr Pasha of Kharisar	Sharikhan Isarkari of Kharisar	Mr & Mrs P R Harcourt-Brown	Breeders & N & M Harcourt-Brown

Name	Sex	DOB	Sire	Dam	Breeder	Owner
Sundowner Fluorescent	b	21.10.72	Bondor Moon Mist	Kissakhani Fleurette	Mrs J E Day	Breeder
Lawkhan Kinkeesha of Khonistan	b	30.10.71	Ch Khinjan Lorcah	Torikhan Demelza	Mr Lawson	R Wilson & I Hodgson
Khivan Blue Korrianda	b	10.5.73	Khinjan Bangaruk	Khivan Mero-Bibi	Mrs B P Maling-Arnold	Breeder
Azrakhan Carah	b	26.6.72	Azrakhan Blue Jet	Khanabad Suhaili of Azrakhan	Mrs A MacQueen	R F Ellis
Saringa's Andante	b	5.6.70	Ch Horningsea Tiger's Eye	Rifka's Kazinga	Miss J Dove	Breeder
Moonswift Moonglade	d	15.12.72	Ch Moonraker of Moonswift	Moonswift Mhirdhana	Mrs D Bowdler-Townsend	M Lancashire & Mrs J Arkill
Jalaluddin of Hazuki	d	22.4.69	Tajeer Khan of Tarril	Suki of Rabiouw Wahad	Mrs H Kinread	Miss M Hardy
Amudarya Shalar	d	1.11.73	Ch Amudarya The Pagan	Amudarya Shakila	Mrs A Paton	Mrs L Aldous
1977						
Taiwara Saroya	b	18.1.72	Horningsea Sarelko	Ch Miyasht Chare Toqmar	Mrs M Barlow	Mr & Mrs R King
Blond Emblem of Kethligarne	d	22.4.70	Veldspringer Ali Bin Aziz	Faizabad of Kethligarne	Mrs F Whiteley	Mr A S Reynolds
Oregano Tarragon of Karnak	d	15.1.75	Ch Koolaba Horningsea Eboni Earl	Pandora of Khyber	Mr & Mrs J D Tait	Mr & Mrs C K Thornton
Millionairess of Moonswift	b	22.7.72	Ch Moonraker of Moonswift	Ch Bondor Sayonara of Fiazabad	J Edmonds	Mrs D Bowdler-Townsend
Amudarya Shastri	b	27.6.72	Ch Amudarya The Pagan	Amudarya Shakila	Mrs A Paton	Miss J Nicholls
Oregano Angellica of Sharazah	b	15.1.75	Ch Koolaba Horningsea Eboni Earl	Pandora of Khyber	Mr & Mrs J D Tait	Mr & Mrs D Arris
Izmars Cherokee of Davlen	d	22.9.72	Ch Hajubah of Davlen	Ch Miyasht Empress	Mrs A Doe	Mr & Mrs B Percival
Bondor Lady Marika	b	28.8.71	Ch Bondor Dera Ghazi Khan	Bondor Cinnamon	A Brooks & E Swallow	Mrs J Robertson
Balkasha Barabbas	d	9.4.76	Ch Amudarya The Pagan	Ch Tarril's Azuur B'Har	Mr & Mrs J Dryden-Bell	Breeders
Netheroyd Basil Khan	d	23.7.72	Netheroyd Prince Luti	Netheroyd Regal Venus	Mrs I M Morton	Mrs S M Howard
Ashihna Charmayana	b	29.2.76	Ch Amudarya Shalar	Charikar Doman of Tsyreba	Mrs M Hitchens	Breeder
1978						
Khelzar Marsh Mist	b	25.3.74	Ch Khinjan Lorcah	Rasma Sarobi	Mr & Mrs Hunt	Mr & Mrs J Thompson
Chayakhan Khamsin of Khonistan	d	12.5.74	Khonistan Bondor Kohendil Khan	Vanathan Chaya	Mrs P Lewis	R Wilson & I Hodgson
Peshewar Rashna	b	10.9.73	Montravia Bondor Bolero	Ch Horningsea Salome	Mrs J Wright	Mrs O E Simpson
Korechie Oriana	b	9.9.72	Ranamedi Kaimaakan	Follymon Moonrocket	Mr & Mrs F J Davies	Mrs L M Loder

Name	Sex	DOB	Sire	Dam	Breeder	Owner
Fiazabad South Sea Maiden	b	7.4.74	Ch Amudarya The Pagan	Ch Bondor Sayonara of Fiazabad	J Edmonds	P W Hughes
Alyshan Ysabel	b	14.11.72	Ch Alyshan Hassan Shabbah	Alyshan Calypso	Mrs C Sturgeon-Walkden	Breeder
Tuttlebees Moon Star	b	7.10.71	Montravia Bondor Bolero	Rhani of Alraschid	N E Butcher	Mrs S Miles
Horningsea Balubianca	b	13.3.71	Khinjan Banzai	Horningsea Kashka	Mrs M M Dods	Mr D S Hawes
Dominic Rajendea	d	20.11.72	Travimas Pinchpenny Shangrila Khan	Sheba Rajendea	Mrs M E Carvell	Mr & Mrs T Hall
Sikandra's Ahalya of Oolyghan	b	18.5.73	Ch Ranjitsinhji of Jagai	Jandou's Demeter	Mrs V Howard	Mrs J Holden
Camasu Darius	d	19.7.71	Debrazza of Davlen	Koolaba Mirjawa	Mrs C Pritchard	Mr & Mrs D Pomeroy
Pooghans Dalarna	b	7.7.70	Taraza of Pooghan	Zazah of Pooghan	D McCarthy	Mrs I J Dyke
Tuttlebees Stargazer	d	29.9.73	Ch Alyshan Hassan Shabbah	Rhani of Alraschid	N E Butcher	Mrs S Miles
Kaskarak Khubara	b	26.10.74	Ch Sacheverell Zukwala	Nosilla I'm A Smartee	Mrs L Race	Breeder

1979

Name	Sex	DOB	Sire	Dam	Breeder	Owner
Badakshan Pink Pearl	b	26.3.72	Ch Khanabad White Warrior	Badakshan Tiger Lily	Mrs A Adams	Miss A C Brown
Koolaba Zanek Tarf	d	6.4.74	Ch Koolaba Horningsea Eboni Earl	Ch Koolaba Tajma Zai	Mrs B Taylor	Mrs B Obo
Kohsan's's Mr Inigo Jones	d	11.7.71	Ch Khanabad White Warrior	Kohsan's Adriana Pamir	Mrs J F Symonds	Mrs M A Pickard
Boggi Wahid of Chizel	d	31.1.74	Ch Ranjitsinhji of Jagai	Penelope of Anzani	Mrs P Hallam	Mr & Mrs B Hallam
Zharook Sugar'n'Spice	b	22.2.77	Moonswift Mozart	Sarik Shahara	Mrs P A Latimer	J Lacey
Bondor Shades of Serenade	b	21.10.72	Ch Bondor Azim Khan	Bondor Cinnamon	A Brooks & E Swallow	Breeders
Pasharif Pindari of Darralls	d	15.12.75	Ir Ch Yawl Pasharif	Pasharif Pharahna	Mrs M J Davies	Mrs D C Gurney
Ashihna Rikarlo	d	29.2.76	Ch Amudarya Shalar	Charikar Doman of Tsyreba	Mrs M Hitchens	B Aldous & Mrs M Hitchens
Sacheverell Madam Zinnia	b	9.10.75	Ch Koolaba Horningsea Eboni Earl	Sacheverell Zelda	Miss M J C Booth	Breeder
Khorlynton Kirjatharba	b	9.11.75	Ch Khinjan Lorcah	Ir Ch Karima of Khamora	Mr & Mrs P Johnston	Breeders
Mirsamir The Druid	d	27.2.77	Ch Amudarya Shalar	Ch Pooghans Dalarna	Mrs I J Dyke	Breeder & Miss J S Knight
Bluestone Rocket of Zudiki	d	2.6.76	Zudiki Smokey Tiger	Zudiki White Velvet	Mrs Garnet	Mrs J E Brown
Kharisar Zoe	b	12.9.74	Ch Khinjan Lorcah	Kharisar Czarina	Mr & Mrs P R, N & M J Harcourt-Brown	Breeders
Anakharas Talisman of Tashmahn	d	10.6.75	Izmar's Red Eagle of Jerbel	Candelli's Gara Yaka	Mrs J K Ayers	P Barton

Name	Sex	DOB	Sire	Dam	Breeder	Owner
Saringa's Jeramiah	d	4.9.75	Ch Saringa's Abra Cadabra	Ahmedazi Dainty Dinah	Miss J Dove	Breeder
Ratheeli's Hooked Again	b	15.3.73	Shah of Ilurose	Kovalan Zilla	Miss P E Mullins	Misses P E Mullins & G M McBride
1980						
Izmar's Enchanting Empress	b	28.8.74	Ch Alyshan Hassan Shabbah	Ch Miyasht Empress	Mrs A Doe	H J McAthy & Breeder
Karnak Juniper	b	17.3.78	Ch Amudarya Shalar	Oregano Rosemary of Karnak	Mr & Mrs C K Thornton	Breeders
Karnak Shamrock	d	17.3.78	Ch Amudarya Shalar	Oregano Rosemary of Karnak	Mr & Mrs C K Thornton	E Szyczewski
Yarrumghan Double Delight	b	14.3.78	Ch Amudarya Shalar	Carina of Pooghan	Mr & Mrs R Murray	Mrs J M Mather & Miss J Shaw
Harlextan Dick Deadeye	d	8.12.73	Ch Sacheverell Zukwala	Takabbor Joao	Mr & Mrs G M Parsell	Mrs C Parsell
Saringa's Jemimah	b	4.9.75	Ch Saringa's Abra Cadabra	Ahmedazi Dainty Dinah	Miss J Dove	Breeder & R Rangarajan
Severndene Marionette of Landhavi	b	26.6.77	Ch Moonswift Moonglade	Severndene Sensation	Mrs E E Fryer	Mr & Mrs M Lancashire
Koolaba Hareeb	d	27.11.76	Ch Koolaba Horningsea Eboni Earl	Izmar's Elegant Empress	Mrs B Taylor	Mr & Mrs T Hall
Kharisar Nicomedes of Phinjani	d	2.1.77	Ch Kharisar Karibh Khan	Carnelian of Kharisar	Mr & Mrs P R, N & M J Harcourt-Brown	Mr & Mrs N R Beckett
Mashour Kataghan Khan	d	5.11.74	Kushra Ben Jashmal	Jahmeel Euragem	B J Farnell & Miss J A Singleton	Breeders
Montravia Kaskarak Hitari	d	14.11.78	Ch Sacheverell Zukwala	Nosilla I'm A Smartee	Mrs L Race	Mrs P Gibbs
Koh-I-Noor Dagmar	b	25.3.74	Ch Amudarya The Pagan	Montravia Ashara	Mrs G I Atkins	Mrs D Pullin
1981						
Montravia Dun-Dun v Bornia State	d	12.9.77	Clyde v Bornia State	Amouret v Bornia State	Mrs E Buma-Planten	Mrs P & Miss M Gibbs
Karnak Bay of Imrahn	d	17.3.78	Ch Amudarya Shalar	Oregano Rosemary of Karnak	Mr & Mrs C K Thornton	Mr & Mrs J H Thompson
Kharakhan Columbine	b	9.12.73	Ch Khanabad White Warrior	Ch Khanabad Peach Blossom	Mrs G D North	Breeder
Kharakhan Lorah Rose	b	6.7.77	Ch Koolaba Horningsea Eboni Earl	Ch Kharakhan Columbine	Mrs G D North	Mrs C Allward-Chebsey
Zensu Jacinth of Sacheverell	d	30.6.77	Ch Sacheverell Zukwala	Bondor Rum Coke	Mrs L Ellis	Miss M J C Booth
Khorlynton Keltic Karibou	b	16.11.79	Ch Amudarya Shalar	Ch Khorlynton Kirjatharba	Mr & Mrs P Johnston	R J Kirkham
Sacheverell Kanika of Saxonmill	b	10.10.76	Ch Koolaba Horningsea Eboni Earl	Sacheverell Zelda	Miss M J C Booth	Mrs R A Hall

Name	Sex	DOB	Sire	Dam	Breeder	Owner
Pasharif Pashtu Khan	d	22.5.75	Khinjan Banzai	Pasharif Pandora	Mrs M J Davies	Breeder & D J Whittingham
Harlextan's Mad Miranda	b	7.10.76	Ch Sacheverell Zukwala	Harlextan's Mad Margaret	Mr & Mrs G M Parsell	Mr & Mrs M J Wilson
Khamseen Mannetass of Landhavi	d	23.8.75	Ch Moonswift Moonglade	Khinjan White Chiffon	Mr & Mrs J Arkill	Mr & Mrs M Lancashire
Sundowner The Witch from Mirsamir	b	25.11.78	Ch Mirsamir The Druid	Sundowner Fable	Mrs J E Day	Mrs I J Dyke & Mr & Mrs B J Jones
Ashihna Raoul	d	19.5.79	Ch Oregano Tarragon of Karnak	Ch Ashihna Charmayana	Mrs M Hitchens	Mr & Mrs C Amoo & Breeder
1982						
Sharazah Milwalki Stroller	d	3.2.78	Ch Koolaba Horningsea Eboni Earl	Ch Khinjan Angelique of Sharazah	Mr & Mrs D Arris	Breeders
Barnesmore The Baron of Landhavi	d	22.2.79	Ch Moonswift Moonglade	Ch Pahari Chirkari of Barnesmore	Miss E Martin	Mr & Mrs M Lancashire
Kharakhan Black Rose	b	6.7.77	Ch Koolaba Horningsea Eboni Earl	Ch Kharakhan Columbine	Mrs G D North	Breeder
Lizzi of Kharisar	b	27.5.76	Ch Kharisar Karibh Khan	Gemima of Solanara	Mr & Mrs S Smith	Mr & Mrs P R & N Harcourt-Brown & Mrs M J Wood
Izmars Dizzy Dolly	b	25.10.76	Izmars Jerimiah	Izmars Empress Messalina	Mr & Mrs M Doe & K Sinclair	Mrs P M Dollman
Sana's Star Personality	b	10.11.76	Ch Tuttlebees Stargazer	Ch Tuttlebees Moon Star	Mrs S J Miles	Breeder
Bondor Gypsey Cassanova	d	8.2.76	Ch Sacheverell Zukwala	Bondor Belle Of The Ball	A Brooks & E Swallow	P T Luty
Kharisar Solomon of Sharikhan	d	1.9.77	Ch Kharisar Karibh Khan	Kharisar Czarina	M & Mrs P R & N Harcourt-Brown & Mrs M J Wood	Mr & Mrs F J Severn
Sharazah Blackberry Silk	b	18.3.80	Ch Amudarya Shalar	Ch Oregano Angellica of Sharazah	Mr & Mrs D Arris	Breeders
Davlen Flame Of The Forest	d	23.6.79	Moonswift Mysabu	Tarril's Chura B'Har	Rev D Ford & Miss H Barnes	Breeders
Moonswift Mitsouko	b	23.3.78	Ch Moonswift Moonglade	Ch Millionairess of Moonswift	Mrs D Bowdler-Townsend	R J Kirkham
Zendushkas Pan-Celli	d	30.10.75	Ch/Am Ch Huzzah Excelsis of Horningsea	Zendushkas Pandora	Mrs N K Hitch	Mrs K Howard
Harlextan's The Mad Nun	b	14.10.78	Ch Amudarya Shalar	Harlextan Mad Margaret	Mr & Mrs G M Parsell	Miss J Hough

Name	Sex	DOB	Sire	Dam	Breeder	Owner
Shushma from Amudarya	b	28.6.75	Ch Amudarya The Pagan	Samala of Shubenka	Mrs W Hack	Mrs A Paton
Montravia Mazar Samba	d	23.3.79	Montravia Shah Rahja Myzana Magic	Montravia Tiger Lily	Mrs P Gibbs	Breeder
Malcas Minerva	b	15.3.77	Ir Ch Yawl Pasharif	Ch Amudarya Phara	Mrs C Buck	Mrs S A Harris
Karnak Chillie	d	17.3.78	Ch Amudarya Shalar	Oregano Rosemary of Karnak	Mr & Mrs C K Thornton	Mr & Mrs J Longson
Montravia Mazar Rozanna	b	23.5.78	Montravia Mazar Safari	Trisheba Cleopatra	Mr & Mrs B Tibble	Mrs P Gibb
1983						
Portia from Izmar	b	9.5.80	Ch Kharisar Karibh Khan	Ch Izmar's Enchanting Empress	H J McAthy & Mrs A J Doe	P T Luty & Mrs A J Doe
Sharikhan Khadine of Brandeswood	b	17.8.78	Ch Kharisar Karibh Khan	Sacheverell Madam Zenita of Sharikhan	F J & Mrs J Severn	Mr & Mrs P F Wright
Tuttlebees Mooncrazy of Oolyghan	d	16.6.75	Ch Alyshan Hassan Shabbah	Rhani of Alraschid	N E Butcher	Mrs J Holden-Ereira
Amudarya Khashushma	b	17.5.79	Amudarya Shura	Amudarya Khashma	Mrs A Paton & Mrs J Rimes	Mrs A Paton & Miss I Nicholls
Ivanhoe Camelot from Alyshan	d	10.4.74	Ch Alyshan Hassan Shabbah	Vectensias Golden Girl	Mrs J Carter	Miss A M Cork
Warrenoak Timpani	b	9.4.76	Zanavars War Lord	Farcroft Viceroy Alshain	Mrs M A Boydell	Breeder
Sharazah Star Shooter	d	18.3.80	Ch Amudarya Shalar	Ch Oregano Angellica of Sharazah	D & Mrs V H Arris	Miss E Holmes, J Murray & Mrs M Morris
Playfere's Petticoat Wag at Harlextan	b	20.3.82	Ch Karnak Shamrock	Ch Harlextan's Mad Miranda	M J & Mrs J Wilson	G M & Mrs C Parsell
Koolaba Alexander of Sacheverell	d	1.1.81	Ch Sacheverell Zukwala	Ch Koolaba Tajma Zai	Mrs B R Taylor	Miss M J C Booth
Katree Miss Schiapparelli	b	22.10.80	Ch Karnak Shamrock	Koolaba Jhalal	Mrs K Fulford	J Bland & Mrs E Bishop
Kaskarak Gigolo	d	2.6.80	Ch Moonswift Moonglade	Ch Kaskarak Khubara	Mrs L Race	Breeder
Shechem Santinella	b	2.6.79	Gardwright Damascus from Shechem	Tashkend Wild Gypsy Girl	Mr & Mrs J Hill	R & D Savage
Sandokhan Mr Maestro	d	15.12.77	Ch Kharisar Karibh Khan	Kindina Magic Mistress of Sandokhan	J J Berry	Breeder
1984						
Isfahan Feisal Ibn Sadiq of Kushbudar	d	2.6.81	Isfahan Dta Ha Da Sadiq	Isfahan Marinda	Mrs J Wonnacott	Mrs H J Miller
Davlen Tijuana Silk	b	21.3.81	Ch Davlen Flame of The Forest	Gift Of Gold of Davlen	Rev D Ford & Miss H Barnes	Breeders & Mrs G Haywood

Name	Sex	DOB	Sire	Dam	Breeder	Owner
Karnak Thyme	d	17.3.78	Ch Amudarya Shalar	Oregano Rosemary of Karnak	Mr & Mrs C K Thornton	J & Mrs V Whittaker
Barnesmore Imperial Wizard	d	22.2.79	Ch Moonswift Moonglade	Ir Ch Pahari Chirkari of Barnesmore	Miss E Martin	Mrs L Race
Maljan Golden Samarina from Sharazah	b	26.5.81	Ch Sharazah Milwalki Stroller	Maljan Sheba Fleur	Mr M Vaile	Mr & Mrs D Arris
Tuohi-Tikan Loiske at Mirsamir	b	17.2.82	Fin Ch Ismails Uffah	Int/Nordic Ch Tuohi-Tikan Tulitukka	Anna Leena & Pirkko Konttinen	Mrs I J Dyke
Gilzye Sarkari	b	14.12.79	Ch Amudarya Shalar	Gilzye Andromeda	Mrs M Harris	Miss H & R Bartram
Saxonmill Black Currant	d	18.4.82	Ch Karnak Shamrock	Ch Sacheverell Kanika of Saxonmill	Mrs R A Hall	Mrs S Weston
Gardwright Bibi at Shanshu	b	19.4.81	Ch Amudarya Shalar	Koolaba Eye Of The Tiger	Messrs Gardiner, Wright & Darby	Mrs B McClark
Karnak Blazing Star	d	25.8.82	Ch Amudarya Shalar	Oregano Rosemary of Karnak	Mr & Mrs C K Thornton	Breeders
Moonswift Majidque	d	23.3.78	Ch Moonswift Moonglade	Ch Millionairess of Moonswift	Mrs D Bowdler-Townsend	Miss S Hudson
Gardwright Damascus from Shechem	d	13.10.77	Ch Amudarya Shalar	Dietrich from Alyshan	Messrs Gardiner & Wright	R Savage & Mrs D Hill
1985						
Lissue Storm Cloud	b	16.2.81	Sarik Senator	Zensu Sheer Sensation	A & Mrs J S Blackwell	Mrs E Wyatt
Kharakhan Black Hussar	d	6.7.77	Ch Koolaba Horningsea Eboni Earl	Ch Kharakhan Columbine	Mrs G D North	M & Mrs J Smith
Gentleman Jim from Tazieff	d	10.4.78	Zendushkas Golden Sun	Peenkande Pollyanna	Miss P Kingsnorth	Mrs C P J Heal
Landhavi Love Bug of Dalparva	b	5.6.81	Ch Barnesmore The Baron of Landhavi	Ch Severndene Marionette of Landhavi	Mr & Mrs M Lancashire	Mr & Mrs B Waistnidge
Khonistan Selina	b	1.8.78	Ch Chayakhan Khamsin of Khonistan	Ch Khanlidar Zuzini	Messrs Walker & Wilson	Mr & Mrs S Moon
Khelazar Moonlight Satin	b	25.11.77	Ch Moonswift Moonglade	Tarakhan T'sarina	Mrs S A Neal	Mrs B Yardley
Sharazah Night Gambler	d	30.5.82	Ch Sharazah Milwalki Stroller	Ch Oregano Angellica of Sharazah	Mr & Mrs D Arris	Breeders
Davlen The Godfather	d	21.3.81	Ch Davlen Flame Of The Forest	Gift Of Gold of Davlen	Rev D Ford & Miss H Barnes	Mr & Mrs Merriman
Kaskarak Giselle	b	2.6.80	Ch Moonswift Moonglade	Ch Kaskarak Khubara	Mrs L Race	Mrs D M Greenfield
Karnak Jasmine	b	28.8.83	Ch Zendushkas Pan-Celli	Ch Karnak Juniper	C K & Mrs B Thornton	Breeders & A & Mrs P Ledger

Name	Sex	DOB	Sire	Dam	Breeder	Owner
Khorlynton Keltic Krusader	d	16.11.79	Ch Amudarya Shalar	Ch Khorlynton Kirjatharba	Mr & Mrs P Johnston	J & Mrs E McMorris
Melleck Extravaganza	b	16.1.82	Ch Amudarya Shalar	Alyshan Estelle	Mrs T Harper & Mr & Mrs B Hedge	Breeders
Zoyford The Baroness	b	6.3.80	Ch Chayakhan Khamsin of Khonistan	Tainui Maid Marion	Mrs J Ash	Mrs O Simpson & Mrs A J Lane
Shullimar Rainbow Warrior	d	24.9.80	Ch Karnak Shamrock	Kamiren Canterbury Belle	Mrs J Speck	E Szyczewski
1986						
Ratheeli Jadu	d	9.7.80	Ch Balkasha Barabbas	Ch Ratheeli's Hooked Again	Misses P E Mullins G M McBride	A M Cleak
Mahogonny Moon of Jhansi	b	25.4.83	Ch Barnesmore Imperial Wizard	Khorlynton Keltic Kween	Mmes J Bracegirdle L Aldous	R M Allison & R J Kirkham
Zendushkas Pekoe	d	15.11.79	Zendushkas Beau Dazla	Zendushkas Pansy	Mrs N K Hitch	Breeder
Kaskarak Kochise	d	28.10.82	Ch Barnesmore Imperial Wizard	Ch Kaskarak Khubara	Mrs L Race	Ms J A Singleton & R W Littlewood
Viscount Grant	d	23.10.84	Ch Sharazah Night Gambler	Ashihna Charmaine	Mrs & Mrs C Amoo	Breeders
Hashtana Lucy Limelite	b	22.7.80	Severndene Starbound	Sasmar Megan Estelle of Hashtana	M G & Mrs H Forrest	Breeders
Bondor Lilac Wine	b	26.1.83	Ch Karnak Shamrock	Bondor Naughty Marietta	A Brooks & E Swallow	Breeders & J Cox
Amudarya Shh Y'Know Who	b	17.11.80	Amudarya El Kyrias Y'Made In Sweden	Ch Shushma from Amudarya	Mrs A Paton	Breeder
Ifmaraf Go-Man-Go	d	15.1.78	Ch Amudarya Shalar	Zudiki's Kismit at Ifmaraf	I & Mrs M Fisher	Breeders
Yarrumghan Miss Dior	b	3.1.80	Ch Amudarya Shalar	Moonswift Music Mistress	Mr & Mrs R Murray	K F & Mrs O Noble
Wilbus Fleur-Dy-Lys of Bowentree	b	2.11.81	Ch Gentleman Jim from Tazieff	Tatianna of Bowentree at Wilbus	Mrs L Busby	Mrs D Waterman
Palamedees Anaja of Calamayor	b	25.8.83	Ch Karnak Shamrock	Khanabad Winter Fashion	Miss A C Brown	Mrs T A Grist
It/Int Ch Joe Mirzabad	d	3.12.80	Int Ch El Khyrias Hazztafer	Swe Ch Adjaian	Ms C Hjerpe	Ms H Bruton
1987						
Barakhel Forever Free	b	1.4.84	Barakhel Flying Dice	Iroka from Jahadi	Miss M A Berry	S V & Mrs A E Jewell
Ellistine A Star Is Born	d	23.12.83	Ch Isfahan Feisal Ibn Sadiq of Kushbudar	Shullimar Mabellyne of Ellistine	Mr & Mrs R E Morgan	W R & Mrs M Clifford
Khamseen She's A Devil	b	9.9.82	Ch Montravia Kaskarak Hitari	Khamseen Coochie-Coo	Mr & Mrs J Arkill	T & Mrs K Lancaster
Jhansi Indiana Opium	b	2.10.84	Ch Karnak Shamrock	Ch Moonswift Mitsouko	R J Kirkham	Breeder
Lissue As You Like It	b	20.7.82	Ch Koolaba Alexander of Sacheverell	Zensu Sheer Sensation	A & Mrs J S Blackwell	M J & Mrs E Wyatt

Name	Sex	DOB	Sire	Dam	Breeder	Owner
Xerkhan Apollo	d	4.8.83	Ch Oregano Tarragon of Karnak	Kentenes Trend of Xerkhan	B P Filson	D & Mrs L Turner
Cihela Clarkia	d	21.10.78	Ir Ch Yawl Pasharif	Ch Korechie Oriana	Mrs L M Loder	Mrs M L Davies
Sacheverell Alexis	b	2.4.82	Ch Koolaba Alexander of Sacheverell	Ch Sacheverell Madam Zinnia	Miss M J C Booth	Mrs C Mahn
Saxonmill Black Iris	b	18.4.82	Ch Karnak Shamrock	Ch Sacheverell Kanika of Saxonmill	Mrs R A Hall	Mrs H Crossfield
Solomon's Seal from Karnak	d	16.5.85	Ch Ashihna Raoul	Karnak Cinnamon	Mrs B Thornton & Miss Y Duckworth	Mrs J Mackay & B Gilchrist
Montravia Kazar Kascade	d	28.2.84	Ch Montravia Kaskarak Hitari	Ch Montravia Mazar Rozanna	Mrs P Gibbs	R Bartram & Breeder
Izmar Lucrezia	b	31.7.83	Ch Kharisar Nicomedes of Phinjani	Ch Portia from Izmar	Mrs A Doe & P T Luty	Mrs A Doe
Gilzye Talikhan	d	14.12.79	Ch Amudarya Shalar	Gilzye Andromeda	Mrs M Harris	Mr & Mrs T Green
Montravia Holy-Man	d	25.12.83	Ch Montravia Kaskarak Hitari	Montravia Dutch Delight	Sqn Ldr & Mrs P & Miss M Gibbs	Breeders
Ioniok Lucy Whatapoppit	b	20.8.84	Warrenoak Wild Viking	Ioniok Royal Gem	Mrs H M Northrop	Breeder
1988						
Karnak Mulberry	d	8.4.85	Ch Saxonmill Black Currant	Karnak Fern	Mr & Mrs C K Thornton	Mr & Mrs A Ledger & Breeders
Izmar Rebecca	b	15.6.82	Ch Kharisar Karibh Khan	Izmar's Hannah	Mrs A Doe & P Luty	M & Mrs J Griffin
Hashtana Red Alert	d	22.7.80	Severndene Starbound	Sasmar Megan Estelle of Hashtana	M G & Mrs H Forrest	Breeders
Ratheeli Mahzuzh	b	20.7.84	Ch Zendushkas Pekoe	Ratheeli Jarab	Misses P E Mullins & G M McBride	Breeders
Bondor Hot Gossip at Karandikar	b	24.8.81	Ch Karnak Shamrock	Ch Bondor Shades Of Serenade	A Brooks & E Swallow	Mrs W Bastow
Katree Miss Henna	b	11.12.84	Katree Lord Eboni	Mandy from Alyshan	Mrs K Fulford	L J & Mrs K Fulford
Weetoneon Dark Zaleta	b	2.11.84	Ch Karnak Shamrock	Weetoneon Mazelda	Mrs A E Lacey	Breeder & E Szyczewski
Sanstas Rum Truffle	b	29.2.84	Ch Saxonmill Black Currant	Gilzye Azuree	Mrs S Weston	Breeder
Izmar Alibech	b	31.7.83	Ch Kharisar Nicomedes of Phinjani	Ch Portia from Izmar	P Luty & Mrs A Doe	Mrs G Hughes
Zoyford Christmas Carol of Khonistan	b	30.11.81	Ch Chayakhan Khamsin of Khonistan	Tainui Maid Marion	Mrs J Ash	R Walker & I Hodgson
Sacheverell Zorro of Zarzakos	d	29.9.81	Ch Zensu Jacinth of Sacheverell	Ch Sacheverell Madam Zinnia	Miss M J C Booth	D & Mrs C Brooks
Bondor Some Like It Hot	d	24.8.81	Ch Karnak Shamrock	Ch Bondor Shades Of Serenade	A Brooks & E Swallow	Mrs S L & Misses C & A McDonald

Name	Sex	DOB	Sire	Dam	Breeder	Owner
Metewand Iezerai	b	15.9.83	Altombet Aristocrat at Metewand	Metewand Opo Noni	Mrs A Mathers	Breeder
Xerkhan Aurora of Taltonia	b	4.8.83	Ch Oregano Tarragon of Karnak	Kentenes Trend of Xerkhan	B P Filson	B W & Mrs R Talbot
Xerkhan Adonis	d	4.8.83	Ch Oregano Tarragon of Karnak	Kentenes Trend of Xerkhan	B P Filson	Breeder
Tazkindi Pharoah's Gold	d	29.8.85	Ch Kaskarak Kochise	Tazkindi Imogen Soroyel	K & Mrs S Ashley	Miss J A Singleton & R W Littlewood
Lissue A Winter's Tale	d	20.7.82	Ch Koolaba Alexander of Sacheverell	Zensu Sheer Sensation	A & Mrs J S Blackwell	C J & Mrs L P Bovey
Palamedees Anishka of Desertwind	b	25.8.83	Ch Karnak Shamrock	Khanabad Winter Fashion	Miss A C Brown	T & Mrs K Lancaster
Sadé Solace	b	25.4.86	Ch Sharazah Night Gambler	Ashihna Charmaine	Mr & Mrs C Amoo	Breeders
Wilbus Hanukah	b	19.6.85	Shullimar Super Trouper at Tazieff	Kanjanelli Ku-Mari of Wilbus	A P & Mrs L M Busby	Breeders
Shanshu Casa Biere from Khados	b	13.3.83	Ch Gardwright Damascus from Shechem	Shanshu Tulsa At The Top	Mrs B M McClark	Mr & Mrs D E Johnson
Jahadi Achill	d	26.7.82	Kunta Kinte von Katwiga from Jahadi	Nausikaa's Djamani from Jahadi	D & Mrs L James	Breeders
1989						
Zharook Scarlet Flame	b	3.4.85	Ch Barnesmore Imperial Wizard	Ayisha's Seductress from Zharook	R E & Mrs P Latimer	Ms E O'Connor & T Thomas
Sharazah Sir Vivor	d	30.4.86	Ch Sharazah Star Shooter	Ch Maljan Golden Samarina from Sharazah	D & Mrs V H Arris	Breeders
Sharazah Shannon	b	9.12.87	Ch Viscount Grant	Ch Maljan Golden Samarina from Sharazah	D & Mrs V H Arris	Breeders
Calamayor Ra	d	29.11.86	Ch Barnesmore Imperial Wizard	Ch Palamedees Anaja of Calamayor	Mrs T A Grist	Breeder
Davlen Tamarisk	b	21.11.85	Ch Shullimar Rainbow Warrior	Ch Davlen Tijuana Silk	Miss H Barnes & Mrs G Haywood	Mrs A J Kennedy
Gilari Goldstrike	d	18.5.84	Ch Barnesmore The Baron of Landhavi	Sana's Bewitching Star of Gilari	Mr & Mrs C H Cross	Breeders
Sashkan Me And My Girl	b	12.6.87	Dk Ch Boxadan Junior Jumper	Ch Shechem Santinella	R & D Savage	Breeders
Ghinja La Peregrina	b	2.12.85	Shullimar Super Trouper at Tazieff	Wilbus Emma Gee at Ghinja	G E & Mrs H J Darnley	Breeders
Gardwright Gloria	b	25.5.84	Ch Gardwright Damascus from Shechem	Gardwright Ginger Rogers	Messrs Gardiner & Wright	Breeders
Khorramabad Fire Fox	d	18.11.82	Zensu Storm Spirit	Ch Izmars Dizzy Dolly	Mrs P M Dollman	Breeder

Name	Sex	DOB	Sire	Dam	Breeder	Owner
Dalparva Mr Bojangles	d	1.7.86	Ch Barnesmore Imperial Wizard	Ch Landhavi Love Bug of Dalparva	Mrs M Waistnidge	J Larden & B Waistnidge
1990						
Am Ch Sumava's Haidalla at Sumahari	b	21.2.85	Sumava's Firang Souvenir	Shahrana of Grandeur	J J Vidorreta & T Sanchez	Mrs S M Virgo & R Rechler
Deja-Vu of Khamis	d	8.4.83	Ch Sharazah Star Shooter	Khamis Ajeda	A D & Mrs J Muir	F Folkman
Kaskarak Quincy Quartz	b	14.10.84	Ch Barnesmore Imperial Wizard	Kaskarak Chaquenta	Mrs L Race	Breeder
Asian Earl at Shalazsar	d	25.4.83	Ch Barnesmore Imperial Wizard	Khorlynton Keltic Kween of Panjsher	Mmes J Bracegirdle & L Aldous	Miss R Livesey
Tazkindi The Sunrizer	d	29.8.85	Ch Kaskarak Kochise	Tazkindi Imogen Soroyel	K & Mrs S Ashley	Miss C A Bagshaw & J T Pursell
Isfahan Zardalu-Maleke	b	11.8.86	Palamedees Perseus of Badakshan	Isfahan Marinda	Mrs J Wonnacott	R Jamrozik
Katree Miss Jhalal	b	26.10.88	Katree Wolfie	Miss Cleo from Katree	Mrs K Fulford	L J & Mrs K Fulford
Padaki Qala-E-Shah	d	21.4.85	Ch Jahadi Achill	Padaki Earth Wind And Fire	P D & Mrs D Kirwan	Breeders
Karnak Turmeric of Jazar	d	28.8.83	Ch Zendushkas Pan-Celli	Ch Karnak Juniper	Mr & Mrs C K Thornton	E & Mrs C Farebrother
Lorahs Silver Winged Fantasy	b	10.3.83	Ch Amudarya Shalar	Ch Kharakhan Lorah Rose	Mrs C Allward-Chebsey	Breeder
Maximillion of Zudiki	d	9.9.82	Ch Ifmaraf Go-Man-Go	Zudiki's Lolita	D W Brown	Mrs S Gill
1991						
Dalparva Imperial Daughter	b	1.7.86	Ch Barnesmore Imperial Wizard	Ch Landhavi Love Bug of Dalparva	Mr & Mrs B Waistnidge	Ms J Williams
Hot Ginger of Azrams	b	23.7.86	Akirams Prince Zaren	Birkhall Key Of The Door	Mrs D K McKnight	Breeder & J Robertson
Chardhuri Chianti for Drishaun	d	16.1.85	Ch Barnesmore The Baron of Landhavi	Severndene Spellbinder of Chardhuri	A & Mrs C Charles	M & Mrs A M Lancashire & Mr & Mrs Sharman
Palamedees Kallista	b	3.11.87	Ch Jahadi Achill	Palamedees Ariana	Ms A C Brown	R Bartram & Breeder
Khardains Midnight Satin	b	3.10.85	Karnak Burdock of Ilinga	Khardains Lady Karla	J & Mrs P L Crack & Miss J A Overton	J & Mrs P L Crack
Zandahar Shadow Play	d	29.7.85	Ch Koolaba Alexander of Sacheverell	Ashihna Rosanna of Zandahar	Mrs G Adams	Mrs G Chilton & D Adams
Tianze Kalvados	d	24.2.85	Ch Barnesmore Imperial Wizard	The Gentle Touch of Tianze	Mrs J Harnett	Breeder
Fin Ch Mandrills Myltha Izmar Tragband	b	23.5.86	Fin/Swe Ch Punapaulan Malahi	Fin/Swe Ch Taikatassun Ebony	R P & Mrs L Soderman	Mrs A Doe, J Watson & A Brace
Khamis Zubedar	d	12.9.85	Ch Karnak Turmeric of Jazar	Dizzy Heights of Khamis	Miss J F Leitch	A Learmonth
Lokhandar Barberry Bey	d	6.8.86	Ch Karnak Mulberry	Rochander Morning Glory of Lokhandar	K R & Mrs F M Hadfield	Breeders

Name	Sex	DOB	Sire	Dam	Breeder	Owner
Birkhall It Happened Twice	b	22.7.85	Ch Bondor Some Like It Hot	Jazar Flirti Gertie of Birkhall	Mrs S Misses C & A McDonald	Breeders
Ghinja Popinjay	d	2.12.85	Shullimar Super Trouper at Tazieff	Wilbus Emma Gee at Ghinja	G E & Mrs H J Darnley	Breeders
1992						
Sochera's Indigo Wizard at Jimellree	d	8.10.88	Katree Lord Eboni	Gardwright Grace	Mrs S Erskine	Mrs E Wilson
Ratheeli Murshadah	b	20.7.84	Ch Zendushkas Pekoe	Ratheeli Jarab	Misses P E Mullins & G M McBride	Breeders
Harlextan Piara at Saxonmill	b	21.4.88	Ch Saxonmill Black Currant	Ch Playfere's Petticoat Wag at Harlextan	G M & Mrs C Parsell	Mrs R A Hall
Zareenas Fire Cracker	b	29.7.89	Ch Khorramabad Fire Fox	Chardhuri Pina Colada	Mmes E & B Yardley	Breeders
Harlextan Mad Masala	b	21.4.88	Ch Saxonmill Black Currant	Ch Playfere's Petticoat Wag at Harlextan	G M & Mrs C Parsell	C & Mrs S Winters
Harlextan Mad Mullah	d	21.4.88	Ch Saxonmill Black Currant	Ch Playfere's Petticoat Wag at Harlextan	G M & Mrs C Parsell	Mrs J Harnett
Harlextan Padishah	d	21.4.88	Ch Saxonmill Black Currant	Ch Playfere's Petticoat Wag at Harlextan	G M & Mrs C Parsell	D & Mrs L A James
Kynerman Andromache	b	18.4.88	Ch Karnak Mulberry	Ch Saxonmill Black Iris	Mrs H Andrews	Breeder
Sashkan Diamond Lil	b	12.9.88	Dk Ch Boxadan Junior Jumper	Ch Shechem Santinella	R & Mrs D Savage	Breeders
Zoreba Indian at Gardwright	d	24.4.87	Ch Kaskarak Kochise	Jhansi Chinah Rose	Mrs L Cheetham	C Gardiner & K Wright
Jahadi Bosch at Wilbus	d	30.4.86	Ch Jahadi Achill	Palamedees Persian Pearl from Jahadi	D & Mrs L A James	A & Mrs L Busby
Diaquiri from Khamis	d	13.1.88	Khamis Zabardast	Cheguevar Golden Ember	E Cowan	J & Mrs L Walls
Badakshan Persimmon	b	24.10.86	Isfahan Khushamad	Palamedees Pandora of Badakshan	Mrs A Adams	Mrs D E Jones & A P Saltern
Drishaun Delores	b	17.8.89	Ch Chardhuri Chianti for Drishaun	Khamseen Free As A Bird	M & Mrs A M Lancashire	Mrs A M Lancashire & Mr & Mrs Sharman
Izmar Tragband Finnigan	d	19.10.88	Int/Nord Ch Choice Be A Pepper Ch/Fin Ch Mandrills Myltha	Izmar Tragband	Mrs A Doe, J Watson & A Brace	Mrs A Doe & J Watson
1993						
Karaburan Jelly Roll Morton	d	5.6.90	Karaburan Count Baisey	Sacheverell Anoushka of Charadelle	D M, Mrs E & Miss R Boyd	Breeders
Amanrha Miss Ayesha	b	2.6.89	Ch Solomon's Seal from Karnak Imrahn Sea Mist of Amanrha		Mmes M Hawarden M Thompson	A Margetts

Name	Sex	DOB	Sire	Dam	Breeder	Owner
Izmar Tragband Finnishing School	b	19.10.88	Int/Nord Ch Choice Be A Pepper	Ch/Fin Ch Mandrills Myltha Izmar Tragband	Mrs A Doe, J Watson & A Brace	Miss S Jackson & Mrs A Doe
Sadé Hi-Ranger to Sharazah	d	7.11.90	Ch Sharazah Sir Vivor	Ch Sadé Solace	C & Mrs J Amoo	D & Mrs V H Arris
Jhansi Calandre	b	9.12.87	Karachi Khan	Ch Jhansi Indiana Opium	R J Kirkham	A & Mrs S Charlton & Breeder
Am Ch Pahlavi Pandemonium	d	17.7.86	Am Ch Pahlavi Puttin' On The Ritz	Am Ch Pahlavi's Jemima Alarickhan	S & Mrs V Babylon & Ms K Wagner	I & Mrs M Keelan
Birkhall The Infidel at Kirghiz	b	26.11.90	Ch Izmar Tragband Finnegan	Jazar Flertie Gertie of Birkhall	Mrs S & Misses C & A McDonald	J & Mrs E Clark
Amudarya Thanks A Million	b	29.4.89	Ch Karnak Mulberry	Amudarya Shaffire	Mrs A Paton	Breeder
Karaburan Pretty Boy Floyd at Shirobana	d	9.3.89	Ch Saxonmill Black Currant	Karaburan Cleopatra	D M, Mrs E & Miss R Boyd	C & Mrs L Bovey
Sadé Sovereign	b	7.11.90	Ch Sharazah Sir Vivor	Ch Sadé Solace	C & Mrs J Amoo	C & Mrs M F J Pascoe
Tianze Bewitched	b	8.10.87	Ch Tianze Kalvados	Omayyak Taboo	Mrs J Harnett	Breeder
Anzani Silver Fox of Khonistan	d	2.12.86	Ghinja Polar Diamond of Anzani	Anzani Istria	Mrs B Appleton	R Wilson & I Hodgson
Krishan's Kribensis at Learael	b	4.1.89	Ch Ashihna Raoul	Krishan's Forest Flower	Mrs J Lloyd	Mrs J P Lear
Dalparva Regal Raider of Hashtana	d	1.7.86	Ch Barnesmore Imperial Wizard	Ch Landhavi Love Bug of Dalparva	Mr & Mrs B Waistnidge	S Forrest
Allahabad Karnak Benaries	d	12.10.87	Ch Karnak Mulberry	Ch Karnak Jasmine	Mr & Mrs A Ledger & Mr & Mrs C K Thornton	Mr & Mrs Lewis & Mr & Mrs Ledger
Kharisar Rhia at Cloudside	b	27.4.91	Ch Saxonmill Black Currant	Coastwind Apphia at Kharisar	Mr & Mrs P R & N Harcourt-Brown & Mrs M J Wood	W Moore
1994						
Zharook Hooked On Love	d	20.8.90	Zharook Heaven Help Us	Zharook Love Affair	R E & Mrs P A Latimer	Breeders & Mrs C Campbell
Kaskarak Khobra	d	28.5.91	Mogell Memphis	Ch Kaskarak Quincy Quartz	Mrs L Race	Miss J Singleton & Breeder
Sadé Regina at Ifmaraf	b	7.11.90	Ch Sharazah Sir Vivor	Ch Sadé Solace	C & Mrs J Amoo	I & Mrs M G Fisher
Lazakhan Abdullah	d	4.11.88	Ch Shullimar Rainbow Warrior	Ch Izmar Rebecca	M & Mrs J Griffin	Breeders
Brandeswood Harrier	b	4.10.89	Ch Karnak Blazing Star	Karnak Betony of Brandeswood	P F & Mrs J Wright	Breeders
Am Ch Anasazi's Testarossa	b	23.10.87	Am Ch Pahlavi Son Of A Witch	Anasazi's Nicole of Naphtali	I & Mrs M Keelan	Breeders
Allahabad Brodie	d	17.2.92	Ch Izmar Tragband Finnegan	Allahabad Karnak Kaley	Mrs P Ledger	A M & Mrs P Ledger
Amshura Nijinsky	d	15.4.91	Ch Izmar Tragband Finnegan	Amshura Madam Gaye	Ms S Evans	Breeder
Selim Bey of Lokhandar	d	22.3.91	Ch Lokhandar Barberry Bey	Amudarya Shaphira	Mrs B Londos	K R & Mrs F M Hadfield

Name	Sex	DOB	Sire	Dam	Breeder	Owner
Amudarya Shushila	b	23.2.92	Ch Izmar Tragband Finnegan	Amudarya Shushma's Image	Mrs A Paton	Mrs A Paton & Ms S Pinnock
Shadia Kimara from Marnadee	b	15.7.88	Jhansi Avalon	Davlen Dawn Till Midnight	W C & Mrs Bell	M Ord
Zareenas Fire Dragon at Severndene	d	29.7.89	Ch Khorramabad Fire Fox	Chardhuri Pina Colada	Mrs B & Miss E Yardley	Mrs E Fryer
Shaybani The Duke	d	16.12.92	Ch Izmar Tragband Finnegan	Shaybani Acaena	Miss E Sutton	B & Mrs A Clegg
Karaburan Be Be King	d	21.2.91	Karaburan Count Baisey	Sacheverell Anouska of Charadelle	Mr, Mrs & Miss Boyd	Mr & Mrs Woodward & Miss Boyd
Bondor I Am What I Am	b	12.2.91	The Charmer of Bondor	Obadar Miss You Mights at Bondor	A Brooks & S Smith	Breeders
Sochera's Diva from Gardwright	b	20.4.90	Mr Felix from Katree	Gardwright Grace	Mrs S Erskine	C Gardiner & G Wright
1995						
Khawari Serenade	d	23.6.90	Ch Solomon's Seal from Karnak	Karnak Linden	Mr & Mrs B Gilchrist	Breeders
Amudarya Shashkia	b	23.2.92	Ch Izmar Tragband Finnegan	Amudarya Shushma's Image	Mrs A Paton	J M & Mrs C A Astle
Sumahari Starlight	b	8.4.92	Ch Sharazah Sir Vivor	Ch/Am Ch Sumava's Haidalla at Sumahari	Mrs S Virgo & R Rechler	Mrs S Virgo
Karandikar Wicked Lady	b	3.3.89	Ch Chardhuri Chianti for Drishaun	Ch Bondor Hot Gossip at Karandikar	Mrs W Bastow	Miss M Niedzwiedz & Mr F P Mallinson
Kulute Miles Ahead	d	6.8.89	Ch Viscount Grant	Zandahar Pineapple Poll	Mrs D Coates-Waite	Mrs D Coates-Waite
Gezancol Dirty Diana	b	16.6.89	Ch Calamayor Ra	Ch Izmar Alibech	C & Mrs G Hughes	Breeders
Izmar By Moonlight of Meredith	b	3.4.91	Ch Saxonmill Black Currant	Izmar Tragband Choice Finnish	Mrs A Doe, J Watson & A Brace	Mrs T Schofield
Mogell The Texan	d	14.11.87	Ch Kaskarak Kochise	Landhavi Lafayette	Mrs S Ellis	Miss C Pearce
Moonswift Medici	d	8.11.89	Ch Barnesmore Imperial Wizard	Moonswift Muna at Altside	Mrs D Bowdler-Townsend	Mrs L Race
Xerkhan Echo	b	17.6.91	Ch Sharazah Sir Vivor	Xerkhan Nemisis	B Filson	Mrs J Parsons
Gezancol Smooth Criminal	d	18.6.90	Ch Calamayor Ra	Ch Izmar Alibech	Mrs G Hughes	Mrs S A Harris
Hashtana Red Revolution	d	29.8.91	Ch Barnesmore Imperial Wizard	Ch Hashtana Lucy Limelite	S Forrest	Breeder
Sashkan Miss Siagon at Karianca	b	8.7.90	Ch Lissue A Winters Tale	Sashkan Black Velvet	R & Mrs D Savage	Mrs C Street
Regal Lilly of Zendushkas	b	24.2.92	Zendushkas Rubas	Firemont Azida	Mrs J Carter	Mrs S Keree-Bartolo & Mrs N Hitch
Karaburan Tina Turner	b	13.6.90	Ch Saxonmill Black Currant	Karaburan Cleopatra	Mr, Mrs & Miss Boyd	Mr & Mrs T Green
Tejas Sahuara	b	5.9.91	Ch/Am/Ir Ch Pahlavi's Pandemonium	Ch/Am/Ir Ch Anasazi's Testarossa	I & Mrs M Keelan	Miss N & Mrs L Bishop
Moonswift Mhirtara at Altside	b	8.11.89	Ch Barnesmore Imperial Wizard	Moonswift Muna at Altside	Mrs D Bowdler-Townsend	D Traversari & C Greenwood

Name	Sex	DOB	Sire	Dam	Breeder	Owner
Tejas Conquistador	b	5.9.91	Ch/Am/Ir Ch Pahlavi's Pandemonium	Ch/Am/Ir Ch Anasazi's Testarossa	I & Mrs M Keelan	M Gadsby & Mrs A Doe
Ir Ch Metewand Mimico	d	12.8.90	Dk Ch Boxadan Junior Jumper	Ch/Ir Ch Metewand Iezerai	Mrs A Mathers	Breeder
Wilbus Kharjeem of Phinjani	d	12.6.91	Katree Lord Sanderman at Obadar	Ch Wilbus Hanukah	A P & Mrs L Busby	N R & Mrs J Beckett
Drishaun Danielle	b	29.8.91	Ch Chardhuri Chianti for Drishaun	Ch Jhansi Indiana Opium	M & Mrs A M Lancashire	Mr & Mrs A J Charlton
1996						
Melleck Impresario	d	18.4.92	Mogell Memphis	Melleck Fairytale	Mr & Mrs B Hedge & Mrs T Harper	Mr & Mrs S Cogdell & Mrs K Bingham
Karnak Damiana	b	25.9.90	Dan Ch Boxadan Junior Jumper	Karnak Rosemary	C K & Mrs B Thornton	M & Mrs J Day & Mrs B Thornton
Khamis Bhi-Candlelight	b	8.11.94	Khamis Zabardast	Khamis Silvery Moon	Miss J Leitch	Miss J Leitch & M Cocozza
Saxonmill Rum Tum Tigger	d	19.10.93	Ch Karaburan Jelly Roll Morton	Ch Harlextan Piara at Saxonmill	Mrs R A Hall	Breeder
Sashkan Georgie Girl	b	17.11.93	Ch Karaburan Be Be King	Ch Sashkan Me And My Girl	R & Mrs D Savage	Breeders
Bellapais Touche Turtle	d	6.7.92	Ch Karaburan Pretty Boy Floyd at Shirobana	Weetoneon Dark 'N' Devoted	M J & Mrs E Wyatt & Mrs C Bustin	M J & Mrs E Wyatt & Mrs V West
Bondor Its A Kinda Majic	b	20.6.92	The Charmer of Bondor	Obadar Miss You Nights at Bondor	A Brooks & S Smith	J Lacey
Rochander Phaleg	d	22.3.91	Ch Lokhandar Barberry Bey	Amudarya Shaphira	Mrs B Londos	Mrs S Kemp
Sashkan Eboni 'N' Ivory	d	12.11.93	Ch Karaburan Pretty Boy Floyd at Shirobana	Sashkan Black Velvet	Mr & Mrs R Savage	Mr & Mrs K R Andrew & Mrs I J Dyke
Melleck Hitchiker	d	15.9.90	Bowentree Orka at Japapa	Kunduz Gentle Star of Melleck	Mr & Mrs B Hedge & Mrs T Harper	Mr & Mrs S Cogdell
1997						
Karnak Sassafras	d	25.9.90	Dk Ch Boxadan Junior Jumper	Karnak Rosemary	C K & Mrs B Thornton	Mrs J Shallcross, Mrs B Thornton & P Broxton
Calamayor Thor	d	6.3.90	Ch Ellistine A Star Is Born	Ch Palamedees Anaja of Calamayor	Mrs T A Grist	Mr & Mrs G Stevens
Cloudside The Ringmaster	d	3.3.95	Ch Saxonmill Rum Tum Tigger	Ch Kharisar Rhia at Cloudside	W Moore	Mr & Mrs P Barnett
Jhansi Touched By Magic	b	31.10.93	Davlen Master Of The Game	Jhansi Magie Noire of Zindajan	R J Kirkham	Breeder & M Higginbottom
Calmayor Glyndwr	d	6.3.90	Ch Ellistine A Star Is Born	Ch Palamedees Anaja of Calamayor	Mrs T A Grist	Mr & Mrs R Clifford & Mrs T A Grist

Name	Sex	DOB	Sire	Dam	Breeder	Owner
Drishaun Djudgement Day for Bichoux	d	22.5.93	Zharook Scarlet Pimpernel	Ch Drishaun Delores	Mrs A M Lancashire	Mrs J A Noble & D Wilcox
Am Ch K'Amour Seafarer Summerwind BBE	b	22.5.92	Am Ch Summerwind Renwick Mass Appeal	K'Amour Summerwind N'Ice N'Easy	Mr & Mrs C Piette, R Sutton & N Madden	Mr & Mrs S Mottershaw
Punapaulan Into Araki	d	11.9.95	Swe/Fin Ch Genesis Beyond The Clouds II	Fin Ch Punapaulan Runo	Dr R Aho	K & Mrs A Sinclair
Zelzah's French Connection at Bozwood	d	8.10.92	The Charmer of Bondor	Zelzah's April In Paris	Mr & Mrs J Newman	Mr & Mrs T Carr
Sashkan Incognito	d	18.11.92	Ch Karaburan Pretty Boy Floyd at Shirobana	Sashkan Black Velvet	Mr & Mrs R Savage	Mrs P Woodward
1998						
Cotton Velvet to Sharazah	b	7.10.93	Ch Sharazah Sir Vivor	Nanak Chantelle at Trickash	J Ashwood	Mr & Mrs D Arris
Izmar Now Or Never	b	27.7.94	Ch Izmar Tragband Finnegan	Ch Tejas Conquistador	Mrs A Doe	Mr & Mrs R Morton
Saqlawi Standing Ovation	b	18.12.93	El Khyrias Veni Vidi Vici of Saqlawi	Izmar Tragband Finnishing Touch	Mrs J Davies	Mrs D Greenfield
Amudarya Sholti of Zadal	d	23.2.92	Ch Izmar Tragband Finnegan	Amudarya Shushma's Image	Mrs A Paton	Mr & Mrs J Bunney
Saxonmill Jennyanydots	b	19.10.93	Ch/Ir Ch Karaburan Jelly Roll Morton	Ch Harlextan Piara at Saxonmill	Mrs R A Hall	Breeder
Melleck Hellraiser	d	15.9.90	Bowentree Orka at Japapa	Kunduz Gentle Star of Melleck	Mr & Mrs B Hedge & Mrs T Harper	Breeders
Ratheeli Zazzah	b	17.4.89	Ch Koolaba Alexander of Sacheverell	Ch Ratheeli Mahzuzh	Miss P Mullins & Miss G McBride	Breeders
Sadé Beryk	d	5.1.96	Ch/Ir Ch Karaburan Jelly Roll Morton	Sadé Laeci	Mr & Mrs C Amoo	Breeders
Tulak Indecent Proposal	b	9.12.95	Ch Saxonmill Rum Tum Tigger	Lissue Salom of Tulak	R & Mrs V McCormack	Breeders
Kajaki Jumping Jack Flash	d	26.6.91	Harlextan The Flasher	Harlextan Jay Jannah	Mrs S Cronk	Breeder
Ratheeli Hajur	d	3.5.92	Ch Tianze Kalvados	Ch Ratheeli Mahzuzh	Miss P Mullins & Miss G McBride	A M & Mrs P M Cleak
Am Ch Seistan Hearts Afire to Freecloud	b	10.3.93	Am Ch Jorogz Heartbreaker	Am Ch Atavi's Seradrift	Mr & Mrs Thompson	M Cocozza

Bibliography

The Afghan Hound Year Book Published by Peter Harcourt Brown, Alnwick, Northumberland NE66 4HR

Hall, W L **The Afghan Hound** London: John Gifford Ltd, 1971

Harrisson, Charles **The Afghan Hound** London: Popular Dogs Pub Co Ltd, 1971

Miller, Constance O **and Gilbert**, Edward M, Jr **The Complete Afghan Hound** New York, USA: Howell Bookhouse Inc, 1965

Niblock, Margaret **The Afghan Hound: A Definitive Study** Edlington, Lincolnshire: K & R Books Ltd, 1980

Turner, Trevor, BVet Med MRCVS, *ed* **Veterinary Notes for Dog Owners** London: Popular Dogs Pub Co Ltd, 1996

West, Geoffrey P *ed* **Black's Veterinary Dictionary** 18th ed London: A & C Black, London.

AHA   Afghan Hound Association

List of Abbreviations

Am Ch	American (United States) Champion
BIS	Best In Show
BOB	Best Of Breed
CAC	FCI Challenge Certificate. Counts towards the title *Champion* in any country where dog shows are run under FCI regulations.
CACIB	International Challenge Certificate. Counts towards the title *International Champion* in countries where dog shows are run under FCI regulations.
CC	Kennel Club Challenge Certificate. A dog needs three of these under three different judges to become a champion in Great Britain.
Ch	Champion (Great Britain)
Dk Ch	Danish Champion
FCI	Fédération Internationale Cynologique. Canine governing body in several European countries.
Int Ch	International Champion
JW	Junior Warrant
Su Ch	Swedish Champion
Nl Ch	Dutch Champion
Nord Ch	Nordic Champion. A dog with CACs from Sweden, Norway and/or Finland.
Nu Ch	Norwegian Champion
RBIS	Reserve Best In Show
RCC	Reserve Challenge Certificate

Useful Addresses

The Kennel Club

The Kennel Club
1–5 Clarges Street,
London W1Y 8AB

The Kennel Club Junior Association,
c/o The Kennel Club

Afghan Hound Breed Clubs

The addresses of breed club secretaries change frequently, but you can find out the address of the current secretary from The Kennel Club. Afghan Hound breed clubs are as follows:

Afghan Hound Association
Afghan Hound Club of Scotland
Afghan Hound Club of Wales
Afghan Hound Society
   of Northern Ireland
Birmingham Afghan Hound Club
East of England Afghan Club
Midland Afghan Hound Club
North Eastern Afghan Hound Society
Northern Afghan Hound Society
Southern Afghan Club
Western Afghan Hound Club
Yorkshire Afghan Hound Society

Veterinary Matters

British Association of Homoepathic
   Veterinary Surgeons (BAHVS),
Alternative Medicine Centre
Stanford-in-the-Vale
Faringdon
Oxon SN7 8NQ

Handling

The Junior Handling Association,
Mrs E Cartledge
Ryslip Kennels
Bracknell
Berkshire

The United Kingdom
   Dog Handler's Association
Mrs J Hurley
Fralex
Middleton Road
Winterslow Salisbury

The Dog Press

Dog World	**Our Dogs**
Somerfield House Wootton Road	5 Oxford Road
Ashford	Station Approach
Kent TN23 6LW	Manchester

Index

Abscesses 128
Agility 160
Aggression 109, 116, 167
Alternative medicine 186–188
Alyshan (Mrs C Sturgeon-Walkden) 12
Anal gland impaction 191
Anzani (Mr & Mrs A Appleton) 10, 29
Arthritis 198
Artificial Insemination (AI) 168–170
Artificial respiration 198–199
Australia 63–64
Austria 63–64
Auto-immune disease 199

Barbille (Mrs D Hall) 10
Belgium 64
Bell-Murray type (desert) 7–9
Bletchingley (Mrs P Riley) 9
Bloat 199
Boarding kennels 129
Body 94, 98–100, 104
Bottle feeding 179–180
Breed standards 91–106
Breeding 162–170
    In-breeding 164
    Line breeding 163
    Outcrossing 163–164
Breeding terms .115
British kennels, contemporary
    (alphabetical) 39–59
Brood bitch .165–166
Bursitis 199–200

Caesarean section 178
Canada 64–65
Cancer 200
Canine Viral Hepatitis 189
Carloway (Mrs S Devitt) 14–16, 61
Castration 111
Cataracts 200
Challenge Certificates (CCs) 145
Chaman (Miss M Sharpe) 9
Champions, Afghan Hound 212–235
Character, see Temperament
Characteristics 94–95
Cheyletiella 195

Coat 94, 102, 104–105,
                                        112–113, 165
    Care, see Grooming
Colitis 202
Colour 94, 102, 104, 115
Conformation 100
    Croup/fallaway 101
    General outline 100
    Topline 98, 100, 103
Conjunctivitis 200
Constipation 200
Cuts and abrasions 200
Cystitis 201
Cysts 201

Demodectic mange 195
Denmark 66–67
Dental care 192
Diabetes 201
Diarrhoea 201–202
Diet, see Feeding
Distemper 189

Ears 94, 96, 103
    Grooming 135, 138–139
    Health care 192–193
Eclampsia 179
Elderly, Care of, see Old age
Epilepsy, see Fits and seizures
Entirety 115
Entropion 191
Euthanasia 210
Eyes 94, 96, 103
    Care of 193
    Ulcers 202
Exercise 108, 123, 153
Expenses 110
Exporting semen 170

False pregnancy .172
Faults 94, 102–105
    Disguising faults 149–150
Feeding 120–123
    Puppies to seven weeks 118
    Problems 122–123
    Supplementary feeding 179–180

Feet 91, 94, 104
Festive periods 132
Finland 67–68
Fits/seizures 191, 202–203
Fleas 194
Forequarters 94, 98, 114
France 69–70
Fronts, *see* Forequarters

Gait/movement 94, 102, 104–105,
                               115, 150–151
    Angulation, importance of 103
    Pacing 103
    Trotting .103
General appearance 94–95, 103
Gestation period 171
Ghazni (mountain) type 8
Gingivitis 203
Greyhound type 7
Grooming 133–143
    Bathing 136–138
    Coat texture and colour 133–134
    In pregnancy 173–174
    Junior coat 135–136
    Maintenance coat 142
    Problems 142–143
    Puppy coat 134–135
    Show coat 136–142
Grass seeds 203

Hair balls 203
Handling 148–149
Harvest mites 195
Hawaii 72–73
Hazuki (Mrs H Kinread) 10, 28
Head and skull 94–96, 103, 112–113
Health care 186–210
Heart attacks 203
Heart disease 203
Heatstroke 203–204
Hindquarters 91, 101, 114
Hip dysplasia 191
Holidays 128–131
Home nursing 187
Homeopathic medicine 186–188, 198
Horningsea (Mrs Marna Dods) 16–18, 65

Immunisation, *see* Vaccination
Importing 34–38
    Balai Directive 35
    Quarantine 34–35
Imports into the UK 36–38

Inertia 178
Insurance 116–117, 186
Italy 73–74

Jagai (Mr & Mrs R Gie) 11
Japan 74–75
Judging 105–107
Junior handling 151–153

Kennel Cough 190
Khanabad (Mrs M Niblock) 18–19
Khinjan (Mrs A Hattrell) 12, 28
Khorrassan (Miss E Snelling) 9, 32
Khyber (Mr & Mrs D Walmsley) 10
Kidney disease 204
Koolaba (Mrs B Taylor) 11
Kushra (Mr A Hedges & Mrs H Morgan) 10

Landhavi (Mr & Mrs M Lancashire) 13
Laryngeal paralysis 204
Legs 94–95, 98–101, 104
Leptospirosis 189
Lice 194
Liver disease 204
Lure coursing 156–160

Making provision in your will 210
Mastitis 178–179
Mating 166–168
    Mismating 168
Metritis 178
Moonswift (Mrs D Bowdler-Townsend) 11–12
Movement, *see* Gait/movement
Mouth .94, 97
    Bite 94, 97, 103, 105, 114

Nail care 193–194
Neck 94, 98, 104
    Neck patches 141–142
Nervousness 95, 111
Netherlands 76–77
Netheroyd (Mr & Mrs Abson) 9–10
New Zealand 77
Norway .77–78
Nutrition, *see* Feeding

Obedience .160
Obesity 123
Oestrus 166
Old age 207–210
Ovulation 166

Pancreatic insufficiency 204
Parvovirus 189
Poisoning 205
Poland 79–80
Pooghan (Mr & Mrs D McCarthy) 10, 31
Portugal 80–81
Pregnancy 171–174
    Care in pregnancy 171–174
    Palpation 172
    Scanning 172
    Signs of 171–172
Progressive Retinal Atrophy (PRA) 191
Prostate gland problems 205
Puppies
    Breeder 110
    Choosing a pet puppy 116
    Choosing a show puppy 112–115
    Development 182–183
    Dog or bitch? 111
    Feeding 118
    Settling in 117–118
Puppy Head Gland Disease 205
Pyometra 185

Quarantine, *see* Importing

Rabies 34–35, 189
Racing 154–156
Registrations 211
Rescue dog 116
Rifka's (Mrs C Race) 10
Ringworm .195–196
Road traffic accidents 205–206
Roundworms 196
Russia 81–85

Saddle 112, 134, 136, 138,
                                    140–143
Saluki type 7
Saringas (Miss J Dove) 13
Season, In, *see* Oestrus
Security 110
Sharikhan (Mr & Mrs F Severn) 13, 27
Showing .144–153
    Show equipment 146–147
    Types of British show 144–146
Size 94, 102
Socialising 125

South Africa 83–84
Spain 84–85
Spaying 110–111, 172, 184–185, 201
Sticky puppy 206
Stings (wasp and bee) 206
Streptococcal infection 168
Stud dog 164–165
    Sperm testing 165
    Stud fees 165
Supplements 121, 173

Tail 94, 101–102, 104, 114
Taiwara (Mr & Mrs R Barlow) 10, 33
Tapeworms 196–197
Tarril (Mr & Mrs S Pollock) 12
Teeth 94, 97, 135
Temperament 94–95, 108–109, 112
Temperature
    Ambient 174
    Body .175, 188
Thyroid, underactive 206
Ticks 194–195
Training 123–128
    House 118, 124–125
    Lead 125
    Ring 145–146

United States of America 87–90

Vaccination 165, 182–184, 188–190
Veterinary surgeon
    Choosing 186–187
    When to call 175–179
Vishnu (Mr & Mrs C Harrisson) 10
Vomiting 206

Warts (pappillomas) 206
Weaning 180–182
Whelping 175–179
    Aftercare of the bitch 184–185
    Box 174
    Equipment 174–175
World Congresses 160–161
Worming 165, 182

Zardin 8, 91
Zygomatic arch 96